RADICAL OTHERNESS

GENDER, THEOLOGY AND SPIRITUALITY
Series Editor: Lisa Isherwood, University of Winchester

Gender, Theology and Spirituality examines the gendered nature of theology and spirituality. Volumes in the series explore a range of topics, often employing materialist and radical readings and frequently questioning the notion of gender itself. The series aims to expand the boundaries of theology and spirituality through an engagement with embodied knowledge and critical praxis.

RADICAL OTHERNESS

Sociological and Theological Approaches

Lisa Isherwood and David Harris

ACUMEN

© 2013 Lisa Isherwood and David Harris

First published in 2013 by Acumen

Acumen Publishing Limited
4 Saddler Street
Durham
DH1 3NP

ISD, 70 Enterprise Drive
Bristol, CT 06010, USA

www.acumenpublishing.com

ISBN: 978-1-84465-721-6 (hardcover)
ISBN: 978-1-84465-722-3 (paperback)

British Library Cataloguing-in-Publication Data
A catalogue record for this book is available from the British Library.

Printed and bound in the UK by CPI Group (UK) Ltd, Croydon, CR0 4YY.

CONTENTS

PREFACE

This book started life as a timely conversation between two colleagues from diverse disciplines: sociology and feminist theology. It would seem an unlikely conversation but both were fascinated by the concept of otherness, a concept that in different ways is central to both their disciplines. So the conversation turned into a book dialogue in which otherness is explored from a number of political and cultural stances. Further, in this conversation we hope that the strengths and the weaknesses of each other's disciplines become highlighted. Certainly the authors have attempted to discover how the dance of these two disciplines can push the other forwards in a mutually supportive way.

It is our experience that many people come to universities because they are interested in finding out more about other people. Of course, they also want qualifications and to improve their chances in the labour market, but attempting to understand others is a common human interest. People might be particularly attracted to social sciences or to theology because of this interest in others. At the same time, they often find that they will have to postpone this interest, because they are faced with the need to encounter the traditions of the subject first, various abstract issues that arise, such as the work of particular writers or the need to pursue particular subdisciplines, such as research methods. In these cases, it is a matter of submitting to the interests of the professionals who design university curricula. Although those professionals are well intentioned, it is sometimes hard to see an original interest in others in the middle of more technical or specialist topics.

We consider the book timely because history has shown that during moments of world crisis, such as the one in which we now appear to find ourselves, the creation of others becomes magnified rather than reduced. We need to find someone to blame and someone whom we can articulate as a threat in order to find a focus in a world that seems to be out of control and allowing us no real choices. Further, we are well aware that the creation of others is behind conflict and persecution, so we believe an examination of how this happens and ways in which we might do things differently appears appropriate. Of course, we are both believers that if we get to the bottom of how things are constructed then it becomes possible to construct them differently. The other may become the radical other, a notion that we believe does not assimilate or annihilate the other but rather gives space for the "co-emergence of subjects in relation". (This is a notion we discuss more fully in Chapter 3.)

We have chosen to focus centrally on the issue of otherness, and to introduce more specialist interests in so far as they can be brought to bear. The central issues, for us, include trying to work out how others relate to ourselves, what we might have in common and what separates us. In turn, this leads to problems such as how best to conceive of others or otherness itself. Do we operate best by considering others as much like ourselves, for example, or do we try something rather more ambitious, which is to allow others to be different, possibly radically different, while still retaining their humanity? This looks like a very abstract issue, but we try to illustrate its importance by discussing a range of others, from asylum-seekers, through strangers, to women, considered in their own right, and not how other people wish to represent them.

The book moves from the personal to the metaphysical and at each stage grounds the theory in concrete examples. It begins with an examination of how the stranger, in a sense the personal other, has been articulated in both disciplines and some of the impact of such articulations. The self and what and who are therefore considered "not self" are central questions in both disciplines, as is the follow-on question of how the stranger is to be treated. This involves a wide-ranging discussion moving from Christian notions of hospitality, through the breakdown of social bonds to new ideas of interdependence, risk, trust and apathy, including what this implies in relation to both the virtual other and the posthuman other.

Having introduced the problem, we investigate the issues in more depth in Chapters 2, 3 and 4. In Chapter 2 we look at exploring the important issue of the political rights of others, and the everyday struggles about these rights. Political rights at one end of the spectrum are contrasted with more general debates about how tolerant we should be about the differences that others display, whether these are differences of religious or political belief, or simply choice of dress and leisure pursuit. There are some difficult cases here, and we are not simply preaching at our readers. We show how, by understanding the way in which others are created, we can move to a place of understanding the other as an empowering challenge to the middle, that is, to those considered normal. The issue of embodiment has been a central feminist theological concern and in the examples analysed it is possible to show how "the other" has contributed to a rearticulation of systematic theology.

Chapter 3 pursues the question of how we might be able to find out about others, especially if we want to go beyond the usual range of opinions that we have grown up with. In sociology, this question can turn into a discussion of reliable research methods and the debates about them: options here range from attempting to be scientific and quantitative to encouraging particular kinds of writing about experiences. However, feminist theology attempts to avoid the methodolatry of which Mary Daly speaks through an examining of experience, which, it contends, is in many ways what sociology is measuring in a relational way through networking across many borders and boundaries. This is not to say that feminist theology has not been, and continues to be, grateful for the work that sociologists do because it does provide a starting-point for some theological reflection. This is one way in which feminist theology has differed from some traditional theology; it is no longer interested in arguments for the existence of God, but rather in what kind of world various beliefs in God actually creates. This is where the social sciences are particularly useful.

In Chapter 4 we focus on a major issue, which is much discussed in the media: what might be the effects of widespread consumerism. Issues here range from attempts to reform consumer capitalism on theological grounds to sociological studies of actual groups of consumers and what they might make of their experiences. Feminist theology, coming as it does from a liberation theological base, is concerned that global capitalism is harmful to people and the planet while sociology takes a more balanced view, measuring the goods of such a system against the downside.

Chapter 5 is perhaps the most theoretical, but we think you might be able to see its relevance after looking at the more concrete discussions in earlier chapters. It is an attempt to introduce some of the main themes of feminist and Queer theology, which might contrast quite considerably from conventional views of theology. The logic of the One and the beyond has enabled a religious power structure to be set in place that has "othered" large sections of society over the centuries. It is this issue that many feminist theologians have taken on from a number of directions in order to release what they understand as a fuller flourishing of divine/human nature.

Some of the theoretical struggles of attempting to ground the subject in a secure philosophical basis are also discussed. The chapter ends with an introduction to the work of an important thinker cited in many modern debates: Gilles Deleuze.

In the conclusion, we look back on what we have discussed and consider an issue that might have become problematic from reading the earlier work: the relationship between sociology and feminist theology itself. We started out by arguing that our interest is in the topic of otherness that is shared by these two, and many other approaches. Of course, there is not a perfect overlap, and differences of emphasis are also clear. This might be unusual in student reading, which has recently taken on the convention of appearing to offer simple and fully coherent arguments, sometimes guided by devices such as "signposting", objectives and student exercises, where readers are invited to reconstruct what the authors thought. We want to challenge our readers to do something different: to grasp that there are differences in academic approaches, that these can be fruitful and that there are no simple right answers.

Throughout, the authors have experienced the tension of otherness and this has enriched the writing together. We have deliberately left a sober impersonal writing style to haunt one section, with an exuberant camp style displayed in the other, raising equal and opposite doubts about their value. A poetic sensibility might be seen as evasive for one, but powerfully creative for the other. We come from different backgrounds in terms of discipline as well as being diverse human persons and not just minds without bodies. All of these have provided challenges and moments of enlightenment as people and, we hope, as academics. It is perfectly acceptable for academics to disagree and argue, and this certainly does not mean that there is any personal disrespect or competition being displayed. All academics say that they want readers to engage critically with what they have written, but it is unusual for two writers to demonstrate critical engagement with each other's work. Given the topic of this book, it seems entirely appropriate that they should interact in this way, and we hope you agree.

ACKNOWLEDGEMENTS

Dave Harris would like to thank the librarians at the University of St Mark & St John, Plymouth, for their invaluable assistance.

INTRODUCTION: RADICAL OTHERNESS –
A SOCIO/THEOLOGICAL INVESTIGATION

Sociologists claim that their work, to put it bluntly, will replace the ideal-ist speculation of philosophers. It is a measure of the discipline that soci-ologists do not even mention theologians in the same breath, believing, it seems, that their metaphysical ranting is way beyond the pale and not even worth consideration. All the "founding fathers" saw a need to break with religious and metaphysical conceptions to found a new rational disci-pline to study the modern order. The sociological claim is seen at its most explicit in the work of the young Karl Marx, who declared he had found a more reliable method for investigating the material practices that lay behind social life and the abstract ideas that held them in place. Marx saw this as a political rather than philosophical endeavour.

This raises an issue, incidentally, of the role of Marxism and other more recent theoretical work: to what extent is it sociology? Marxist perspectives, by and large, have been incorporated, perhaps rather tactically, as in the claim that Marx was a founding parent, despite the claim raised above that Marxism also replaces sociology. As with feminist theology, below, other disciplines, strictly speaking, have been incorporated into the sociological canon to stave off critique. A boundary problem arises quite frequently and it is addressed in a way that is almost certainly not coherent or consistent. So, for example, various linguistic approaches claiming to replace sociol-ogy altogether, whether based on Wittgenstein, Hans-Georg Gadamer or variants of discourse theory, have been discussed here as aspects of soci-ology. Advocates of those approaches have similarly found themselves having to cooperate or break with other trends in sociology (largely the empirical investigations). This is the result of a series of pragmatic conven-tions, probably emerging from the professional academic need to retain the boundaries of sociology in order to protect business as usual, while also maintaining a political radicalism. This combination of the radical and the professional and scholastic has been analysed in more detail by Harris (1992) for the subdiscipline of cultural studies.

Another "founding parent", Max Weber, also shared a concern for concrete social practices that are to be analysed using particular methods. He argued that the course of history displays such a series of unintended consequences and ironies that any speculative attempt to impose an overarching order is doomed to fail. His best-known example is an analysis of the way in which ascetic Protestantism, ostensibly rejecting material success in favour of a notion of predestination, became adopted in practice as a work ethic justifying hard work and primitive accumulation, which, ironically, did much to develop early forms of capitalism (Weber 1985).

These initial arguments and many that followed have been very important as critiques but it is now almost impossible to assert that they have actually managed to develop empirical methods without any lurking philosophical assumptions that might be used to investigate material practices. At first sight Marx does appear to offer ways to develop empirical methods – for example, using statistics to measure poverty in Britain – but this too depended on theorizing, if not philosophizing, of the complex totality producing those empirical data. Whether Marx ever actually broke with Hegelian or Kantian (or even Judaeo-Christian) categories is still a much disputed topic and religious commitments are found in the most technical discussions.

If it were not to be merely descriptive, and to break effectively enough with rival disciplines such as economics and psychology, sociology had to concern itself with the conceptual status of its key terms, especially "the social". The desire to rely solely on material investigation has been tempered by an acknowledgement that empirical methods are combined with, or at least informed by, ontological and epistemological positions in the various paradigms on offer. If speculative philosophers have been naive about material practices then sociologists have been naive about philosophical argument. Philosophers may have uncritically applied their speculation to lived realities but sociologists have also uncritically used philosophy to justify what they think they are doing. And theologians are still nowhere in sight!

THE CHALLENGE OF OTHERNESS

While relations towards and between other people have been a defining concern of studies of the social, the danger was always that sociological generalizations would obscure radical notions of Otherness (capitalized to distinguish it from the mundane kind). What might be called mundane otherness would predominate: a form of licensed or limited otherness that actually preserved the "imperialism of the Same", to use Emmanuel Levinas's terminology (see Bergo 2011). For example, other people could be seen as offering variants of conventional identities – "deviant" ones, or simpler ones – which left central categories intact as the norm. Empirical sociological categorization can easily subsume difference as an extreme value or "outlier" on some agreed variable. These notions of "normal" behaviour have theoretical and political implications. The most recent crisis for sociology has come from new accounts of the modern, perhaps the postmodern, which tend to emphasize the decline of the traditional social patterns and social bonds and thus raise doubts about the whole strategy to manage otherness as variants of similarity.

However, the more mundane problems of otherness have run like the proverbial scarlet thread through much applied sociology, although not quite in the same terms. Here, the argument is that applied sociology encounters the issues of otherness whenever it studies the social groups and networks in which individuals are enmeshed. Thus we find discussions using such terms as solidarity versus exclusion, for example, or communities and outsiders. These terms clearly link with the general debates about otherness briefly discussed above. Those general debates tend to focus on persistent social divisions such as those of class, gender or "race", but there are more concrete solidarities and divisions to consider as well.

Sociologies of deviance (in this case criminal activities) often reveal a similar dialectic between the identities of selves and the irruptive potential of others, for example. Early work on juvenile gangs in the USA revealed that the "criminal" values of members were best understood as an inversion of official values; an inversion is a limited kind of otherness sharing the same agenda as official values but "upside down". Even professional criminals such as Chicago gangsters shared goals with straight businessmen, although they differed about the means to achieve them (Merton 1968). More individualized work suggested that convicted criminals actually shared many mainstream values as well, to such an extent that they needed "techniques of neutralization" (Sykes & Matza 1957) to try to explain to their straight selves what their deviant selves had been up to. Émile Durkheim's analysis of exclusionary rituals such as criminal trials shows the main benefits for most of the onlookers consisted in having their official values confirmed and socially supported (see Lukes 1975). These analyses suggested that criminality was at least integral to official values, maybe tightly connected to, and inherent in, those values, and was deviant only in terms of the chosen means to achieve those values; criminality inhabited normality as necessary otherness, as it were. Some Queer theory (Dyer 2002) implies as much for sexual identities.

Other applied work indicates some of the unintended consequences of one of the main social bases of selfhood: membership of a community. Community membership is often seen to be a "good thing" in current policy (as long as the community in question is an approved one and not, say, a paedophile ring), but all belonging has its disruptive aspect: the exclusion of others. Notorious cases, such as the Nazi *Volksgemeinschaft*, show this clearly, but there are more everyday examples as well. The working-class "lads" studied by Paul Willis (1977) forged strong bonds of solidarity with each other and with their fathers, and these were sufficient to maintain their identities against a school system that attempted to devalue them. But this solidarity had its costs, including the exclusion of others such as women or members of ethnic minorities; a strong, rugged masculinity supported values of persistence, stoicism and self-respect but, almost by definition, others lacked these qualities. Willis suggests that even the blanket rejection of schooling (as "poofy") was a cost, since "the lads" went off into manual labour relatively uneducated, more or less as the system intended all along.

Paradoxes like this haunt community regeneration policies. People in one local Plymouth community draw strength from seeing themselves as different from those in a neighbouring one, even though local administrators are oblivious to these differences and both lie in the same administrative area. Participation policies in sport attempt to build solidarity among participants but unwittingly import exclusion as well. Some heterosexual male sports teams bond by excluding and ridiculing women and gays, or at best by dealing with their challenges in various heterosexual hegemonic discourses, and anyone can see the genuine hostility generated by rival fans at local "derbies" and the sense of solidarity it engenders among those who belong.

Social relations, where individuals orient themselves to the actions of others, have been defined as the central subject matter of sociology by one of its founding parents, Weber. The other founding parents clearly demonstrate such concerns in their work too, although possibly in less direct ways. Durkheim, for example, thought of the problem in terms of the relations between the individual and society, where society takes on a certain externality, a reality *sui generis*, an abstract otherness. One major theme turns on the dangers of excessive individualism, as people somehow become detached from the social world of others and become excessively egoistic or anomic: in extreme cases, this would produce suicide. Marx's early work, at least, focused on the problems of an alienating social and economic system that had the paradoxical consequence of making people feel other than they really were, so to speak: they were alienated from themselves, from their key human activity (work, but not capitalist wage labour), and from their "species being".

The same general concerns can be detected after only a slightly tweaked reading of the work on methodology in sociology as well. The general insights have been provided by attempts to classify the social sciences in terms of how they conceive of others: Jürgen Habermas (1987) has pointed out that some sociological approaches see other people in a very restricted way, more or less as carriers of data, while others allow an increasing number of autonomous human characteristics. Some studies based on questionnaires, standard tests or norm-referenced attitude scales clearly fall into the first case; every other quality or characteristic of the respondent is ignored except for those that are being measured or tested, and it is assumed in particular that respondents are unaware of the purpose of the research, unable to respond in any subjective way to the questions. Perhaps we should say unable to respond in a positively subjective way, since even questionnaire-based studies usually allow for "noise".

At the other extreme, methods and techniques such as life history or various kinds of ethnographic study seemed to offer a much more rounded picture of the other. The researcher tries to engage in normal conversation with others, to treat them as full human beings, and to try to understand them using techniques similar to those that one would use to understand one's friends and fellows. These techniques have been slightly amended in some accounts, to make them more self-consciously related to various theories in different ways: to use them to develop "grounded theory" (Glaser & Strauss 1967) or "theoretically informed ethnography" (Willis & Trondman 2000).

This apparent respect for others can be slightly misleading, however. It is certainly true that the earliest forms of ethnographic study were unable to distance themselves very far from colonialism, despite some of the good intentions of the ethnographers themselves (it is also fair to say that some leading ethnographers were still Eurocentric, if not racist). There are also a number of criticisms of ethnographic fieldwork that imply that, despite the apparent era of cooperation and collaboration between researcher and researched, there is still a disguised power relationship that reduces otherness at the final stage: John Elliott (1986) notes that as soon as a researcher leaves the field, they engage in a "knight's move", and the subjective creations of their collaborators become mere "data" after all, used to support a professional academic's argument. Pierre Bourdieu (2001) was to call this "symbolic violence".

A recent set of poststructuralist arguments make rather similar points about ethnographic work and the crucial, yet undisclosed, role of the writer. Writers manage otherness in order to accomplish the well-known ethnographic aim of making the strange familiar and the familiar strange. Patricia Ticineto Clough (1992), for example, suggests that ethnographic researchers write up their results using various conventions of realism to do so. These conventions deliver a "knowledge effect" to the reader, which can include a sense of pleasurable yet safe involvement in the lives of others. Subjects of the study can become exoticized, or used in some other way as a resource for reading pleasures. A blunter critic, drawing upon different resources, once referred to this tendency as "zookeeping" (Young 1975: 64).

Bourdieu (2000a) has discussed the dilemmas in a particularly acute way. In general, the difficulties in understanding others in conventional social science research have been glossed by various assumptions. One is that other people can be understood as expressing certain social and psychological laws when they act. This comes through in a vulgar form sometimes, when social commentators assume that members of other societies are particularly religious, saturated by religious values, affected in every detail of their lives. We have already hinted at another assumption: that subjects are "cultural dopes", completely unaware of our purposes as researchers, innocently behaving "in the field", as we take notes and then attempt to generalize. Bourdieu has described what really happens: the ethnographer encounters people who are willing and able to manage their own otherness, to describe their own behaviours in terms that researchers will understand.

James Clifford (1993) has done much to question another major assumption: that those living in the field are somehow uncontaminated by ideas, beliefs and cultures from outside. Indeed, that is almost a definition of a "field" for some ethnographers and anthropologists. However, there is a long history of such "contamination", such as the case of the legendary Native American Tisquantum or Squanto, who, speaking good English, greeted the Pilgrim Fathers soon after their arrival. He had learned English after staying for some while (involuntarily) in England, and had probably learnt an agricultural technique while travelling through Spain, planting small fish with maize seeds to ensure fertility. This technique saved the pilgrims during their first season and has been celebrated ever since at Thanksgiving.

These sorts of debates have left even the most workaday sociologists in full awareness about the problematic nature of others. To paraphrase and simplify considerably, we all now know that it just is not easy to make assumptions about others. We also know that in many cases we have pre-decided the nature of others, reproducing a range of political and social values as we do so; others have been defined as simpler, inferior versions of ourselves, more or less as colonial administrators have always done. Finally, we now realize that relations between selves and others are problematic. Just as others can no longer be neatly categorized, especially as many of them refuse to stay obediently in their confined fields, so selves are no longer as simple and organic as they once were.

Important but "difficult" theorists such as Jacques Lacan are often seen as central to the topic, with his re-reading of Freudian themes such as the Oedipal scene and the "mirror phase" as universal stages in the development of the modern individual subject (see Althusser 1977a). Lacan and other theorists have been critically taken up by feminists in particular, for example the contributors to *Screen* (1993), and involved in substantial debates, including the processes by which women become "other". Lacan was to argue that very general and important social and cultural mechanisms – the Symbolic order itself, no less – coded, at a deep level, male conceptions of the world. The very structure of language was patriarchal, much as Sigmund Freud had argued that male sexuality was central to the processes of the development of the personality itself.

Lacanian views defined women in terms of a "lack" (not necessarily their fault): lacking real biological penises and other male tackle and lacking a clear and apparently simple link to the possession of symbolic penises as well. The wielder of the symbolic penis controlled cultural and linguistic power. The struggle of feminists to overcome the blocks to full emancipation in such work had put the whole issue on the agenda, and we discuss some in later chapters. For example, if the Symbolic is so phallogocentric, there is a need to rescue some non-Symbolic or pre-Symbolic form of communication before women were so dominated, and this has been found in Bracha Etting-er's "matrixial" or Julia Kristeva's pre-semiotic "chora", usually located as a potentiality in the pre-Oedipal infant. There might even be a realm removed altogether from the phallogocentric actual, which has led other feminists to follow Gilles Deleuze into positing a virtual femininity, as we shall see.

This response led to a generally applicable one: women were not defined simply in terms of something they lacked compared to dominant groups but were other. Characteristically, this conception of women led to a social dichotomy, a political and cultural split, but masculinity also owed rather more to it than was acknowledged: "Femininity, suggests Shoshana Felman, should be conceived as 'masculinity's uncanny difference from itself. It inhabits masculinity as Otherness, as its own disruption'" (Jervis 1999: 129).

The last point is pursued in some detail in the work on identities in modernity, postmodernity, late capitalism, or advanced societies, depend-ing on one's stance. To simplify considerably, the old social supports for a unified and relatively simple self have weakened and dissolved. Families and communities have declined, work has become much more fragmented, religious beliefs multiply, we travel and become familiar with other cultures and even adopt some of their ways, while others travel and live alongside us, at least in our larger cities. Culture and identity have become much more relative and flexible, or "nomadic", and, as a result, relations between self and others have become much more complex.

Given the warning above, it is no surprise that the relations between sociology and feminism, and then feminist theology, can be considered ini-tially in terms of the many debates about the relation between the more concrete and the more theoretical wings of sociology. Certainly feminism has played a major part in some of the more abstract struggles over Other-ness and its cultural and linguistic underpinnings. Feminism has also made more mundane social theory well aware of its limited conceptions. Even the most critical theorists, such as Habermas or Michel Foucault, Nancy Fraser (1989) tells us, tend to privilege male conceptions of areas of life such as work, and to invoke basic binary oppositions to describe the relations between, say, work and family life. Most sociologists would have encoun-tered Luce Irigaray (1985) and her insistence that binary oppositions are insufficient to explain gender differences, since women, or the female, are not one thing but many.

In order to grasp some of the more obvious implications, it might be helpful for sociologists to see this sort of argument as the familiar one invoking concrete complexity against abstract generalizations and reductions of various kinds. This is an argument found in conventional sociology among all the founding parents. Even Marx, who is commonly seen as one of the most reductionist, criticized rival theories precisely for their positivist abstractions. Classically, the commodity, for example, was by no means a simple object but a complex combination of familiar exchange value with a unique use-value, and the simple categories of political economy simply failed to acknowledge this complexity. As a result, they fell into ideology, both in the political and methodological senses.

Complexity is found in much more contemporary social theory too, such as in the attempts of Anthony Giddens (see Craib 1992) to operate with different levels of analysis between a virtual level of potential social material ("rules and resources") and a more concrete "structurated" level of social life, and by the introduction of a Weberian complicating factor, the unintended consequences of behaviour.

In other words, confronting abstract theories with complex analyses is a familiar procedure in sociology, and feminist analysis has done much to elaborate such confrontations. Again, sexuality and sexual identity are major fields for such analyses, especially in those more recent developments that consider sexuality itself to be a performance (such as Butler 1990b) and that insist that there are no simple stable identities and fixed oppositions.

However, a sociology of complexity has its own difficulties as well. This has been demonstrated in areas such as political life. Some theoretical tendencies push towards a politicization of every aspect of social life, for example. Foucault might be a representative of these tendencies, but there are earlier ones in "conflict theorists", Marxist variants, and some examples in discourse analysis. Extending the notion of political tendencies like this helps to fight off those "centred" readings of social life, including those found in classical social theory, which wants to privilege particular political divisions or processes; class struggle for Marxists is the classic example. However, it is clear that the analysts involved are actually fairly disinterested in many such examples, and tend to focus on the politically more significant ones: not class exclusively, but very often other "big" issues such as gender, "race" or disability. Thus, to paraphrase some of the critics, disputes between neighbours over a hedge could be seen as a "political" issue in the abstract, but no one really bothers to analyse the power–knowledge links involved. In other words, there is some suppressed theoretical argument wanting to privilege some processes after all.

There is perhaps only one approach in sociology that devotes itself to teasing out the full complexities of the most routine and mundane activities, such as the negotiation of understandings involved in calling your friends on the telephone. This is ethnomethodology, or conversation analysis (see Atkinson & Heritage 1984). Even this approach was intended to have some general theoretical implications, however, not least in rebuking classical sociological theory for ignoring these everyday processes involved in the construction of social order. More recently, it is noticeable that examples chosen for such detailed analysis have tended to focus on conventional "big" issues after all, as in Eve Chiapello and Norman Fairclough's (2002) attempts to marry up Marxist critique and linguistic analysis to produce the hybrid "critical discourse analysis", which focuses on matters such as the peculiar discourses of middle-management as they do ideology in practice and in detail.

The issues identified so far turn on where to find and how to study mundane otherness. What of radical Otherness? "Radical" in this term can mean "politically radical", but also "conceptually radical", a kind of otherness that transcends the mundane, some deeper and more significant kind of otherness, something structured into social life itself that cannot be managed in the usual way.

We have briefly examined Irigaray's argument for such Otherness, but there are also other approaches (the difficulties of avoiding terms such as "other others" are hard to avoid). Thus for some Marxists, the main social classes in capitalism were certainly becoming radically different in terms of their political interests and their whole consciousness. For example, the working class was the only genuine universal class with some perception of universal interests, while the bourgeoisie could never escape their own immediate interest and the ideological perceptions based on them. Other Marxists (such as Antonio Gramsci) saw class struggle in fundamental terms too, as the main classes struggled to impose quite different and hegemonic visions of social and political life on each other. Marx himself argued (Marx 1875) that there was a need to smash the bourgeois state and all its apparatuses and do away altogether with liberal conceptions such as "a fair day's work for a fair day's pay".

The same tendencies towards radical alternatives can be found in feminist activism too. For women to truly celebrate their otherness, the arguments might go, a radical break with patriarchal conceptions and practices is required. Families might be abandoned, together with parliamentary democracy, private ownership, work, patriarchal forms of organization, conventional sexual identities, conventionally gendered childrearing practices and so on. A theoretical claim to privilege might well accompany these arguments, as in early versions of "radical feminism", an approach that argued that gender differences were fundamental, pre-dating all the other main axes of division such as social class (see e.g. Firestone 1993; and we discuss Grosz in Kontturi & Tiainen 2007 in Chapter 2).

These arguments involve a well-discussed difficulty, however, in that mundane and concrete practices have somehow to be seen as manifestations of more fundamental theoretical differences. Everyday struggles between bosses and workers have to be seen as class struggle, or domestic disputes about budgets as some symptom of underlying resistance to patriarchy. In most of these cases, a two-level model is being deployed: quite often a "surface-depth" metaphor. While events on the surface might be complex and concrete, deeper and more fundamental issues lie beneath. Actual struggles are mere "epiphenomena" in Marxist formulations, specific effects of deeper processes: this has been argued very clearly in Nicos Poulantzas's (1975) account of the emergence of middle-class groups, Stuart Hall and Tony Jefferson (1976) and their account of youth cultures as "symbolizing" real political tensions between classes and generations, or Valerie Scatamburlo-D'Annibale and Peter McLaren (2003), to take a recent argument connecting "race" and class.

The problem lies in deploying the two-level argument consistently and transparently. Barry Hindess and Paul Q. Hirst (Hirst 1977; Hindess & Hirst 1975) argued that this connection could not be made without dogmatism or foundationalism. Their arguments were based on close readings of major theorists in sociology, including the founding parents. The point was that a theoretical construct, designed to answer theoretical problems and produce theoretical knowledge, was often made to fit theoretical systems in incoherent ways. The problems increased when we tried to stretch this concept to fit complex empirical cases, since that always involved a selection of empirical features. Deleuze's (2004) critique of conventional thought relying on dubious analogies or dogmatic judgments makes the same point. This is fundamentally the structure of religious language; all two-level arguments are theological. This is a sign of weakness for these critics.

There was a political imperative involved as well. "Centred" readings that insisted on a privileged place for certain concepts and certain struggles disqualified others, as Foucault argued. Foucault wants to ask: "What types of knowledge do you want to disqualify ...? Which speaking discoursing subjects – which subjects of experience and knowledge ... do you then want to 'diminish' ...? Which theoretical-political *avant-garde* do you want to enthrone?" (1980: 85). However, there is a dilemma awaiting, what might be called "Foucault's fork". To reverse the terms of his question, once the old agendas are abandoned, which types of knowledge would qualify? All types? Should the activities of all speaking and discoursing subjects be considered equally worthy of Foucaldian analysis, even the mundane competitions to take turns in telephone conversations as in ethnomethodology? Foucault seems to resist; it would make his work look "fragmentary, repetitive and discontinuous", a mere scholarly indulgence, "a typical affliction of those enamoured of libraries, documents, reference works, dusty tomes, texts that are never read ... [an addition to the] ... great warm and tender Freemasonry of useless erudition" (*ibid.*: 79).

This sort of poststructuralist challenge only deepened into full-blown postmodern scepticism towards all metanarratives. Such scepticism has undoubtedly had an effect on sociology. To be sure, social theorists have managed to reply to postmodernist critique with some effect. For example,

Peter Dews (1987) and Seyla Benhabib (1984) are among those who have identified a metanarrative inside postmodernism itself. Habermas has been a leading critic of the implicit conservatism in a position that seems to gleefully predict the end of social critique (e.g. Habermas 1984). Others, such as Axel Honneth (1985), have identified a preference for the local and a decisionistic "aversion against the universal": he, and others, have suggested that postmodernists have cheerfully dismissed or "forgotten" sociology before actually studying any of it (see also Harris 1996). It is possible also to see postmodernists, especially French ones, accustomed to a role as a public intellectual, unable to resist the temptation to comment on socially significant problems, and thus finding themselves having to refer to sociology after all – or a common-sense version of it. Other sociologists (especially Giddens 1991, or Beck 1992) have attempted to rescue the central concepts of sociology, while amending and adding to them to develop a sociology of modernity or late modernity as involving a lot more flexibility than classic modernist societies and a whole new set of problems, from globalization to risk.

For other sociologists, any attempt at theoretical resolution appears to have been abandoned altogether. The drive towards "relevance" in higher education has meant that sociologists often now find a home helping to solve much more "practical", political or policy-based problems. What this means is that other people now set the agenda, deciding which problems to reinvestigate, which ones are significant and so on, and also helping to fix an appropriate level of enquiry, sometimes even an appropriate methodology. In some ways this must be a relief, and, of course, sociological contributions are extremely useful. Nevertheless, this kind of decisionism means that there is unlikely to be any investigation of anything radical, let alone radical otherness. There is enough work to do at the mundane level.

There is also the issue of the audience for radical analysis. Social theorists have always argued for some relevance for their views outside mere academia. In the 1960s and 1970s, there was some basis for the view that social theory actually informed radical practice. It has always been a problem for British radicals to link with activists because there is no radical political party on the left to bring them together. Instead, radical sociologists comforted themselves with a view that they were contacting working-class militants in various ways, including helping to teach them social theory in expanded universities (including, or possibly especially, the Open University in the UK). As other radical movements and groups developed, so sociological analysis could be adjusted to theorize their practice as well, especially in the case of militant women, black activists or various minority activist groups. Again, this sort of commitment helps to fix and limit, to stabilize, the whirlpool of the "post-" critiques.

However, such links and ties proved to be fragile. First, the classic activism of working-class militancy declined. At the same time, analysts discovered other aspects of working-class culture of which they disapproved, such as racism and sexism, which, curiously, were never particularly addressed or grasped by theory, as epiphenomenal for example. An apparent decline of socialist regimes and the triumph of international capitalism globally also had an effect. Other radical groups, such as women or black activists, did not really seem particularly keen to accept theoretical advice from outside, but developed their own critiques and pursued their own combinations of theory and practice. As a result, social theory now finds itself largely confined to the university, where scholasticism, incorporation and domestication are possible fates that await.

In what follows, sociological argument and analysis should encounter a different tradition in feminist theology. There will be some points of contact, given that feminism did much to bring the discussion of radical Otherness to the sociological agenda and that theological traditions are hard to shake off. There will also be differences, perhaps touching on different levels of analysis or different methodologies: in everyday discussion, sociologists often think of theology as abstract and limited by excessive commitment to privileged concepts, while theologians see sociologists as philosophically naive, unreflective and reductionist. At the same time, there is every reason, from the outside at least, to believe that feminist theology still remains able to undertake critical analyses for good sociological reasons as well as theoretical ones. It does still seem to retain a powerful social audience and agent. Although it clearly has to negotiate difficult institutional times and the incorporation that those threaten, it still seems better able to exploit liberal beliefs, such as the defence of free speech and open criticism. These are enshrined in theology itself, and in the Christian tradition, possibly, and not just in what seems to have been a temporary commitment in higher education.

THE WORD BECAME FLESH AND DWELT AMONG US?

The theologian stands before a wealth of sociological theory with very few tools at her disposable, and for this feminist theologian the tools themselves may only enable the building of yet another patriarchal edifice since they have been fashioned in the furnace of male centeredness and possibly even a will to power that is at odds with much that feminist theology stands for. Of course, theology does have revelation, scripture tradition and hope! However, what it has been slow to admit is that the central statement of faith mentioned above – that the divine itself came and lived on earth and this changed things – has always relied on "theories" to make it intelligible to the world in which believers have declared that faith and, as mentioned, they have for most of Christianity's history been male theories. Theology has even been prey to language games for the sake of male focus, as the phrase from John 1 illustrates. It is now commonly accepted by scholars that "the word" is a translation and co-opting of the Sophia/wisdom of the Hebrew Bible, a female concept of deity who dwelt among her people in the market square, where she mucked in and urged their empowerment, their embodying of her wisdom in the everyday business of their lives, and indicated they lived the power of the divine in all its messy incompleteness and all its potential power to transform. In the words above, Sophia becomes Logos and the power is fundamentally shifted. The Logos is the pre-existent word of God emanating from above and beyond, commanding all into existence with God rather than gently nurturing all into life as Sophia wisdom was imagined to do alongside YHWH. Logos becomes the yardstick and the way in which love is to be understood: a harsh master. So we cannot just simply read, and the tools of interpretation can lead us into slavery. The point is that theology has never been very good at "reading itself". It has relied on other disciplines to enable it to be read and, as we shall see, this has not always been a very productive reading. As we see from the central declaration of faith – which may indeed have set us into a freedom of being that had no place for projections of destructive "otherness" and the exclusions that come with such projections – when spoken as "the word" it becomes almost a central hub in the creation of exclusions. We are no longer Sophia's beloved engaging with her wisdom in our lives for the expansion of the human and non-human world, but rather the children of God, who can never be as he is and can never in this life reach any kind of perfection, for it is now perfection that has become the guide by which we are judged. There is a hierarchy with all the exclusions that speaks of, rather than a radical inclusion based on the wisdom that is innate in all that lives and breathes: wisdom imbued with the *Ruah* of desire whispered at the dawn of time and alive in the chaos of those beginnings.

As well as hierarchy there is also a distance, one that theologians have assumed as their privilege. As they associate themselves with the distanced, declaring Logos, this has led to theology from ivory towers clothed in the comfort of elaborate metaphysics removed from the messy realities of life. From this safe distance much theology has forgotten that a theology based in Christian incarnation is an ever-changing reflection on action, instead of a set of fixed abstract codifications that lend themselves to power and privilege. I have for some time argued that incarnational theology can never lend itself to certainty; the God who abandoned the heavens in favour of enfleshed existence gave up the assurance of good/correct and perfect outcomes and instead embraced risk as central to the divine unfolding. In grounding theology in incarnation I am declaring for the God who, we are told in the Prologue of John's Gospel, pitched his tent among us: a tent, not a house; a moveable dwelling, one fit for the walk; one that expands and changes shape with the winds of change, best understood perhaps as the breath of the Spirit. It was this incarnation who became God in community/God in society/God in creation. The gospels show us Jesus becoming the Messiah through walking with, being affected by, marginalized communities and individuals. Marcella Althaus-Reid (2005) believes that the life of Jesus presents us with a communitarian reading of rupture that challenges us to move beyond a nostalgic dwelling place from where we remember past utopias or promised kingdoms and propels us into an ongoing process of imagination and creative engagement. It is not the task of theologians to heal the rupture that the divine incarnate made; rather, it is our task to continue the discontinuity. In other words, counter to some traditional theology, which longs for a move back to the place it all began with perfect human beings cloned in the likeness of an unchanging father God, feminist theology looks to move and change, to open more and more to the ever-unfolding and continually revealing ground of being with all its instability.

So what, if anything, does feminist theology have by way of tools and alliances that may make it a productive dialogue partner for sociology and, in this dialogue, a useful contributor to understanding the world and notions of otherness? Perhaps very little other than its own history, based as it is in the experience of being outside, and therefore a method grown from at times bitter experience and resolutely grounded in counter-readings and expectations of transformation. This expectation is based in the bodies of people who live differently rather than in a place of beyond and a time yet to come. So at first glance it would seem that feminist theology relies on, indeed rejoices in, otherness and difference, for it is here that transformation is thought to lie, not in bodies conforming to the heavy weight of a patriarchal society. It would, however, be misleading to suggest that feminist theology has always got this right or that it, indeed, has it right now. There are ongoing debates, begun in bitter anger, that feminist theology was, and remains, a white discourse developed and perpetuated by white, middle-class women who cannot see beyond their own noses. The interesting point here is that while middle-class privilege was viewed as only white, the middle classes of colour could almost speak with impunity. In its early days feminist theology did not enter the sexuality debates with gusto, fearing, I suppose, that like the women's movement before it, a label of lesbian activism would be attributed that in theological circles would immediately signal its demise. Was this understandable caution or further marginalization and "othering"? Many have claimed that feminist theology remains more comfortable in discourses about gender than in conversations about sexuality, as can be seen by the move into Queer theory of some who were previously content with the methods of feminist theology. Queer theory, they believe, gives more flexibility in areas of identity than even feminist theology could do. This, of course, has both an upside and a downside; after all, if we can no longer speak of women and men as categories then how do we politicize the violence done by one to the other, or the exclusions based on genitals that still appear to be prevalent in the wider world? The debate is a fierce one and at times feminist theology appears to fall back into essentialism in defence of what is, in fact, a political observation: that in many cultures and many situations, to be a genital female is more dangerous, less advantaged or lower down in hierarchies. However, it is also true that Queer theology has enabled many new voices to emerge in the creation of theology simply through the questioning of rigid categories. Now we can have "trans-" voices of many descriptions as well as cross-species conversations that, while perhaps not being generated by Queer theorists themselves, have been enabled by the questioning of the distinctiveness of categories.

Perhaps only a limited number of things can be said about feminist theology: the first that it has enabled an array of methods to be used in theology that were previously unknown within that discipline. For example, like liberation theology, it incorporated Marxist methodology into the way it created theology. Indeed, while some claim that liberation theology itself was never Marxist enough, others claim feminist theology to be too Marxist. Whatever the truth of these claims it is easily demonstrated that Marxist theory has allowed feminist theology to make a large impact in many areas of doctrinal theology and through into the ethics that spring from it. This is clearly demonstrated by those authors within the classic period of feminist theology who, when writing on Christology, always insisted it had to be ethical. The days of substance and essence had, in their minds, been superseded by praxis: praxis based in some ontological reality, less fixed than it once was, but nonetheless tested in the lives of people (Brock 1988; Heyward 1982; Isherwood 1999). This concrete demonstration had to be political and not merely what one might call moral; for example, the sexual activity of people became less important than equal pay and cash cropping. If it had ever been doubted that theology needed a context and one that could be understood and concretely analysed, feminist Christologies argued strongly that this had been a false understanding of Christianity. In absolute terms, the point of feminist theology became to create theology that would no longer attempt just to understand the nature of God but to radically change the world. Contexts became crucial and the way was open for the huge impact that the messy lives of people would make when taken seriously as the stuff of theology. It also meant that theology needed a conversation partner that was good at the analysis of contexts if it was not to fall into the realms of make-believe. That is not to say that it wishes to give up on its utopian visions and dreams, but that it needs the tools of other disciplines to help it realize them in concrete situations. Its conversation partner for many centuries has been philosophy, but feminist theology, while engaging with this discipline, understood very early that it had to tread with care in this realm of patriarchal worldviews and spectacular theories. The Word in this context may not have the weight of religious justification but nevertheless in many cases writes phallic discourse in stone.

Second, within its contextual theology feminist theology has been good at bringing many, but by no means all, to the table for making theology together, and this is because it is open to change; nothing is written in stone because the experiences of women and men and, increasingly, the planet have an ongoing impact on the way in which feminist theology unfolds. While it has made mistakes in this area, it has grown and continues to do so. It is this reluctance to write in stone that has been a cause of criticism from more traditional theology, which confuses this with lack of direction and no guiding principles. Feminist theology, on the other hand, sees this as a strength, believing that it is not possible or desirable to fix the unfolding nature of the divine within and between us in a set of rules and principles. Perhaps there is hope here for a new way of understanding otherness and even radical otherness.

Third, related to the issue of context is the way in which feminist theology in the branch that is body theology has enfleshed the context in a way that was perhaps missing prior to its intervention. Sociology also had its "turn to the body", as we shall see in Chapter 2, partly as a methodological issue and partly as a realization of excessive disembodiment and a focus instead on beliefs and consciousness. Bodies matter to many feminist theologians and this changes most things. It does not allow the luxury of grand theories because there are always bodies in the conversation that will challenge or disprove most grand theories. At its best, feminist theology invites multiple bodies to the table and, while they are indeed representatives of a variety of "others", they often do not inhabit the space of otherness since their presence as dialogical partners challenges that complete distance. It has also been found that when women begin to talk of children, home, illness and even bread-making (as with the women of Northern Ireland and the Republic of Ireland exchanging soda-bread recipes at the height of the Troubles), the frightening and abject other tends to dissolve. Real bodies in the development of discourses make a difference and feminist theology has found they also make a difference in the creation of theology; an incarnational theology should not be surprised by this but it still seems to be, and still wishes to control which bodies, if any, can be part of the debate. This may be a philosophical sticking point or even a psychological one, since the latter has demonstrated over the years that some men tend to be more cut off from their physical bodies than some women so, because men have created most theology to this time, it may not, then, be at all surprising that bodies pay little part in incarnational Christianity.

BIBLE, DOCTRINE, TRADITION AND "I WILL BE WHAT I WILL BE" (GEN. 32:32–3)!

Much traditional theology has accepted the more fixed interpretation of Genesis 32, which reads "I am what I am", an interpretation that has fed neatly into a Hellenistic reading of Christian theology. In this reading we have the God who is what he is and a world that has to fit or perish. There is no room here for otherness; as the history of Christianity has shown, the other has often paid the ultimate price for a reality it did not create. Black people, witches, homosexuals, indigenous folk, and transgendered and transsexual people did not place these identities on themselves; it was the dominant narrative of the Christian West that defined them and made them other. This otherness may, at times, have been exotic but it was always as Kristeva (1974) would say, the abject: that which could not be tolerated and was actually also unthinkable; that which had to be expelled from society and from thought categories.

As a feminist theologian I regret the day that the Jewish background of the Jesus movement lost out to the dualistic hierarchical thinking of Greek philosophy, which took the place of those who lived as though other realities were possible and even desirable. The dominant interpretations of Christianity have found it hard to think beyond the identity of baptism, which has acted almost as a mould for personality and ways of thinking, the notion underlying much Christian thought being that it is possible to train people to be good Christians, a designation that has often appeared to have very little variation within it. This worldview emanates from the view of an unchanging Alpha and Omega deity who is what he is and knows what he likes. Sociologists may well view this as the ultimate philosophical statement, the declaration of reality based on no empirical evidence at all. After all, hermeneutical attempts to recover the historical Jesus hardly count as science. Indeed, much of how people actually live is disregarded under the doctrine of original sin; if we live this way it must be bad!

Theologians, even the most liberal among us, tend to give a passing glance to the Bible and there is much material there to make the theological world other than it has been. Genesis 32 is just one example of where a different starting-point is possible. This passage does not actually read "I am what I am" but rather "I will be who I will be", and it is a statement made in the midst of a struggle, a fight between a named person (Jacob) and a stranger who appears terrible and even terrifying in "his" otherness, almost beyond all that humans may know, an angel. They exhaust one another in this struggle and the human has a wound inflicted that means he is unable to walk as he once did, but there is no real conclusion to this struggle and the name asked for by the human is as open-ended as the struggle "I will be who I will be": no commitment there to essence or newness but an open flow of becoming in answer to a question that sought fixedness. Far from setting anything in stone, least of all the God who is commonly understood to be the angel in this story, there are endless possibilities placed in the telling; there is agency but openness to the movement of becoming that is relational. Relational and far from simple, there is struggle and even menace in this becoming for the divine and the human. Threat is ever present and there is no satisfaction in the end. Indeed, we may even say there is no end. No name is ever given and the human is left physically changed: not crippled, but not able to walk as he once could. The encounter has actually meant that his relationship with his body has been altered and he is set a challenge to incorporate this into the future of physical landscapes. How is he to navigate his way now? The encounter with this stranger has left him less sure-footed and it may be argued more aware of his own body and environment, which now has to be considered when making a journey. Further, of course, Jacob also undergoes a name change, to Israel, a name signalling that he has striven with God and with men. It is something to ponder that this struggle with God and man resulted in a change of name: a change, perhaps, in how one sits in the world, given the importance names are felt to have in many cultures and particularly at the time of the story. Yet the angel, God, remains a form of becoming, not a fixed identity through a naming. In many ways this is a representative of what Rosi Braidotti calls nomadic subjectivity, because this becoming is capable of taking form and engaging within concrete contexts but remains fluid and untamed. There is a note of defiance and energy in the "I will be what I will be" that is not present in "I am what I am", which seems more resigned and static.

Braidotti (1994) has been used by feminist theologians because she puts the movement, the fluidity, back in this stale and stagnant thing we call doctrine and even tradition. She is not the fiddler on the roof declaring tradition to be the saving grace of all; rather, she is the strong voice calling for the resurrection and pilgrim people to regain their courage, to move and to become, rather than to cling on to the past as if it were a life raft in a stormy sea. Of course, the notion of subjectivity as a nomadic venture has appealed to women because it is precisely the so-called "nomadic" state of their bodies that has placed them under suspicion in theology, coming off badly when held up against the ever-unchanging God, the Alpha and Omega, the same yesterday, today and tomorrow. Women's bodies do not do this! And, of course, later on the early psychologists were to claim that neither did the female mind. Hence women may not be able to be holy but they could not be moral either: no surprise there for theologians, who had always claimed that to be the case. The obvious changes in a women's body and the apparent ability to change her mind and change the rules if people were being excluded and discriminated against was what the fathers of various descriptions found so distasteful and untrustworthy about women. Braidotti (*ibid.*) declared that nomadism is a way for women to develop and hold their subjectivity: she will be what she will be. What a gift this was to feminist theology!

While feminist Christology allowed praxis to take the place of essence and thus the notion that one may become rather than be statically made, the other biblical/doctrinal source that may help with this question of otherness is incarnation. An event, that of God fully inhabiting flesh, is understood within Christian doctrine to fundamentally change the world: to offer redemption from a fallen state to one of transformed grace. This doctrine has been fixed in stone after many attempts to understand it differently by the early Church and this fixing has meant that Greek metaphysics won the day and an event meant to transform has become a yardstick by which to measure worthy and unworthy lives and to judge those lives for eternity. In terms of the question of otherness, what it has done for the best part of 2,000 years is make humans and most certainly the created order the other in relation to the mono-revelation of the once and for all son of God. Of course, as the notion of human power became more prevalent in the creation of doctrine around this revelatory event, control of lives and knowledges became tighter. We have only to think of the persecution of scientists by the Church over the ages to realize that the mono-revelation did indeed create a mono-world. In case we believe this is now a thing of the past, we have decided in this book to consider the issue of mono-thinking in later chapters. A worldview was created that could not bear, indeed would not bear, any deviation from its placing one life as a central indicator of all lives and the workings of the universe itself. Bluntly put, everything was otherness and even the saved who may see God after death could never be more than "less other" at that happy event.

Luckily, of course, mono-dialogue, even when it is divine by decree, has cracks appearing in what we may call the underside of the received history. There have been many sects that have challenged the total otherness of God from the created order, for example the Shakers, but even in what may be called the mainstream, mysticism of various kinds appearing at different times of history has been a space in which even union with the divine has been experienced as possible. It has often been a radical space and one that needed careful navigation if its practitioners were to survive; not all avoided the flames though. It has to be noted that even mysticism has not always been viewed as challenging any essential doctrines about the otherness of the divine from the created order. However, in more recent times, with liberation and Queer theologies, different methods of interpretation have emerged that allow a very different picture to take shape: a picture in which Christians have experienced a oneness that at times appears not to have otherness within it yet at the same time allows for difference. Far from changing the mystic beyond recognition, it has sometimes been the case that the divine is changed into uncommon shapes and personas. All the edges seem flexible and it is even the Godhead itself that can be viewed as a nomadic subject within the experience of the mystic encounter: once more the "I will be who I will be" of more ancient times and not the solidified tyrant created under the pressure of Greek metaphysics. This will be explored later in the book.

Even the more traditional interpretations offer challenges for the notion of otherness as, for example, with the idea that Christ may in some form dwell within us. This indwelling is, of course, not quite the same as the oneness of which mystics speak since there is always a distance between self and the Christ within. It is not an uncommon phrase within Christian writing to read "not I but Christ who dwells in me". Here we see a concept more akin to giving hospitality to Christ within the self than a radical transformation of the self through this indwelling. What kind of stranger within might this be, then: not the self but not totally other perhaps? Augustine referred to the divine spark within, which he felt was all too often extinguished by selfish desire, so are we here faced with a notion that there is a real core self, an indwelling, that is known to us but often alien in our actions. This stranger within, which is such a deeply Christian concept, finds resonance with some postmodern thought. For example, Sara Ahmed (2000a) suggests that in recognizing one we do not know, we literally enflesh "the beyond". What kind of beyond, I wonder, is the stranger of the incarnation suggesting to us in the recognition of it? Certainly a beyond; indeed, it may well be argued, an infinite beyond. Not perhaps one of Greek metaphysics, as previously believed, but one of the endless possibilities of quantum thought, which is making its presence felt in theology.

The medieval women mystics offer us a challenging set of experiences in relation to the notion of otherness within. Women such as Margery Kempe (see Isherwood 2004) would have been under the influence of affective piety, a form of devotion much advocated by the Franciscans; this devotion encouraged the devotee to imagine themselves in the scenes from Christ's life, not just in their minds but also in their bodies. Margery was very good at this and attended the Virgin Mary in the stable when she was giving birth to Jesus. As a mother of fourteen, Margery has empathy for the young girl and brings her mulled wine and soft cloth in which to wrap the child. There is nothing too out of the usual there, perhaps, but, as we shall see later, Margery and many of the other women from this period crossed gender, sex and material metaphysical realities in their affective or mystical devotion. Many paid with their life, which tells us a great deal about how important Christianity has historically felt it is to limit gender and sexuality through very clear-cut divides and lines. This theologian wonders at the power of both: that a religion fears the transgressions; further, of course, that a religion of incarnation does not abandon itself to the full potential of incarnational thought.

Some of the possible reasons for this have already been mentioned, namely the imposition of Greek dualistic metaphysics at an early point of Christian development. However, what is now opening up as an area of consideration is the mentality, not just culturally, of the people who engaged in the development of Christian doctrine and tradition. The great fathers of psychology have not been a great help to women until relatively recently, with the likes of Freud, perhaps, just endorsing the fears of the Church Fathers that women have no morality and are more easily swayed by fleshy/earthly/material concerns such as children and fair play. Even psychologist of child development Lawrence Kohlberg declared that women can never reach the highest peak of morality because they are indeed more programmed than men for the home and domestic morality, which in itself is quite inferior to the morality needed for the world, which requires action carried out from dispassionate and disconnected notions of duty and absolute right. Of course, there have been other views expressed by people such as Carol Gilligan (1982), Jessica Benjamin (1983) and Nancy Chodorow (1979), who have pointed out that what they call a more relational psychology in women in fact has benefits for society and should not be viewed as just fit for the home. Their work has had an impact in feminist theology, which has itself developed a more relational understanding in Christology. However, in recent years the psychotherapist and artist Bracha Ettinger (2006) has suggested an even more daring notion of relational psychology, which she places in what she calls the "matrixial borderspace". Some work in feminist theology has been done on her ideas but the full impact of this work if taken seriously has not been explored and I hope to bring her insights to parts of this book (see Chapter 3). It may be the case that she can highlight notions of otherness in those little explored words of the Virgin Mother, "blessed in the fruit of my womb". Words that may, in the light of matrixial borderspaces, remove Mary from the place of passive acceptance to the ground of empowered radical otherness through that real, yet ignored, creative borderspace.

The authors have always suspected that a fruitful and challenging conversation may be possible between sociology and theology that does not rely on the co-opting of one by the other. We shall see!

1. OTHERNESS, OUTSIDERS AND LARGER TENTS

This chapter begins with some examples of mundane otherness and its role in interaction. The mechanism here that relates selves to others has been described by various symbolic interactionists. Charles Cooley (1972), for example, coined the phrase "looking-glass self" to describe ways in which our sense of self is clearly related to the perceptions and reciprocal actions of others; indeed, we develop a "social self" almost completely oriented to the real or imagined actions of others. George Herbert Mead developed a cluster of concepts, first splitting the "I" and the "me" (a more reflexive and more objective notion, respectively, of the self), and went on to describe the general mechanism for learning how to orient oneself to the actions of others. One "takes the role of the other" in imaginative play, assuming a reciprocity of perspectives so that if we can experience a situation in a particular way, we can assume it must be experienced like that for others too. Others with most contact with us (both quantitatively and qualitatively) can become "significant others", an idea that lives on in the currently fashionable talk of "role models". As our experience grows, we can construct a "generalized other" to orient ourselves towards the actions of strangers: this, in turn, gets incorporated back into the "me". It is easy to see functionalist assumptions here too that the levels and dimensions will be smoothly integrated.

SCHUTZ'S "STRANGER"

Alfred Schutz's (1971) famous essay on the stranger describes very well the disorientation that can arise when encountering others. All individuals have a stock of knowledge that guides their own action and helps to interpret the actions of others. These tend to be deeply established in particular communities, to such an extent that they are taken for granted, and they have been maintained over generations. Newcomers to those communities experience a double shock: their own stocks of knowledge and recipes seem inadequate for the first time, and the actions of those in the host communities become problematic for the first time. Schutz says that these problems do not present just as a matter of temporary social dislocation that can be fairly rapidly overcome after a period of suitable resocialization. What is involved is a whole problem of knowledge and how to reflect on it.

Considerable changes in orientation are required for immigrants. They have to abandon the "natural attitude", which has governed personal and social action unproblematically in the past, and adopt what looks much more like the "scientific attitude", a matter of attempting to become detached, to adopt an impersonal centre for the deployment of knowledge, and to be prepared to subject common sense to new tests of adequacy. Schutz is curiously unhelpful about how the shift from common sense to scientific attitude can take place, in fact, here and elsewhere in his work, and in this essay he seems to offer us only the metaphor of "a leap".

Understanding is possible in the Schutzian framework, which draws upon Husserlian phenomenology. Strangers are likely to find themselves in social situations with individuals from the host community in which shared understandings can develop. Schutz insists on the importance of face-to-face communication here, since such encounters can deliver a sense of sharing subjective time or duration. As a result, each participant can see how typical chains of action are established, since participants can be observed responding to objects and a common environment, and the actions of the host individuals. Phenomenological processes are invoked , sharing objects in horizons and generating common thematizations based on them, while making reasonable inferences that if an individual appears to act like oneself then there is a suitable "reciprocity of perspectives". As an aside, the process seems remarkably similar to what Ettinger describes as "matrixial" understandings (Ettinger 2007), although she emphasizes the presymbolic dimensions.

One application might have been the integrationist policy towards race relations that dominated post-war Britain. The idea was that by preventing segregation of jobs and housing by law, immigrants and hosts would be forced to mix and, eventually, share duration and develop intersubjective understandings. There are studies that suggest that this policy worked, and that face-to-face contact provided many more paths to understanding than, say, the indirect knowledge of immigrants that was available to residents of predominantly white areas, provided mostly by television coverage. It might be interesting to revisit the issue. However, social mixing is by no means easy to engineer from above. There have been, for example, attempts to engineer limited forms of contact such as sports facilities that permit the genders to share subjective time together. Here, a number of serious barriers appear to remain, including a number of sexist discourses or hegemonic-masculine ideologies and practices (see Elling *et al.* 2003).

For most of us, most of the time, we are drawing upon a stock of knowledge and a system of relevances of which we are barely aware. They serve, as we saw, as a set of recipes for action and interaction, or, to use a more modern analogy, programs. There are opportunities even in ordinary life for us to develop "we-relationships", or even "thou-relationships", where the other is treated as a fully developed subject. "We-relationships", in particular, develop in social relations of intimacy with a great deal of shared subjective experience.

However, most of the other apparent individuals in our social world are outside such relationships. They are "typifications", and here Schutz wants to refer deliberately to the work of Weber, who suggested that the "ideal type" was the basis of sociological method as well. The term has been much debated and discussed but we can characterize it as a theoretically informed model of the other person. Unlike the conventional, positivist sociological models, which are often statistical or empirical generalizations, though, Weber insisted on the "ideal" quality as well, referring to a theoretical and philosophical judgement about what is essential. Schutz (1972) actually has done a great deal to extend unclarified Weber's conceptions of social action, using phenomenological terminology.

Returning to the personal level, however, individuals in the naturalistic attitude operate by allocating other places in sets radiating out from ourselves at the centre of our subjective world. The distance from ourselves reflects the degree of anonymity that we use in our typifications. Thus relatives might be understood in terms of fairly detailed typifications, while the postal service operative (to use one of Schutz's actual examples) can be understood in terms of a basic minimal and undetailed form of typification: we only need enough to know about our postal service operative to be able to regulate the minimum interaction with them every morning.

Bourdieu's more sociological contributions are in some ways more radical. For example, Bourdieu wants to refer to an unconscious "habitus" instead of Schutz's sedimented stock of knowledge, implying definite social organization (see e.g. Bourdieu 1993, 2000). The habitus arises from initial socialization and manifests itself not only in thought but in typical ways of behaving and conceiving of bodies. One result is that it is extremely difficult to reflect upon the impact of the habitus in describing more conscious activities, principally, for Bourdieu (1986), matters of social "distinction", including and excluding others. These appear to be spontaneous, taken-for-granted, naturalized. Even the most acutely reflexive philosophers, such as Kant, have only rediscovered in thought categories based on these unconscious perceptions and judgments (*ibid.*). No doubt, if we wished to be more aggressive in this discussion with theology, we might suggest that the categories of theology are similarly grounded, and, no doubt, theologians would reply that this work is typically reductionist and "sociologistic".

It is undoubtedly true that much traditional theology relies on a limited stock of (not even knowledge) belief. It is, after all, 150–170 years ago that methods were accepted for examining the Bible, methods that suggested that the words within it were not necessarily literally true. This is a very short period of time for the more conservative Christians, and those of a less conservative nature but who find that the world described within biblical literature serves their position and sense of themselves (usually white Western males), to wake up to new possibilities and realities. The claims of sociologists may appear reductionist but, when addressing certain types of theology, they have a truth in that traditional theology feels unable to move out of a tight circle of what it understands as revelation. As more contemporary theologies are demonstrating, these revelations have served the powerful more often and more completely than they have ever served the marginalized. Further, they have also served to create and expel "others", those whose only crime is that they ask questions of the revelation, those received knowledges and beliefs that may upset the solid, fossilized and power-laden structures that have sprung up from them. This has been demonstrated by many feminist and liberation theologians who examine the way in which religion has played a large and, at times, motivating role in colonization. There was never any intention of dialogue with the received knowledges and wisdoms of the colonized; their understandings were simply labelled primitive, marginalized, at times punishable by death, and wiped out.

Recent work by Marion Grau (2012) carefully outlines how this strategy was not simply one of ignorance, as has often been said, but was intimately tied in with economics and greed. Many indigenous religions had a high regard for the ecological resources of their lands and an intimate relationship with those resources and creatures. In order that capitalism, the bedfellow of colonizing religion, may exploit and abuse the world's resources, those religions that protected them and gave humans a more realistic perception of their place in the world had to be marginalized and those "primitives" who followed them made to be "other" in the most grotesque ways (*ibid.*: 15). We know that in France, up to the 1960s, human zoos were a great attraction, with the "primitives" being on display for the civilized to be both thrilled and disgusted by them (Chrisafis 2011). It is becoming clearer in theology that the unconscious habitus therein has not always led to the redemption of the world but rather destruction of civilizations, religions and environments on a massive scale.

Feminist theology also has to guard itself from this trap. Having started life with very destabilizing and, therefore, apparently new questions based in different knowledge bases, that of lived experience and the body, there is always a danger of feminist theology falling back on received orthodoxies. The most obvious and constantly challenged one is essentialist in nature, when many feminist theologians argue for the unique experience and even nature of women. In the early days this assumed that woman was a single category but there is now recognition that such a stance, which underpinned the notion of global sisterhood, was at best naive. The tension, however, still remains as a category of women is needed in order to have a feminist critique, but one should always guard against this itself fossilizing into received wisdom. We discuss this issue in later chapters.

Bourdieu suggests that the contents of the stock of knowledge in question can be understood as functioning as if they were stocks of capital, hence the term "cultural capital". This clearly introduces a dimension of social inequality, especially a notion of social class, since cultural capital is distributed as unequally as economic capital. Those from elite backgrounds acquire more, and far more useful, stocks of cultural capital.

In one of his most famous works, Bourdieu (1986) suggested that these stocks underpin organized systems of tastes and values, or "aesthetics". To be very brief, the "popular" aesthetic judges the value of cultural activities on the basis of whether or not they deliver immediate emotional reward and permit immediate participation. It is no accident that the "high" aesthetic defines itself in opposition to these values, and stresses instead the delights of cool, detached and rather academic considerations of matters such as form rather than content. There are also correspondingly different stances towards the body and pleasures of the flesh. Bourdieu's empirical work in France suggests that these two aesthetic dispositions are evident in the differing tastes expressed by people from different social classes in cultural areas such as diet, exercise, film, music and sport. There is a current study of modern Britain that attempts to replicate some of this work and has found problems (Bennett *et al.* 2008). The issue of the "cultural omnivore", able to cross boundaries, is also still much discussed (see Warde *et al.* 2007).

Bourdieu further suggests that these differences are played out in education as well, and that those from non-elite backgrounds are being judged against the high aesthetic and, hardly surprisingly, found wanting (Bourdieu 1988). The judgements in education turn on matters such as accent, written style and "bodily hexis", including the extent to which one feels comfortable in one's body. This has obvious implications for the ways in which non-traditional students are treated as "others" by academic hierarchies. The process operates at the unconscious level so that structures of judgment underpin and inform in unrealized ways more formal systems of assessment and grading, for example. Bourdieu is also a pessimist about the possibilities of reform. The accumulation of cultural capital enabling one to move away from the popular aesthetic is inevitably a slow and painful business (Bourdieu 1986). Even those who have acquired some insights, say through university education, are liable to remain socially marginal, rather as in the figure of the autodidact; they can never deploy the high aesthetic fluently and apparently naturally, especially when new cultural developments require judgement. It is easy to see how judgements like this are connected to the reproduction of social class differences: there is a constant process of defining self against others in terms of social class, and social-class dynamics drive processes of othering, and constantly renew and energize them.

It is possible to see the same processes at work with the other main social divisions too. Much work suggests that masculine hegemony is constantly instantiated in all sorts of areas where the genders meet, especially, perhaps, in sport (see e.g. Burgess *et al.* 2003; Collins [2002] also shows how women can resist). Dana Berkowitz (2006) shows how both ultramasculine and ultrafeminine "fronts" are constructed in the rather extreme example of a sex shop as customers encounter each other. We might have an account of a relational process of local solidarity and exclusion, a micropolitics of otherness.

We can expect the process of differentiation to affect intercultural differences as well. Bourdieu himself began life as an anthropologist, trying to explain the dynamics of the Algerian or Kabylian habitus (actually, a cluster of habituses). One of his best examples turns on the understanding of the calendar for Kabylians, as a contrast with Western rational notions (Bourdieu 2000). The very "otherness" of this understanding confounded anthropological attempts to subdue it with academic categories.

SIMMEL'S "STRANGER"

Georg Simmel's ([1908] 1950) essay on the stranger is only brief, but it encapsulates many of the issues raised so far. Simmel also refers to immigrants and their relations to host societies, referring to the Jews in Germany as examples. The social relations between immigrants and hosts are an interesting combination of "distance and nearness, indifference and involvement" (*ibid.*: 404). Rather like Schutz, Simmel points out that immigrants can never fully feel at home since they do not share the deeper cultural and social commitments and beliefs of their hosts, but they get much closer than visitors do. The good side of this situation is that strangers are able to pursue a more objective and detached stance, and this has economic benefits (e.g. permitting trade), and social benefits (e.g. being able to avoid partisan positions). The bad side arises from suspicions of lack of commitment, disloyalty, even subversion from within.

Simmel argues that these combinations of intimacy and distance are actually widespread in modern societies as well, although possibly to a lesser extent. Even lovers are aware that their relationship is both special and unique to themselves and also part of "something more general ... [applying to] an indeterminate number of others" (*ibid.*: 408). There is a growing sense that the general is becoming more important than the

27

special and unique. Simmel suggests that immigrants know this better than anyone else.

We discuss the issue of the modern asylum seeker later, but there is some sociological work on relative movements within social systems by "natives". Earl Hopper (1981) examines the socially mobile, who have come from social class and status origins that mark them as other, and who now find themselves in closer contact with those from another social class or status group. It is not surprising to find that social mobility can bring a considerable number of tensions and social problems based around challenges to identity and belonging. Hopper noticed a feeling of "relative deprivation" and dissatisfaction, which was far more marked when individuals came into contact with members of adjacent social groups (*ibid.*). We do not commonly compare ourselves with the life and conditions of the aristocracy, for example, but find comparisons with similar professions much more likely to trigger dissatisfaction and discontent.

More recent studies of social mobility through higher education suggest similar findings. Diane Reay (2003) and others have found that female working-class students entering university exhibit considerable self-doubt and anxiety, feeling that they may have to leave one social class but never fully belong to another. This restricts their ambitions in their choice of university, and may explain the considerable self-doubt that affects many such students: the "impostor syndrome", where working-class students constantly worry that they will be "found out".

THE CONTEXT: MODERNITY

It is possible to go from here to briefly outline some of the themes that will be considered in later chapters. There are many social critics who argued that advanced capitalism or modernity seriously erodes a sense of self or identity. This might well provide the impulses to define oneself constantly against others in the micropolitical everyday activity we have been describing.

The links are clear in Simmel, for example, as has been hinted in the remarks about relations of distance and nearness in society generally. David Frisby's (1984) excellent brief commentary argues that these themes characterize Simmel's sociology in general, which turns on the relations between individualization and group memberships. In particular, patterns of "sociation" in modern society were becoming dominated by the peculiarities of the money system. Money is the most abstract of mediations between people. It does encourage the development of individualism (individual "selves", to revert to the terms of this specific discussion) by helping break the old patterns of dependency (of vassals to feudal lords, apprentices to guildmasters). Most readers will be aware of economic issues surrounding immigration in Western countries, and the primarily monetary way in which the integration of immigrants is discussed. But money also reduces human relations to quantitative and calculating ones, to excessively abstract and indifferent forms. As Frisby argues, Simmel's work bears a clear relation to the better-known works of Durkheim and Weber on modernity, and anticipates the rediscovery of the "young Marx" on alienation, despite important differences with each of these "founding parents".

To summarize these founding approaches very briefly, Durkheim (see Lukes 1975) saw modernity as offering an increased sense of individualism as the old "mechanical" forms of solidarity eroded. In those older forms, conformity was so strongly enforced that individual selves virtually did not exist; the only alternative to full integration into the group was exile and social, if not literal, death. These older forms encounter unsustainable challenges as new societies are encountered and as complexity and diversity increase within territorial boundaries. Developing a new form of solidarity that would encompass the new individualism would be both difficult and urgent. Durkheim saw excessive individualism as a social pathology, ending in "anomie" ("normlessness") or egotism (since social constraints are the only ones that affect human beings, their absence brings insatiable self-centred activity). The solution lay in developing a new level of "sacred" (i.e. indubitable) values and a new set of institutions to support and embed them. This led to Durkheim (1961) advocating a new cultural form of "moral education" in the new state schools of France, among other reforms.

Weber's work is equally well known and picks up on a common concern for the decline of traditional community and its replacement by modern work-like organizations. In Weber's terms, "scientific rationality" dominates social life, replacing older forms of traditional action but also earlier notions of "value-rationality", based on some conception of an ultimate good life (such as Christian ones). Secularization and "disenchantment" ensue as economic and cultural developments embed scientific or calculative rationality. Cultural developments included the paradoxical development of puritanical Protestantism. That Weber disapproved of these trends is apparent in his phrase "the iron cage" to describe future society (Weber 1985). He was also classically pessimistic about the chances of revolutionary resistance despite the occasional surfacing of trends such as charismatic movements.

The work has triggered considerable debate about secularization especially. Current debates in particular consider the rise of various kinds of religious fundamentalism as seemingly integral to modernity after all. In an equally well-known series of debates, George Ritzer (1993) has used Weberian terms such as rationalization and disenchantment to grasp the "McDonaldization of society", sparking off more controversies, which we shall come to when we discuss consumerism in Chapter 4.

To complete this quick review, Marxist analysis of modern, capitalist, societies is also clearly relevant. In the 1960s the "early writings" were rediscovered and translated into English, and they contained discussions of alienation and communism that provoked much discussion. For Marx, people were alienated principally by capitalist institutions such as modern labour, markets and commodities, all of which were then quite new, despite their superficial similarities with forms that had gone before. It was misleading to think of capitalist labour as just work, for example, since work was the general human tendency to interact with the world and with each other for common benefit: labour in capitalism was quite different, involving selling (one sense of alienating) labour for a specific purpose (the production of commodities for exchange and of surplus value). Labourers did not own the fruits of their labour, nor control the production process, and labour itself was a mechanical matter of rational machine-like operations coordinated by some other agency. The only non-alienated society would be communism, with its attractive utopia of proper unspecialized work and its common ownership of capital.

However, Marxist remedies – the abolition of capitalist institutions and their replacement with communist ones – are notoriously idealistic, in several senses. Social revolution might have been imminent in 1848, but Marx himself realized that the moment had passed in 1851, and that social polarization was less likely in modern states (Marx 1852). Social revolution seems even less likely from the current position, promising developments in developing countries notwithstanding. The idealism might lie at the very heart of the concept of communism too, with its view that no further alienating, or at least disempowering, political forces would persist after the defeat of capital: feminists at least would be able to suggest an alternative view. Finally, there is the idealist notion of reconciliation or reunification at the heart of the notion: that it will be possible, come the great day, for all divisions to disappear, for objects to be fully reunited with subjects, selves with others, individuals with communities, personal goals with social ones, for the state to wither away, and for social life to become "transparent".

The founding critical insights have been discussed, modified, combined and applied to more recent conditions. The rationalization, commodification and reification of advanced capitalism have been identified by a number of Marxist critics as having highly personal effects, often after drawing upon Freud. Theodor Adorno et al. (1964) suggest that, in Freudian terms, ego would be minimized at the expense of a socially institutionalized superego. Weak egos would lead to a constant search for some direction, some strong paternal authority, especially for those whose real fathers had already become victims of powerlessness and frustration. The result was the development of "the authoritarian personality", with its vulnerability to strong leaders and vigorous action, including the demonization of outsiders of various kinds.

In the same tradition, but more recently, Christopher Lasch (1982) argues how the same kind of powerlessness arises from the domination of social and personal life by big business and rationalized organizations. This time, the dominant personality type is the narcissist, with an extremely weak, almost absent, sense of core self, which has to be constantly buttressed by self-centred actions including endless consumerism and the inability to form committed long-term social relations with others. Apparently, Freud regarded narcissists as peculiarly difficult cases to treat because there was no "core" reflexive self to mobilize in order to undertake the analysis.

In a much less pessimistic way, and without the same commitment to Marxist approaches, recent analyses of "risk society" or "second modernity" (Beck 1992; *Journal of Consumer Culture* 2001) offer similar analysis. There is something about modern societies that produces flawed and limited individuals who find an emptiness and powerlessness at the heart of their senses of self and identity. This analysis touches upon classic themes in social theory, referring to the decline of the traditional social bonds of class, family and community. Individuals are liberated from those bonds but find themselves adrift. Other bonds might develop to reintegrate people, but these are likely to be general and abstract forms of relationship, based on commodification, a rationalized division of labour or the market. These mechanisms are particularly unsuitable for the social, cultural and personal dimensions of social life, however.

For Giddens (1991), the gap is met with the growth of new sources of expertise, including lifestyle guides and consumer organizations (and sociology). For Ulrich Beck (1992), these are inadequate still, especially in dealing with the big threats to personal security: the emergence of new, deadly and seemingly unmanageable risks, like the threat of eco catastrophe, new diseases and epidemics, new outbreaks of war and terrorism. The problem for Beck is that no one trusts the usual experts any more, probably for good reason because the risks really are new. Individuals are therefore thrown back on their own resources, or rather those offered by the market, for advice on lifestyle. Although not discussed by Beck explicitly, it would not be surprising to find that these resources include the old familiar superstitious distrust of others as responsible for threats from outside.

ONLINE OTHERS

The development of the internet provides an excellent case study of current developments, where technology seems to have raised the same paradoxical possibilities for self and other. The internet probably developed initially as a military form of communication, then an elite academic form, and is clearly congruent with advanced capitalism and the requirement for global communication. It has enabled the development of new forms of capitalist enterprise, including the rapid transfer of finance in what can be called the "weightless economy" or the "economics of nothing" (Ritzer 2007). As with other globalized developments, rich anglophone countries have dominated so far.

Other innovations include the curious ways in which "free" services can still produce economic value, pioneered by internet companies, possibly because the stock market will buy shares in a company on the expectation that it will, one day, charge for its products or make money from its extensive customer databases. Yet there are also really "free" services, provided without charge to the user. These include "open source" software developed by whole groups of coders and available for download: products such as Linux are now serious competitors for Microsoft software. There is also participatory software, like that used to exchange content on the internet. This is cheap and easy to use and it has spawned worldwide take-up (except for those on the nasty end of the "digital divide").

On the one hand, being able to access resources and people worldwide has led to a considerable growth in the potential to develop one's sense of self, and the scope for self-expression. In formal educational terms, for example, it is now possible to access books, electronic journal articles, conference papers and specially designed courses, even in elite universities, to an unprecedented level. No other medium can offer what looks like instant access to a range of materials from Japanese artwork to images of the Dead Sea Scrolls at the click of a mouse button. Many famous academics also have their own websites, enabling a degree of contact with them and their work that was unheard of before, even where earlier and similar technologies were available, such as telephones and faxes. On certain discussion boards and lists, it is possible to actually witness academics in debate with each other and to join in. Sometimes, unlike in face-to-face meetings, participants are eager to contribute their point of view and their questions.

There is a specific possibility of becoming more self-aware that feminist thinkers have developed in particular. Donna Haraway (2003), above all, has done much to argue that the capacity to develop an online avatar provides an unprecedented opportunity to develop and explore one's self (see also Land 2006). An avatar can take on whatever shape, age, gender or physique is desired and, in the interaction between avatars, new possibilities of selfhood develop. In the most obvious case, women can interact with other people while keeping their gender secret, and men can go online as women in order to share something at least of the everyday experiences of women in interaction. Haraway wants to push the argument to suggest that even the boundaries between human beings, machines and animals are far more permeable online than they are in "real life", hence her phrase "cyborg society". There are also multiplayer online role-playing games, and online communities such as *Lambda MOO* (Miah 2000) or *Second Life*. If *Second Life* develops voice-activated chat, as seems quite likely, interaction with a wide range of others while remaining as anonymous as one chooses promises to offer considerable room for easy experimentation, including being able to literally "take the role of the other" and live with it for a while.

Of course, these wonderful opportunities also feature considerable restriction. Online communication is still constrained by the familiar conventions of everyday life. Whether women actually do experiment with their identities or simply reproduce them is unresolved (Herring 2003). Explorations exist of sexuality and sexual display using interactive technology to break the conventions of pornography, especially the role of the male gaze (Kibby & Costello 2001), but these experiments are tiny and insignificant compared with the explosion of commercially produced pornography. At the most detailed level, electronic chat is still rather clumsy and slow. Sometimes the software hesitates or interjects; perhaps the most amusing example concerns online sexually explicit chat that was interrupted by error messages (Marshall 2003).

As a result, being part of an online community is a curious experience. One can learn about all sorts of new relationships and interactions but at the price of having to hide behind an avatar. Liberating possibilities coexist with tedious conventional requests for personal information, classically "ASL?" (age, sex and location), before people will interact. *Lambda MOO* was the scene of what some participants describe as "online rape" (Miah 2000). *Second Life* is capitalist, although some participants were able to organize a virtual demonstration outside the offices of some of the wealthy residents.

There are some implications particularly brought into focus by discussions of online interaction that have been lurking in discussions of sociological theory for some time. The internet is clearly a network and as one uses this network one encounters different possibilities for self and identity. As societies increase in complexity, so the possibilities for developing different partial selves also increase, a point made particularly well by Simmel in fact. This is also a major theme of poststructuralist theory, of course, with its notions of "nomadic subjectivity" (see Deleuze & Guattari 1984), with a destabilized self occupying a number of more concrete positions.

One issue in sociology has been whether or not any "core identity" remains: whether the modern or postmodern self is still a unified entity beneath its various appearances or whether it has been truly distributed across a long series of options. Traditional social theory might want to argue that social class, gender or ethnicity remain as core identities, but the grounds for such an argument seem to have changed nevertheless, as the substantial discussions about the relevance of social class in modern Britain have indicated (Pakulski & Waters [1996] offer a useful summary). One possibility is that these core identities remain crucial but mostly as a focus for political activity, the result of a discourse, rather than for any essential theoretical reason. Political activists of various kinds insist that certain identities remain somehow privileged: "sexual difference" feminists are perhaps the best example (discussed in the next chapter). However, other identities have their claims to privilege too, as we shall see in the Conclusion.

THE STRANGER AT THE GATES

Feminist theology is perhaps indeed the stranger at the gates and in that sense highlights much of the tension with traditional theology and churches in relation to the issue of the "other", the stranger. Classically hospitality and welcoming the stranger, the other, have been central concepts in both theology and Church doctrine, but the reality has been that the ways in which both are constructed has acted as a comprehensive way to both create and then exclude and even eliminate the other. While modern-day feminist theologians have not, to date, been put to the flames, many of their female forebears have been, as have many forms of "other"; the word faggot is said to originate from the use of homosexual men as tinder to get the flames going to burn heretics and witches. This said, it remains true that Christian theology likes to assume a position of hospitality within its theology and doctrine.

In ancient civilization, of course, hospitality was viewed as a pillar of morality and in Israel, care for the vulnerable stranger was a sign that they, Israel, were people of God. The story in Genesis 18:1, where three strangers arrive at the tent of Abraham and Sarah, has a Christian interpretation as a Trinitarian visitation while Jewish interpretation sees the strangers at best as angels signalling that the hospitality given emphasizes the presence of God and promise of blessing. Central to their welcome, of course, was food and drink and this was a theme that was carried through by the early Church Fathers when they considered hospitality. For John Chrysostom, Jerome and others, the belief that Jesus had relied on the bread of others was central to their understanding of hospitality as giving to those who could not give in return and thus was also an important signifier of transcending status boundaries (Pohl 1999: 9). Further, feeding another is a very basic way of recognizing them as fellow humans and offering them some dignity. The Fathers argued that the Gospels themselves were centrally concerned with the notion of *philoxenia*, the love of strangers, and therefore demand that we always orientate ourselves towards the stranger as a way of being Christian. This picture is further complicated by the idea that Christ, while being a stranger reliant on the hospitality of others, was also the ultimate host, giving himself without limit through the Eucharist, another shared meal that signalled the reality of God's kingdom among people as they, in a sense, become one with the host and those partaking with them. This notion has very deep cultural roots. Food and eating have never been simple matters of satisfying hunger, but have always, like other matters of life and death, carried meaning beyond their biological basics. It is this highly symbolic, ritualistic and religious meaning of food that makes it a theological matter. When we look back we see that in primitive society the act of eating symbolized the partaker being eaten by the community and, through sharing food, becoming a companion (*com panis*, shared bread), an equal in that society. This simple and basic act, then, carries historically a great deal of significance; at its heart is a notion of sharing, not exchange, in which subjects are born through the powerful symbolism of food (Falk 1994: 20). Pasi Falk argues that although one became a member of a group self through being eaten by the community and sharing with them, there always remained "an oral type of self-autonomy" (*ibid.*: 21, quoting Parin 1978); there was subjectivity and group identity in harmony through the primitive understanding of food as a symbol. He goes on to argue that with the collapse of the primitive systems, eating changed from an open to a closed activity: from the notion of an eating community to that of a bounded individual eating. In other words, there was a huge shift from food and eating being an inclusive community activity to it becoming one that began and ended at the edges of the individual. In this way, eating and what was eaten lost their communal symbolism and became signifiers of the worth, merit and general status of the individual; they became a sign of the narrowly defined standing of the bounded in individual self. Falk points out that in the nineteenth century, communal eating reappeared as a sign of utopia; that is, for a short while it regained its equalitarian communal symbolism.

The shift in understanding of the symbolic nature of food leads to a crucial shift in the place of the individual in relation to others. There is much more emphasis on the bounded self, which, in terms of Christian theology, can be understood as personal salvation: the relationship between an ethereal God and the self-defined individual. In broader terms, this individual sense also disconnects people from the wider community and leaves them vulnerable, indeed primed, to be genocidal consumers, by which I mean their bounded selves need things and the cost is not counted; there is no "eating community" to which they are attached and so only a bounded self to be served.

Falk suggests that "the decline of the ritual significance of the meal manifests itself not only in the shift from food to words but also in the informalization of the reciprocal speech acts – into conversation in the modern sense of the term" (1994: 34). Falk's understanding may shed light on the differences between Protestant and Roman Catholic meal significance; Protestant theology moves the saving significance from the communal meal to the word in the book – a speech act, not an embodied act of community. This is reflected in the space that the Reformers made available for the welcome of hospitality. In emphasizing the value of ordinary life, the Reformers also undermined the mystery that had been part of the Christian understanding of hospitality and welcome. Also, of course, the transformation into one community through sharing was replaced by acceptance of the interpretation of the word, which meant that those with different interpretations were not welcome. This is not to suggest that the Eucharist community prior to the Reformation had been one big welcoming family, but rather that at the symbolic level something significant was changed and with it the notion of welcome strangers and "others".

As Chrysostom and Jerome realized, hospitality can be an act of resistance not just to status but also politically in a broader sense. Strangers are often vulnerable and sometimes by the very act of welcome we open a new vision for what society may be. An act of welcome can be a small gesture signalling a world of transforming possibilities. Some contemporary theologians have begun to understand this in the broad political sense and have linked it to their Eucharistic understanding of a meal where all are welcome.

Monica Hellwig (1992) has argued that the way in which we view the "hunger of the world" should always be within the context of the Last Supper, which was, as she sees it, the foundational meal of Christianity. The context for it was one of oppression and the act of communal eating was a commitment of ultimate fellowship of the kind that would be embodied through these continued acts of eating and radical praxis. We see many instances in the biblical accounts of Jesus and his followers challenging boundaries, even within their difficult political situation, through the company they kept and the bread they broke with that company. It is a traditional theological understanding to see connections between the feeding of the five thousand and the Last Supper. The former is seen to be a precursor to the latter, which is understood to be the ultimate food. I wish to see the connection lying in a radical commitment to feeding the world when we eat from that Eucharistic table. We are compelled to demand fairer production policies, better quality food, more equitable distribution and enough food on all tables. This resistance to world hunger through profit-driven food distribution and production can be where we situate ourselves in acts of hospitality, not just the people in front of us but the whole world present at our table, and in the justice-making we attempt to create, and in acts of relationality beginning at our table.

L. Shannon Jung (2004) believes that we have forgotten the purpose behind the blessing of food and have been satisfied with an impoverished appreciation of eating. For Jung there are very embodied consequences that stem from this impoverishment. Two worldviews emerge: one is holistic and revolves around relationships and sharing while the other is business orientated and involves slicing life up into bits (*ibid.*: 8). In this way, food and eating are performative acts displaying the Christian life and the political side of hospitality within it. Jung here picks up another aspect of hospitality and eating, which is that both the host and the stranger are equally opened to one another in this intimate act; neither has a superior position.

This is a point that Chrysostom was at pains to emphasize: there should be no pride in giving but rather humility.

The welcoming of new communities rather than individuals, of course, presents new challenges. Hospitality is an important first step, but we have to guard against it simply being a generous invitation into one's own home, that is to say, the edges of "one's own home" become the defining boundary of the hospitality; our home needs to be more flexible than normally envisaged. In addition, in these postcolonial days, welcoming certainly does not call for assimilation programmes. What seems to be presented to us is what Paul Ricoeur would call a reading of "rupture". New communities bring with them new ideas and cultures as well as challenges to existing economic systems and the "normality of life". It is not the job of the theologian to heal the rupture, far from it, but it is the theological task to engage with the rupture, to walk with the interruption of everyday life in order to bring to birth new interpretations of life "as is", new ways to express faith and to see everyday reality.

Feminist theology has pointed to the Prologue of John's Gospel (as we have seen), where we are told that God pitched his tent among us. It can be argued, then, that what Christians have declared as the incarnate God is one who has no solid foundations and is not dug in to one position alone, as Church doctrine has often declared. Indeed, using the life of Jesus as an example, feminist theology has said that this god among us in community/God in society became the Messiah, the hope of freedom, through walking with, being affected by, marginalized communities and individuals. This could best be fuelled, one may argue, through the constant engagement with the stranger, the strange, the unfamiliar in which one is asked to expand the tent, to see more of the divine incarnate rather than incorporating the diverse manifestation of the divine into the narrow confines of one's own limited, firm, foundational world.

As receivers of diasporic peoples, not one exodus but many, the opportunity is here for multiple trespasses over our own philosophical, political and economic boundaries. Hospitality, in this context, means changing systems that exclude or that attempt to eradicate difference. More than anything it calls for face-to-face engagement since ideas alone do not change anything and they run the risk of losing real people; the idea replaces the flesh and blood, a place that incarnational theology can never justify occupying. Robert Schreiter considers it the duty of poets and prophets to "capture the rhythms and contours of a community's experience [the poet] and have insight into the ways the community may move [the prophet]" (1998: 28). I would argue it is also the very lifeblood of the incarnational theologian to create theology from this place, so ever new and changing theology, theology in the ruptures that strangers make in our safe worlds.

The twentieth and twenty-first centuries have seen massive population disruptions, perhaps on a scale never known before, and countries are called to be hospitable, but often the response is far from open. Jean Vanier tells us welcome is a sign that we are not afraid, that we do not cling to our own comfort at the expense of others and that we are not insecure or spiritually dead (Vanier 1989: 275, cited in Pohl 1999: 140). It also, of course, calls for the embrace of diversity. What we find though is mistrust and governments that wish us to believe that recent and not so recent newcomers to our country wish to harm us. Christine Pohl warns that even hospitality, however, can lend itself to power-play by keeping the stranger/guest in a position of need, either wilfully or through over-protective hospitality (Pohl 1999: 120). These dual aspects of deliberate stirring up of fear of the stranger or the developing of need in the newcomer are aspects of how we treat people that emerge from deep-seated aspects of ourselves, places that even centuries of Christian hospitality rhetoric have not managed to reach.

THE STRANGER WITHIN

The Christian is always, or should always be, the stranger in a strange land, the one who is able to see with different eyes the culture in which he or she lives in order to embody the counter-cultural revolution that the early Jesus movement felt itself to be. To be a stranger in a strange land in a proactive and counter-cultural way is a risky business and is, I have argued elsewhere (Isherwood 1999), the very essence of an incarnational Christology: one in which Christ is not a fixed eternal absolute but rather journeys with us as the stranger within, the one who is strange to us and makes us strange to ourselves.

For many mystics within the Christian tradition this stranger within has had profound effects on who they understand themselves to be and they have undergone quite profound transgressive changes, understood as truly transgressive when one considers the constraints of both their time and their religion. Michael Warner says religion "makes available a language of ecstasy, a horizon of significance within which transgressions against the normal order of the world and the boundaries of self *can be seen as good things*" (Warner 1993: 15, quoted in Rambuss 1998: 58; original emphasis). This language opens incredible relationships for many mystics with the body of Christ; what at first is a total other – the divine body of the God – becomes the desired body of the intimate lover. Strangely it is not the "otherness" of the lover that attracts in these instances but, rather, the making visible of that internal stranger, that Christ within, in the form of a desirable body that brings about a moving beyond otherness to one degree or another.

Catherine of Siena married Christ and was offered his foreskin as a wedding ring by her bridegroom. The story gets even more remarkable, as the body of Christ crosses genders for Catherine and she is eventually engaged passionately with, sinking into the flesh of, a female Christ, a Christ whom she desires. In these passionate embraces people move beyond the feeling of a distant God and find a union that transcends and transgresses all their known boundaries; their own sense of self is expanded and includes that which was previously excluded. For example, Catherine is able to engage with parts of her sexual self that might otherwise have been "othered" in her everyday life; there is a physical experience for these mystics that takes them to another place. Rambuss (1998: 109) insists that these closet devotions, as he wishes to call them, are "the technology by which the soul becomes a subject" (*ibid.*), a space in which the sacred may touch the transgressive and even the profane. And in that touching of those things once thought untouchable nothing is excluded, so nothing is the other.

The best example of this, perhaps because she insisted on having her story written by a scribe she employed and not through the eyes of some redactor, is Margery Kempe, who places before us the erotic embodiment of moving beyond otherness. What emerges is a relationality based on radical subjectivity (see Isherwood 2004). Margery's experiences with Jesus, Mary and the Godhead are extraordinary. She has sex with them all but, most extraordinary of all, she becomes them all in that amazing sexual play, leading to a greater assertion of her own being and bringing her closer to a full and free life, one that moved beyond otherness. We are boldly told that God himself declared to her "and God is in you and you are in him" (Windeatt 1985: 124) and further that she is wedded to "the Godhead" as a whole, and not just one part of it (*ibid.*: 122). Her descriptions of these encounters are radical because in them we see subjectivity with no persona, and no hidden corners, but simply a raw and gaping laid-bareness of the self in relation to the self/divine with total absence of otherness. Margery shows how a desire for the other/God moves on and develops into an erotic engagement with the divine/self in which there can remain no otherness; all is one and all is connected.

This appears to be radical otherness in which a destabilizing sense of identity also affirms it: a type of nomadic subjectivity. Her edges are expanded but at the same time she moves around her own core in a dance of autoerotic/erotic self-discovery. Of course, in this mutual subjectivity, father, son and spirit all experience their divinity through Margery. The more her identity becomes nomadic, the more her subjectivity is heightened, but this is no mere gender performance. Father, son and spirit are all interchangeable and, as such, go beyond gender categories and into animal, mineral, ether, bread, wine, presence and absence and so much more. Through not losing her identity, but rather cosmically affirming it, Margery moves her world and places before us endless possibilities of inclusion.

Theology, then, may have something in its heritage that runs counter to its normal doctrinal creation and exclusion of the other and, strangely, this heritage could speak to some very modern concerns.

EMBODIED STRANGERS

Ahmed (2000a: 4) says that the alien most certainly assists in the demarcation of space and the policing of borders but also as we recognize the one we do not know we put flesh on the beyond. She also challenges Zygmunt Bauman in his postmodern take on the stranger. He believes that the stranger is to be preserved and celebrated since it is this figure that helps us understand all that we have excluded in modernity. For Ahmed this is indefensible because it gives status to the concept that causes the problems in the first place. She likens it to the Marxist idea of a fetish, whereby the stranger is made into a fetish and has no life of his or her own, but is simply removed from histories and lives and made to carry all that is projected onto a fetish, to carry meaning that is in no way related to the reality of his or her life. This simple yet not so simple arrangement, by which the stranger just *is*, Ahmed feels, is one of the worst examples of a postmodern approach to the other. It makes the stranger's body carry all that by projection: it simply acts to secure and even reveal the "at home's body" in its own being and in the world (*ibid.*: 8). Ahmed is not persuaded by another postmodern suggestion that the stranger is the one created by movements and displacements that, in the postmodern world, make us all strangers. She also has some thoughts to add to Kristeva's claim that we all journey into the strangeness of ourselves and others and by so doing come to a self-discovery. For Ahmed this needs to include a visible identity not just an inner knowing, so she posits the notion of encounter rather than journey. It is in these strange encounters that one meets the stranger, which involves surprise and conflict by necessity: not so unlike our struggle described in the pages of Genesis.

We recognize the stranger, Ahmed suggests, not because they are necessarily from elsewhere or we have not seen them before but because they are already here and they are not belonging, they are out of place. The stranger is one who has crossed the line and come too close. Of course, the theologian might pick up Kristeva in response to Ahmed's suggestion and talk of the god/Christ within who has come too close either in a personal internal encounter or in an encounter with another. We hear very often that Christians respond to the Christ in others. Is this a recognition of that stranger who has come too close? In terms of Kristeva's understanding, this encounter would, for many Christians, be the start of a journey either to a greater understanding of the relational nature of the entire cosmos or, for the more fundamentalist type, to Christ and the ever-unfolding love affair between the person of Jesus and the believer. I suppose both approaches may run the risk of making this stranger fit too well; after all, Ahmed finds the usefulness of the stranger to lie in the fact that they do not quite fit, that they are not quite us but also not entirely alien. The encounter that Ahmed envisages is one of surprise but is also not without conflict, as noted, and so is one that takes place on a body with emotions. This is not a purely philosophical exchange but rather one that takes place at the border of the skin, a place in which bodies are affected by other bodies. It is here that a suggestion of a predetermined body, a fetish, is cast aside when real bodies meet and challenge real bodies. This is the true essence of encounter for Ahmed. It is the fleshiness of the world that opens us to the intimacy, even intrusion of/by the stranger and it is this fleshiness that inhabits us and is inhabited.

Ahmed (2000a: 49) speaks of economies of touch, by which she means the politics of how we touch, who we touch and the power of that touch. While she is well aware that there are bodies that are in place, that is, those that have an intimate connection with social space, and bodies that are out of place, those that are excluded from the body politic, such as children, the enslaved, the conquered and so on, she still wishes to consider ways in which the economy of touch affects the way we are in the world. It could be argued that bodies borrow from other bodies ways to be in the world and that neither body is reduced by that exchange, possibly even if one exchanges with bodies out of place. For Kristeva, of course, it is this border, this place where meeting of bodies is resisted, that creates the abject, that which is vomited out and made into the object, the other. For Ahmed there seems to be an openness to recognizing that strangers know differently to how they are known and in this economy of touch something changes through the challenge and the struggle. For the feminist theologian this is in itself an incarnational struggle and one that challenges the traditional sense of a God who is unchanging, untouched and always complete. The "border" between human and divine is not seen as one that makes the human abject or the divine a mystery; both become a challenge for each other and within that struggle, or even intimacy, new understandings emerge that diminish neither.

The implications of this move in theology can be argued to be far reaching. Just as theology has in the past gone hand in hand with various forms of exclusion from society and colonization because of its ability to create and exploit the other, so too such a move, even in these so-called secular days, may make a difference. We say "so-called secular" since a look at even the most postmodern of our activities at times show roots, certainly long forgotten, in the Western religious heritage so ingrained in our bodies and our societies. One example can be shown, taking up Ahmed's discussion of consumer culture and commodity fetishism (discussed in Chapter 4). Multiculturalism makes it possible for us to believe that we accept difference but still remain part of a nation, but in this case it can be argued that culture is reduced to style alone and the inner person remains committed to a nation but in an unrealistic way, since the culture of that nation is reduced, as we see, to the style of globalization. So in a way the nation becomes a style artefact with little, if anything, of its real heritage at play. Within this arrangement, Ahmed argues that the commodity object, the object of style, allows for an encounter without a face-to-face meeting so, strangely, there

41

are no bodies present as we attempt to adorn ours with style/culture. In this way, she says, the commodity fetish meets the stranger fetish (*ibid.*: 114). The objects become valued only through detachment from the social reality and lives of those who labour to produce them. The objects stand in for the stranger, whom we almost feel we consume through owing them. So in a strange way we feel we understand and engage with that stranger. Nothing could be further from the truth. The Western consumer is often invited through marketing to "go ethnic", and in this way the stranger is that which is produced, marketed and sold in order to define a commodity object. Ahmed (*ibid.*: 117) argues that this marks a shift from biological to cultural racism, which bell hooks sees as reducing ethnicity to spices, seasonings and all that spices up otherwise dull white culture: a culture that is invited to consume the other through the products, to eat, take in and shit out as disposable waste (hooks, cited in *ibid.*: 120). This kind of consumer culture gives the fantasy that we can become the other and that difference can be incorporated through consumption. Of course, all that happens here is a recasting of the other to fit the Western subject.

Feminist theology has argued that the roots of this form of thinking lie buried in dualistic metaphysical thinking laid down through centuries by the Christian Church. As has been mentioned in the Introduction, this form of thinking allows for distance and for the creation of hierarchies that support that distancing and the creation of the other. For those of us who explore the reality of enfleshed redemption, we are asked, in a deep and disturbing way, what can incarnation offer to challenge this way of thinking that numbs us to the reality of the other, indeed helps us guard ourselves against the other who is not where we are in this hierarchy of redemption? It may seem pointless and useless to use the language of theology in the face of the brokers of advanced capitalism and its global agenda of greed based on the insistence that all that is distinctive in human culture be reduced to nothingness (Ritzer 2007) by the global people- and value-musher. What can theology do when it is well understood by many that the globalization agenda is, in reality, the globalization of poverty, in which the majority never have access to all that we call normal in a civilized society. Further, there is no desire to include all in developed standards of living; indeed, such an idea is almost seen as a threat. The First World still needs the rest of the world, but only the sea, air, nature, materials and space in which to dispose of its waste; it does not need the people. Isherwood (2007) has argued that even those who appear to be benefiting from this genocidal system are themselves victims of it.

Just as Ahmed suggests that the producers of the goods we hope will give us an identity, a culture, meaning are invisible and reduced to nothing, so too we suggest are the consumers of those goods. This is from an incarnational perspective because they have lost the ability to look into the faces of those who produce and indeed into their own "authentic" faces, their own person. The economy of touch even exerts oblivion on those who believe they have the upper hand in this exchange. We too become strangers but the mighty economic system for the moment leads the West to believe that it is the signifier of all that is normal, cultured and civilized. This will not always be the case and so it does seem to be in the interest of all that even the so-called privileged begin to examine the system in which they too are imprisoned.

Christian theology, with its insistence on dualism, allows us to do the necessary damage to ourselves in order that we may make enemies and learn to hate. Traditional Christian theology has been at the heart of disconnection by making people aliens in their own skin. Feminist theology has encouraged engagement with raw/radical incarnation and the vulnerability and bravery to feel and to touch: to understand Christian theology as a skin-on-skin activity, a face-to-face mutual engagement of ever fuller becoming. Dualistic theology rips us from ourselves and cauterizes us, enfeebling our judgement, our heart, our passion, and it is the argument of many feminist theologians that this has been the basis of the genocidal systems we find in place in politics and national economies (more on this in Chapter 5).

Feminist theology has argued that our incarnate brother Jesus did not flee from politics: he was offered the chance to rise above it all through a metaphysical engagement with his own divine nature. Is this not what the temptations of the devil were about? Fly high, control nature, be a *god*. The response was a choice for life: to be involved in the real stuff of everyday living and to find and share the divine amongst his friends (Isherwood 1999). Jesus can be understood as a comrade who, through transgressive praxis, made a hole – created a space, opened up a gap – in what was hitherto understood as reality and invited others to make it bigger. There is no better time than now to make it even bigger, to root deep in one's own divine/human nature and find a way through the maze of misinformation and the temptations to rise above it all through consumption of the right products: products that, in the end, make stranger fetishists of us all.

Isherwood (*ibid.*) has argued for an understanding of incarnation as the flesh becoming word, which enables us to find a voice and to make our desires known; we do not have to conform to agreed absolutes but rather discover where *dunamis* leads us. Further, our bodies and the bodies of others, far from being aliens to us through the basis disassociation that much Christian doctrine has required, become sites of moral imperatives. Those who are starving present themselves as challenges to redress the imbalances in food distribution; those who are poisoned by toxic waste challenge the ethics of business and profit and call into focus the integrity of the planet as well as people; while those who labour under the genocidal reality of advanced capitalism present their bodies as a moral challenge to find alternative economic systems. When the flesh is word, these questions cannot be delayed or avoided by talk of reward in heaven. This rooting of the divine within and between us is a foundational act of resistance to markets and perhaps an unfolding of the hospitality spoken of in the early Church, the hospitality based in an understanding of the Christian as an alien in a strange land, which was understood as central to the way in which the early Christians viewed resources. For them, whatever was a resource was on loan and so should not be built up in order to reinforce a sense of self in this alien environment of an unredeemed world. Rather, they should share all in common, particularly with the poor, as a sign that they were not tied into the private and unyielding routines and acquisitions of this unredeemed world but were instead open to the possibilities of change and indeed the moments when a different world may shine through. In the early Christian world this was seen as the way all should conduct their lives: always open to those around, to face-to-face encounter and the unexpected changes that such may bring. Of course, where this worked it meant that the care of the vulnerable was not placed in the hands of the few, even religious institutions, where it became easier for people to fade from sight and to lose human dignity and connection and rootedness, which gives a meaning-filled place in the world, where it might be said that their embodiment could become diminished.

A feminist incarnational understanding of the Christian tradition does encourage such living so it may have a place in the conversation about strangers, consumerism and people as commodities.

LARGER TENTS AND THE POSTHUMAN

What happens when a human stranger becomes a thing? Earlier in the chapter we discussed virtual reality but the posthuman is possibly taking that further, removing the person from the reality. Actually, we are not in a position to know what a posthuman might be because as yet there is none. However, the term helps us to understand that human nature is viewed by many as flexible enough to warrant the imagination of such a being. It, of course, raises questions of continuity and discontinuity of the human person and, while it may appear to offer much – better health, elimination of genetic diseases and enhanced capabilities – it also opens up questions of invasion of bodily integrity, economic exploitation and even oppression.

When the posthuman is mentioned this usually means either the cyborg or the transhumant, the former being a hybrid embodiment of human and non-human, while the latter is human plus, a humanity that can transcend its own limits. We have become used to humans having parts of animals implanted in order to prolong or enhance life and therefore have moved beyond the sharp distinctions that our recent ancestors would have understood as existing between animal and human. Many understand this as simply the continuation of evolution while others see it as a move back to our distant past, when the connection between animal and human would have been better understood. And, of course, we accept the implantation of mechanical devices into our bodies in order to save or enhance our living. Both these moves have encouraged debates about natural identity and what may happen to a human who is now partially something else through a blurring of boundaries that may cast doubt on free will.

Cyborgs have been designed to liberate humans through additional layers of functioning, be they internal to the human or external. Jeanine Thweatt-Bates (2012: 18) argues that the robot-like function of a cyborg is meant to free humans to think and explore and to feel, but she also cautions that they can threaten human autonomy. Of course, the relationship between the body and the self has already entered the debate with cyborgization both in terms of prosthetics and genetic modifications. It also raises the question of the leakiness of modernity's boundaries between species and categories and symbolizes the generation of new creatures as well as highlighting Western dependency on technology (Graham 2002: 218). The cyborg has no origin and no end; it is a self-creating and self-sustaining mechanism, which is what Haraway celebrates about a cyborg ethic; it is radically immanent. However, some critics of Haraway have pointed out that, without a beginning and end, it has no salvation narrative and thus no moral or mythic imagination to move it beyond a strange form of humanism (*ibid.*: 219). However, for Haraway this removal from beginnings and ends is also a move away from the Christian history that has enslaved the identity and lives of women. In her famous statement that she would rather be a cyborg than a goddess she encapsulates all that she sees as problematic in this world and all that she believes a cyborg future offers. It frees women from the essentialist debates and demand to be "natural" and in so doing removes the teeth of the virtues debate, which sees male virtues as of a higher order than female and, of course, it breaks down the patriarchal divide between human and non-human and the hierarchy of which this thinking is part; it offers an "ontological kinship with the non-human machine" (Thweatt-Bates 2012: 23), which in turn offers a crossing of political and ethical boundaries. The cyborg is not fleeing the body but rather expanding the possibilities of embodiment through non-human and mechanical means. This may, then, be a larger tent that we may embrace in the search for a radical other; this radically immanent other, which is me, is at least a challenge to that quest.

The transhuman, on the other hand, may just be a stretch too far in that search. This is best understood as designer evolution, a space that does not accept any limits to human nature; even the ultimate of death is claimed to be overcome. Those who work in this field speak of uploads, which are meant to contain one's personality, emotions and memories on a chip. This "you" can be given a virtual body in which they could enjoy food, drink and sex or, indeed, a robot body in which they could explore the world. While many who imagine this world also imagine a white male "identity", there are others who move towards a form of postgender with the ability to pick out any traits or biological attributes. Haraway is opposed to this way of thinking and points out that a cyborg has the ability to move beyond culturally constructed forms of gender but still needs a body. For Haraway, a body, albeit a cyborg one, is required to combat dualism. Further, she believes that knowledge also needs a body in which to be experienced and transferred while those who advocate transhumanism believe that gathering data and evaluating evidence are enough: a human knower does not need to be present (*ibid.*: 87).

What happens to incarnation and the ability to encounter the stranger within this posthuman world? Elaine Graham is clear that transhumanism is not about love of life but rather fear of death, which it is attempting to transcend. She finds it an ethically deficient picture of what it is to be human and a limited vision of what human may look like in the future (Graham 2002: 233). Perhaps this is so strange that we are afraid we are looking at monsters rather than an extension of what evolution could be. Is incarnation limited to flesh and blood? In terms of the ability to be moved by encounter and the presence of the stranger it does seem that for the present time it is. However, is the story different with the cyborg, which we could suggest is the example *par excellence* of hybridity, Queer and even postcoloniality? Would it be possible for our posthuman identity to incorporate the divine as one component of an ongoing self (Thweatt-Bates 2012: 149)? Thweatt-Bates does suggest that a cyborg Christ may not be out of the question since it would be partial, temporary, specific and content-dependent and open to ongoing negotiations of human/divine lives. In this way, she claims, it upholds the logic of incarnation and embodiment and troubles the category of human (*ibid.*: 156). So perhaps this embodying of the unknown is a way to bring us face to face with the alien who is, in material terms, a metaphor of ourselves (Graham 2002: 55).

AND SO?

For feminist theology it seems that the stranger, the outsider, is a positive idea and also a challenge. The challenge lies in not making an excluded other from this stranger and the positive is the way in which those beyond the boundaries of our known experience, if not fetishized, expand our tent and make the reality of incarnation ever wider and more fluid. Through a recognition of this stranger who is not other, we come to a more profound understanding of interconnectivity and perhaps even interrelationality. Carter Heyward and others would wish that this carried with it what they term a radical vulnerability, that is, an openness that has no boundaries, one that is transformed through encounter and transforms in the mutual exchange, perhaps, we might now say, of strangeness. Is this strangeness of understanding what the early Christians meant by being an alien in a strange land: one who is always on the margins as a choice, understanding this to be a place that asks for greater inclusivity, an inclusivity that is never stretched enough but one that works towards a redemption – a transformation of the world as we see it? For feminist theology this transformation is not to another world; rather, it is an ongoing process within the world in which we live, the process that always places the Christian on the edge in the place of unlikely encounter, challenge and intimacy.

2. THE POLITICS OF OTHERNESS

It is really only a convention to confine the politics of otherness to this chapter, since there are political implications raised in other chapters as well, such as Chapter 3, on methodology. Clearly, for example, there are implications in how one treats others when attempting to research them: as sources of data, a rational typification, or as fully subjective agents with minimal hierarchies established between others and researchers.

It is also conventional to consider politics as operating at two levels. At one level, politics describes the operation of the state and its various apparatuses, such as the armed forces, the civil service and those organizations regulated by the state, in various degrees of proximity and distance, which might include the media and the education system. Politics at this level both organizes and justifies the use of state power, sometimes itself based on vested interests of well-organized groups such as ruling classes or various elites, including those based on claims to privilege on the grounds of ethnicity or gender. However, following various rejections of such "top-down" accounts of social order, including Foucault's (e.g. Foucault 1977), it is also common to think of politics in a much more extended and elaborated way, to cover more or less any kind of conflict between individuals or groups and ways of resolving it. Famous examples of this kind of politics include identity politics, where various social groups, including youth, struggle to assert themselves and claim their rights. This kind of everyday politics has also sometimes been studied in the form of "micropolitics", describing the jockeying for power and prestige that goes on in modern organizations. Again, connections between these activities and wider social groupings such as class ethnicity or gender have occasionally been established.

THE STATE AND ITS OTHERS

At the macro level, otherness has clearly been a major issue in the exercise of state power and in the ideologies that accompany it. Nazi Germany is the obvious example. The Nazi concept of community, *Volksgemeineschaft*, proposed that a series of similarities united the *Volk* in a way that was far more profound than the arbitrary national boundaries of 1920s Europe. Classically, the similarities turned on the rather mysterious categories of blood, race and soil. These bonds were entirely mythical. Clearly, the same bonds that united people also effectively excluded others, especially Jews, who had "mixed blood", an inferior racial heritage, and no nation or soil of their own. As a result, to be classified as other than a member of the *Volk* was to be damned, not only as an outsider, but as subhuman.

The Nazi state's scientists made those classifications, although earlier systematic attempts to categorize people in terms of "race" had been common in colonial powers such as France and Britain. In those states, ethnic identity was not seen as a matter of choice, but as some kind of "master identity", overriding all the other options. Thus German citizens, who had lived in Germany all their lives, and had even fought for Germany, were occasionally surprised to find that they were Jewish on the grounds of one of their grandparent's supposed racial heritage. These findings would end in tragedy.

The Nazi Reich is obviously an extreme example of the connection between sameness and otherness at the macro political level. Clearly, social bonds can be strengthened by drawing a boundary around a group that unites all those inside the boundary, a very useful outcome if some great national purpose has to be served, such as fighting a war. Unity can be emphasized and dramatized by demonizing all those outside the boundary, who then appear as obvious enemies, either internal or external.

This process is often discussed in terms of stereotyping, scapegoating or witch-hunting. At one level, these activities involve perfectly natural and understandable ways of categorizing people, working typifications that are required if normal life is to be pursued: no one can be expected to develop a fully complex, insightful and empathic picture of the person they meet for a few seconds in the course of buying a coffee at the railway station. However, there are specifics relating to politics that render the general terms less useful, when stereotypes become the basis of political discrimination. After all, as Adorno and Max Horkheimer argued (1979), Nazi stereotypes of Jews were not actually based on Jewish behaviour, but on some deeper notion of the outsider, probably located in the Unconscious. Rather like Freud's neuroses, stereotypes contain a mixture of daily available concrete and specific elements, such as an actual encounter with a person who looks like a Jew or a picture of one, which act as cues to release the deeper Unconscious material. It follows that you do not actually need to hate (real) Jews to become an anti-Semite. "Jews" were turned into political categories that could be used to persecute and kill people because of some underlying authoritarianism in the German people, and because of a specific connection with the main themes of Nazi politics and propaganda, especially themes of heroic "little men" excluded by elite society but able to intuit directly the direction of "Providence". Adorno *et al.* (1964) were horrified to find that authoritarian tendencies were widespread in the American people as well.

The authoritarian personality was to be investigated using the tools of psychological surveying on a large sample (2,000 people). The best brief account of this work is by the Frankfurt Institute for Social Research (1974). Fascism could be described in terms of a particular personality structure (the authoritarian personality), indicated best, after a process of intercorrelating various scales measuring educational attainment, social class and other variables, in scores on a particular instrument. The "F-scale" essentially measured intolerance of ambiguity. The personality mechanisms at work were considered in Freudian terms: for example, as "morbid projection", the "transference of socially taboo impulses from the subject to an object" (Adorno & Horkheimer 1979: 192), a process also known as disavowal. In particular, fear of the outsider is transferred into paranoia and hatred through introjection. In the process of constructing stereotypes, we can also see an echo of the remarks about standardization, positivism and magic (in Chapter 3) as a means to achieve power over the external world: "The closed circle of eternal sameness [in stereotyping] becomes a substitute for omnipotence" (*ibid.*).

Excessive positivity, and a disregard for negativity and critique assists in the development of whole worldviews that are paranoid. All normal individual judgements are assertive, but they particularly need negativity to correct them, and we cannot defeat them simply by pointing out their irrationality or inconstancy. This sort of positivist system building goes on in normal thought too, however, hence "Paranoia is the dark side of cognition" (*ibid.*: 195). The impersonality and ruthless rationality of capitalism underpin the development of authoritarian personalities: after all, it is routine in capitalism to reduce people to the status of objects so they can be manipulated in markets. Education has become incorporated and is now a matter of transferring information and awarding qualifications, and it opposes social theory or philosophical critique, which are seen as mere negativity.

Of course, there is a huge debate among historians and sociologists about whether Nazism was some sort of normal development of, or persistent tendency in, advanced capitalism, or whether it was some special case, based on the contingencies of German history. We might make some progress by trying to define our objects more carefully, to refer to the opening issue in Chapter 3.

Thus Adorno and Horkheimer (1979) saw the same mechanism at work in the notorious witchcraft trials at Salem. The argument here is that the combination of personal responsibility for one's life, and the rational approach to the conduct of affairs, characteristic of Massachusetts Puritans at the time, necessarily involves a dark irrational side as well, normally well repressed, and that surfaced in the waves of denunciation and killing. Once the local magistrates permitted the use of "spectral evidence", the testimony produced by local girls who claimed to have seen spectral demons surrounding the accused, rational discourse was undermined, and full-blown witch-hunting broke out.

Adorno (1973) also singles out the concept of personal authenticity, and his original critique of Karl Jaspers and Martin Heidegger might apply really well to modern variants of the cult of sincerity, even some that might be found in feminism.

> [The] field of association [of the concept "authentic man"] ... is a leftover of romanticism and is transplanted without second thoughts into the contemporary situation ... The categories of the jargon [of authenticity] are gladly brought forward, as though they were not abstracted from generated and transitory situations, but rather belonged to the essence of man.   (1973: 59)

Adorno suggests that there is a central vacuousness in the "jargon" surrounding authenticity, which values sincerity in the speaker, and not the truth in the speech. This appears in the uncritical reception given to (acceptable) emotional statements in particular in autoethnography, and their ability to induce similar emotions in the readers, the "validity of tears" (discussed in the next chapter).

STRANGERS REVISITED: ASYLUM SEEKERS

We discussed the concept of the stranger in Chapter 1. In modern Britain, politicians and their civil servants have openly celebrated Britain as cosmopolitan, "globalized" and multicultural, and have campaigned to attract people from overseas – tourists, visitors, and even residents – to admire the community (Mynott 2000). There is control over immigration, but this is seemingly rational, aimed at managing "community relations" and offering a fair and open basis for all newcomers. There are categories of excluded people, most obviously terrorists, but, to use the current terms, Britain also cannot afford to subsidize people who come here just to take advantage of the social security and benefits system while pretending to be refugees: first called "bogus asylum seekers", then just "asylum seekers".

Official policy is still fundamentally based on "a notion of national community which has always racialised certain newcomers" (*ibid*.: 315), despite the euphemisms and categories that attempt to disguise the situation. In particular, "the multiple and confusing definitions of community have a central thread to them: they are actually about race" (*ibid.*: 319). For example, recent (Labour government) plans to disperse asylum seekers to "clusters" where ethnic minorities already live is defended as not dumping asylum seekers in areas where they are likely to experience racism (always seen as working-class racism, Mynott points out), but the policy also assumes that "the existing minorities share with asylum seekers the overarching property of a non-white ethnicity" (*ibid.*). It is further assumed that the existing settled ethnic minorities will exhibit no prejudice of their own towards the newcomers and will even support them, saving government finance. The reality includes a punitive approach to asylum seekers as they wait to be processed by a poorly financed system, including allocation to housing, support "in kind", and the withdrawal of all benefits if asylum seekers refuse to cooperate.

Imogen Tyler (2006) addresses the issue directly in terms of cultural politics and offers an analysis that starts to look like the one we saw above on Nazi Germany. Asylum seekers are seen as "abject others", she says. Abjection is referenced to Kristeva's work, where it becomes something that raises fears, disgust, challenges to normal subjectivity and hate, and thus serves to maintain the legitimacy of dominant political systems. As with Jews for Nazis, asylum seekers in Britain are seen as outside the normal political discourse of rights and obligations. They literally have no rights, partly because they are stateless. The state claims sole legitimacy to be able to deny or award rights. The national popular press regularly runs hate stories in a way that extends the stereotypes and this helps the government maintain a sense of constant crisis referring to asylum seekers, and the need to constantly manage this crisis includes policies of "detention, dispersal, electronic tagging, [being denied] access to paid work [and receiving] only limited access to education, health care, social housing and income support" (*ibid.*: 188). For Ed Mynott, the overall picture is one of contradiction, euphemism and constant tactical changes, while for Tyler, there is a more "positive" and coherent stereotype emerging. Phil Hubbard (2005) also suggests that fears of the undeserving stranger are pursued with an unusual intensity in the case of asylum seekers, and that this suggests Unconscious energy, including reactions to the abject, and the connections between the evasive concept of "whiteness" and the "Oedipal family structures and norms".

Finally, Tyler is good for pointing out some of the contradictions of liberal discourses of human rights or empathy that attempt to combat these depersonalizing tendencies. Appealing to universal rights is no good if asylum seekers are denied access to rights. Personalizing strategies to reveal the human being behind the abjection can involve the humanitarian liberal "taking the place of the other", and this "can make it difficult for us to 'hear' those whose place has been taken ... repeating the disavowal of silenced voices by creating a kind of equivalence of positions, between 'us' and 'them'" (Tyler 2006: 195). There is also the danger of generalizing the reasons for seeking asylum in the name of some humanist resisting subject. This can "fetishize the refugee by universalizing the condition" (*ibid.*: 197) and "constructing the imagined 'victims' ... as narcissistic figures of 'our own' political hope" (*ibid.*: 9).

OTHERNESS IN "NORMAL" EVERYDAY LIFE

Some famous examples of stereotyping in everyday life reveal the same combinations of rational and irrational thinking. Brett St Louis (2004) notes that spectators of athletic events can hardly fail to notice that many of the athletes who make the finals have black skin. This is a significant enough relation to count as quite strong evidence that there is some connection between black skin and athletic prowess. What the spectators then do is supply their own "irrational" explanations: that athletic prowess is somehow connected to various attributed "racial" characteristics – a preponderance of "fast twitch muscle", unusual shoulder joints or lung capacity (in the more "scientific racist" version) or an enhanced physicality, bestiality or natural-ness (in the more vulgar racist versions). More complex explanations are not so apparent or available: that sport is a "sidetrack" for black youths, for example, who are diverted from academic achievement by well-intentioned teachers (Carrington 1983) or that being a member of a minority group can produce high levels of motivation and determination to succeed. Louis Harrison *et al.* (2004) found in their small study that sidetracking and "per-vasive racial stereotypes" persisted among American athletes and coaches and it was often simply assumed that sport was a route for black people. Indeed, many coaches discouraged the participation of white students because they were perceived to be at a disadvantage in selection.

Ernest Cashmore (1987) talks of the "everyday logic of racism", where working-class British inhabitants of Birmingham and its environs clearly have perceived, rightly, that they are the victims of discrimination. They live in poor houses, have low-waged jobs or are unemployed, send their children to underachieving schools and experience high levels of ill health. Then, says Cashmore, the conversation often introduces a racist note, where "immigrants" (and "asylum seekers" these days, no doubt) get blamed for jumping queues for housing, taking the best jobs and flooding local schools. There are plenty of other groups to blame for the discrimination, but "racial groups" emerge as favourite, no doubt because of other highly visible differ-ences that they display: skin colour, dress, language, cuisine and so on. This echoes Adorno and Horkheimer's (1979) view that instead of investigating the causes of the shortfalls, those who are seen to benefit from rationing policies are blamed.

THE POLITICS OF YOUTH

Interest grew in the emergence of spectacular youth cultures in the UK during the 1970s and 1980s, much discussed as a form of symbolic politics, a form of cultural resistance to the authority of parents, teachers, police and, through them, the state (see Harris 1992). At the time, this was a liberating, if possibly apologetic, analysis, opposing the official view of rebellious youth as wastrels or mindless hooligans. In the form of highly visible embodiments, youth reclaimed cultural symbols such as the leather jacket, the British motorcycle and the Italian scooter, or even fetishized underwear, and offered various "inversions" of respectable values (as in endless and sequential inversions of conventional hairstyles) or even ironic commentaries on values such as neatness in the case of Mod style. Their leisure pursuits, often based around music and the consumption of illegal drugs, were seen as countercultural, a hedonistic rejection of "normal" lifestyles and life prospects, especially with hippies. Mods acted out fantasies of classless technocratic futures, bikers imagined a retreat to the old values of British technological superiority, and skinheads recreated, to their own satisfaction, the vanished traditional working-class communities of their childhood.

These particular subcultures probably culminated in the phenomenon of punk, and analysis here began to question the earlier analyses, based on Gramscian notions of cultural resistance. Punk seemed to involve inversions of not only respectable values but those of earlier subcultures too, especially "progressive rock", with its millionaire guitar virtuosi and strong countercultural themes (Hebdige 1979). The mass media had also played a major part in describing, codifying and popularizing various lifestyles. Thus subcultures are "representations of representations" (*ibid.*: 86), rather than coded political protest about social conditions, and their critical perceptions and insights are often widely shared by "straight" society too. Homology arises from an "integral" process of selection and cultural work on an object or item, exposing the "symbolic structures" of which participants themselves may be unaware (which gets very close to the concept of ideology as a complement to standard ethnography) (Willis 1978). Dick Hebdige went on to argue in his later work that all youth subcultures are always both a demand to be seen and a refusal to be watched; they are, to quote the title of his book, "hiding in the light" (Hebdige 1988).

However, it was clear that the usual cycle of resistance and commercial incorporation was working as well as ever. Sarah Thornton (1995) showed how clubbing and the consumption of popular music had split youth into fragmented groups based on consumption patterns that were not likely to form active social groups: audiences or club clienteles rather than subcultures. Even in the earliest days of analysis, youth cultures were recognized as limited politically, offering only "magical solutions" to the serious problems posed by modernization and social change. The argument was pursued in Willis's famous study of working-class male youth at school. They were able to partially penetrate the ideological illusions of capitalism, especially the view that hard work at school would bring meritocratic success in life. At the same time, they were politically limited mostly because they rejected all intellectual activity that challenged their own common sense, including theoretical critique: they remained sexist and racist as a result.

A recent study of modern Britain revealed a considerable decomposition of class aesthetics, with factors such as age, gender and ethnicity affecting taste (Bennett *et al.* 2008). Thus television-watching did not separate the social classes particularly clearly, but it did separate the genders. Social preferences were more marked in areas such as musical taste and less marked in bodily leisure. Overall, there was very little snobbish cultural exclusion from the elite and some limited evidence for a much broader range of tastes and the growth of "the cultural omnivore" (see also Warde *et al.* 2007). In these circumstances, popular culture ceased to be an active boundary generating cultural politics.

Chas Critcher's (2000) account of the "raves" of the late 1990s was able to revive some of the themes of studies of demonized others discussed above. Raves were gatherings with "larger than average venues; music with 120 or more beats per minute; distinctive dress codes; extensive special effects ... and ubiquitous drug use" (*ibid.*: 147). Ravers also offer an alternative to the disciplined body: "the subversion of the ordered, restrained, chemically pure and self-contained body" (*ibid.*: 156) had to be met with a strong social reaction. Thus rave culture "represented a symbolic dissent from dominant discourses about the need to minimise risk through bodily management" (*ibid.*: 156). Social reaction soon emerged. The media gradually became hostile after well-publicized Ecstasy deaths. Raving became subject to a number of increased attempts at legal control at first, featuring "three interlinked but ultimately distinct sub-plots: those of new-age travellers, rave and Ecstasy" (*ibid.*: 151). The punitive effects were probably greater for travellers, but raves were so popular and sustained that some accommodation with them was inevitable. They were licensed, relocated indoors and commercialized, becoming another form of club culture. The authorities lifted restrictions on nightclub hours to permit this transition. Ecstasy use also remained unresolved: massive police action would have been required to outlaw it, and would have resulted in widespread criminalization. Campaigns designed to reintroduce self-regulation for drug-takers emerged, focusing on "harm reduction" and informed choice, rather than punitive measures.

Another recent study shows that the "active feminine sexuality in gaining gender egalitarianism" is apparent in American Goth (Wilkins 2004: 328). It is the case that "strategies of active sexuality (proactive sexuality, non-monogamy, and bisexuality)" appear liberating and anti-mainstream, permit experimentation in self-presentation, and enable "sexual play with multiple partners" and this can avoid stigmatization (*ibid.*: 329). It also bestows a political significance on the scene, sometimes supported by a feminist discourse. However, as signs of partial penetrations and limitations, gender inequalities are present as well; sexy dressing still leaves women subject to "predatory and critical male and female gazes" (*ibid.*). There are still double standards. There are still broader gender inequalities that are unaddressed, and there is the unwitting "reproduction of an ideological system in which romance trumps sex" (*ibid.*). Goths are insufficiently critical of romance, and still operate with some notion of romantic "'ideal' intimate relationships", even though these need not be monogamous as long as they are valid (*ibid.*: 330). Heterosexuality is still the norm, although same-sex relationships between women are permitted; men approve of them but only as long as they are "subsidiary" (*ibid.*).

MODERNITY AND THE POLITICS OF EMBODIMENT

John Jervis (1999) is among those who points out that modernity as a project has paradoxical implications for otherness. On the one hand, otherness is increasingly brought under rational scrutiny, regulated and domesticated; on the other, the other is a necessary presence lurking in the entire project. Modernity is contrasted, sometimes explicitly, sometimes implicitly, with "the primitive"; the rational is contrasted with the chaotic; the civilized with the uncivilized and barbaric; the normal citizen with the dangerous and threatening outsider, the terrorist or the dropout. The concept of the normal citizen is also used to define others that are symbolically threatening, so to speak, such as perverted, or disabled persons.

The discussion of normality developed after a turn towards recognizing the body as an important topic for analysis. It is not just minds that are affected by social processes but bodies too. Certainly, these processes become visible when inscribed on the body (what might be called the "soft" version of the turn to the body), but there is still some debate about whether bodies determine culture or consciousness (the "harder" version); Renée Hoogland's (2002) discussion is useful.

Bill Hughes (2002) has argued that the physically impaired or disabled body is always present as the other of modernity and its project. He seems to have severe disablement in mind, although, as usual, disability is a very flexible concept: as we age, we all experience it and, even in our prime, we are still disabled relative to top athletes or professional intellectuals. The able body acts rather as a fantasy to which people aspire and against which others are arranged in hierarchical order. Even compassion for the impaired "is a hair's breadth from barbarism", since both draw from modernist conceptions (*ibid.*: 581). Postmodernity might offer more flexibility and greater tolerance, Hughes thinks. The movement for rights for the disabled arose from the counterculture and the early challenge to medical authority. It benefits from a tolerance of different kinds of cultures as ways of life, and thus "difference and heterogeneity can become a basis for social relations" (*ibid.*: 578). Disabled people are still not fully accepted as normal, but the dominance of the disciplined able body has been challenged: much has been made, in the press at least, of the importance of the 2012 Paralympics in increasing respect for disabled athletes at least. It is possible that disability will become not "a symbol of disorder and tragedy ... [but] nothing out of the ordinary" (*ibid.*: 579).

In modernity, people rated as disabled were forced to develop a number of strategies to combat the prejudices of the relatively able bodied. Erving Goffman's (1963) study of stigma remains a classic. The stigmatized could sometimes cope with the reactions of the normal by hiding, covering or masking their stigma, for example by wearing a prosthetic, using make-up or clothing, or simply remaining hidden as much as possible. Ingenious variants also included admitting to a more acceptable stigma – such as being poor at spelling – to cover a less acceptable one, such as living with a learning difficulty. Other strategies included various ways of helping normal people adjust to the presence of a stigmatized person by normalizing the encounter as much as possible, managing the disclosure of the stigma, for example, and then insisting that, despite the stigma, normal conversation and interaction should be maintained, managing any embarrassment or hostility on the part of the unstigmatized.

What Goffman omits to consider, however, is a more openly and publicly "political" response, where the stigmatized band together and demand equal rights. The sexually and ethnically stigmatized have shown the way here, but there have also been quite successful demonstrations by wheelchair users who have chained themselves to buses or to public buildings in order to draw attention to the ways in which they are discriminated against. A study of obese people (Honeycutt 1999), for example, outlines various strategies that the obese use to make a claim to normality. These range from the kind of covering strategy discussed above, where obesity is covered by claiming that it is a medical condition, through claims to possess special compensatory powers and abilities that outweigh the stigma, to various political campaigns to end discrimination and claim equal rights. Other examples appear in Chapter 4.

The embodiment of culture can be seen to be at work in current practices of body modification. Nick Crossley has charted a whole series of "reflexive body techniques", which range from brushing one's teeth to piercing one's genitals: in using them "we learn to constitute ourselves for ourselves, practically" (2005: 13). Some of the more challenging examples are discussed below, which are especially good at raising the issue of otherness.

For example, some practices such as tattooing were once seen as stigmatizing; a mark on the body that indicated that one had been a criminal, slave, outcast or member of a dubious profession such as being in the armed services. There are several explanations given for the spread of tattooing and piercing, especially among the young (see e.g. Fisher 2002), but a clear focus emerges on the power of tattoos to show deliberate transgression of parental authority, membership of a particular group, an attempt to demonstrate personal ownership of one's body, the enjoyment in successfully undergoing a challenging *rite de passage*. More political themes are described by Victoria Pitts (1998). Some women in the USA are using scarification techniques on their bodies in connection with "an agency discourse of reclaiming the female body" (*ibid.*: 67). These activities invoke "a state of liminality or bodily ambiguousness" (*ibid.*). There is, therefore, a potential for subversion of and resistance to conventional identities. The carnivalesque is evoked specifically in the "grotesque, vulgar representation[s]" the women carve into their skins (*ibid.*: 71). "[This] new grotesqueness is seen as an improvement over the old, pristine self" (*ibid.*: 76).

Some tattoos have little significance and have been purchased while intoxicated or under the influence of peers or fashion, while others reflect a "body project", where participants attempt to anchor their identities and develop "a coherent personal narrative" (Sweetman 1999: 53). The modified person must participate "as producer, consumer and living frame" (*ibid.*: 64). This can reflect "a form of 'anti-fashion'" (*ibid.*: 58), since the markings are effectively permanent.

There are many other studies of body modification, all of which can help to explain what appears to many of us as bizarre and inexplicable and to thus normalize the threatening other. Debra Gimlin (2007), for example, explains why women choose to have cosmetic surgery. Although the reasons vary between Britain and the USA, they include accounts based on themes of "entitlement, morality, need versus desire, exclusion, autonomy and responsibility" (*ibid.*: 48). Gimlin is still not entirely convinced that these are not rationalizations, however.

Ambivalent public and political responses are gradually leading to a new tolerance, it could be argued. According to Jervis (1999), the development of modernity is wholly on the side of demands for equal rights. Modernity no longer attempts to rigorously police otherness. What has undermined any such attempt is the sheer proliferation of otherness, offering more and more possibilities for what he calls "transgression". This means all of us can experience otherness as a routine matter in our everyday lives (and there are implications for modernist social science in that categories are clearly routinely transgressed as well). These include routine experiences such as participation in the carnivalesque (subversive and ironic elements of which might be detectable, even in the recent official monarchical jubilee celebrations in Britain).

THE FEMINIST BODY

The turn to the body has much more significance for, and impact upon, feminism and feminist theology in that discussions of corporeality have promised a material base for these disciplines. In particular, the female body has been seen as a material substrate for sexual difference, and sexual difference itself has been defined as a key category or approach for particular kinds of feminism. In feminist theology, the idea of feminist corporeality has led to important reworkings of the notion of incarnation, as we have seen, breaking with traditional conceptions that say God was incarnated only once in the body of Jesus. There have been far-reaching implications, for theology and for understandings of otherness, as we discuss in more detail in Chapter 5.

To take feminism first, the problem has been to avoid notions of biological determinism that privilege male bodies as stronger, better adapted, more perfect. One response has been to argue that biological sexual differences are relevant only because they have been used as a basis to develop major social, cultural, psychoanalytic and linguistic systems that have installed phallogocentrism. Male sexuality becomes the centre of whole social systems of kinship and social hierarchies based on them. Maleness becomes the main category against which important social statuses are developed, in a fundamental social and cultural structure of man, male, adult, woman, child (Goulimari 1999). The biological penis has taken on greater significance as the Phallus, the main signifier for some Lacanians, central in the emergence of identity and in the development of the Symbolic. Here, the first struggle has been to undo this "bad connection" between biology and the social, and to challenge these apparently natural and fundamental structures of male privilege wherever they occur, including in Christian texts and practices.

Some of the debates about corporeality show the ranges of options, often within a Deleuzian framework. Elizabeth Grosz, for example (see Kontturi & Tiainen 2007) pursues a Darwinian account of the development of human diversity driven by sexual difference and sexual selection, as an instance of the general Deleuzian emphasis on universal difference and its endless generation. This gets close to a biological determinism: "sexual difference is ontological, the very conditions for the emergence of the human" (*ibid.*: 249), but she is careful to distinguish this from sociobiology and neo-Darwinism. Her argument is pursued in the course of wishing to turn from a main concern with representation in feminism, with its emphasis on identity politics, as in the sort of sociological studies that we have been examining above. There should be, instead, more of a concern with what Grosz calls "reality" (or, more strictly, materialism), as that which precedes representation. Grosz follows Deleuze into denying the centrality of the human subject, and in stressing expression as a matter of communicating

59

form not just subjective intent. She also takes the concept of becoming to introduce themes such as an emphasis on the future of feminism, and urges feminist writers to move away from the initial critical stages.

Ahmed thinks that Grosz's implication that difference just exists makes it look rather like the idea of God, "the cause without a cause" (Tuori & Peltonen 2007: 259). Adopting Deleuzian ontology can avoid political issues so that "it might become 'desirable' for some to talk more about becoming molecular rather than whiteness" (*ibid.*). We need to retain the concept of representation and structure in order to understand how the empirical world coheres in particular ways. We need a language that helps us to explain systematic regularities, as in racism, patterns and distributions, "So I do not think that we can start by talking about acts as things that just happen" (*ibid.*).

Patricia MacCormack (2009), sketching the concerns of a particular Australian kind of corporeal feminism, which would include Grosz's work, explains that the turn to Gilles Deleuze and Félix Guattari is a suitable introduction to philosophy for feminists, since Deleuze and Guattari have already broken with a number of masculinist conventions, including their famous critique of the Oedipal structure in Freud (Deleuze & Guattari 1984). Nevertheless, MacCormack is still critical of a certain residual idealism in the work, and argues, for example, that we need to remember the corporeal dimension when discussing their notion of "becoming-woman": real suffering is a component of empirical womanhood, she argues, easily overlooked in more philosophical discussions.

MacCormack is keen to avoid biological reductionism, however, and says that what is required is a "libidinal body without organs" (2009: 91). Both Irigaray (1985) and Alice Jardine (1985) would see this as dangerously weakening the specificity of women and its ground in their distinct anatomy and sexuality. Irigaray argues that 'To turn the organless bodies into the 'cause' of sexual pleasure, isn't it necessary to have had a relation to language and to sex – to the organs – that women have never had?" (1985: 141). Jardine suggests that experimenting with the body without organs can lead only to the invention of "new kinds of [male] subjectivities" (1985: 223), Desire operating within a deterritorialized brotherhood that threatens to dispense with women altogether.

An extensive debate has developed within feminism around these different options and possibilities. Pelagia Goulimari (1999) offers a complex chart of the debates between Braidotti, Irigaray, Jardine and Michèle Le Doeuf, again based on central terms in Deleuze and Guattari. The options can be summarized as variants of "sexual difference" versus "becoming-minoritarian"approaches, and the implications cover philosophy and politics. No one denies the importance of escaping from phallogocentrism, but the issue is whether feminism should focus on becoming-woman, retaining sexual difference as a key category that underpins every aspect of the "male imaginary". Becoming-woman, in Braidotti's view, is an urgent task, and she means exceeding the options available for women in phallogocentrism beginning with the notion of the "virtual feminine". Women are a particular group who have been systematically denied the possibility of becoming a subject in the first place, and Braidotti thinks this adds an important empirical dimension to qualify Deleuzian abstract possibilities. Her stance would retain the category of woman, which remains as the most important one politically.

One basis for this argument, and for many similar ones about sexual difference, can be found in Irigaray's classic discussion of the female body, especially in the two chapters about the two lips of the female vulva and/or face (Irigaray 1985). We discuss methodological implications of this work in the next chapter as well, but Irigaray describes the anatomical characteristics of these lips: that they are two, unlike the one of the phallus; that they are constantly touching each other, providing opportunities for female autoeroticism that males do not possess; that they express a kind of internally consistent sexuality and sexual pleasure that does not depend at all on penile intrusions, which only interrupt. This special kind of female sexuality provides the basis for intimate relations with all other women and for a flexible form of thinking and recognition in a way that must always remain external and mysterious to men, and seem inferior compared to their binary logic.

At the same time, Irigaray's focus is clearly much more than anatomical, and metaphorical or poetic themes are soon developed. Maggie Berg (1991) discusses some of the earlier criticisms of Irigaray as biologically reductionist or essentialist, but argues for a reading that sees the whole discussion as a rather elliptical and critical allusion to the Lacanian argument that the male penis is readily equated with the symbolic phallus, an example of Irigaray's "ironic mimesis". Irigaray is arguing that it is "impossible to cut the signifier (the lips) free from its habitual referent (the labia) as Lacan claims to do with the phallus" (*ibid.*: 70). These layers in Irigaray's text avoid any kind of simple anatomical determinism, says Berg, while retaining a necessary materialism.

It is likely that sociologists might see this sort of argument as evasive as well as allusive, refusing to state clearly whether anatomy has an effect or not and, if so, how much of one, but there has always been a tension with poststructuralist poetics as a method, as we shall see in the next chapter.

Goulimari thinks that sexual difference options even of this poetic kind still operate within the fundamental binary division between the sexes of phallogocentrism and, politically, this risks both recuperation and political isolation. The same sort of argument is pursued by Queer theorists worried about the limited escape from heterosexuality offered by lesbian practice, which can rapidly turn back into a polarized distinction between butch and femme (Isherwood 2004). Even the "virtual feminine" of Irigaray and Braidotti runs the risk of being established as a new territory, which, as we know from Deleuze and Guattari, then runs the risk of turning into a stratified space: the point is to pursue a tactic that escapes from all territories, a process of "becoming minoritarian".

Goulimari's option involves a permanent process of flow and escape from territory, and this can be seen as a purely abstract possibility in itself, a flight from concrete politics, or an invitation to disembodied, or less embodied, aesthetic politics, where experimental literature develops "minoritarian languages", in the main examples discussed by Deleuze (see Smith 1997). We discuss this option too in the next chapter. MacCormack's preference is for a tactical stance rather than an attempt to prioritize positions philosophically: there is no single face of feminism and "no inherently, transgressive, important urgent cause" (MacCormack 2009: 94), only a rhizomatic territory characterized by heterogeneity. There is a need to reconcile abstract French theory with corporeal struggles, producing "fleshly poststructuralist feminism" (*ibid.*: 95) .What should drive embodied struggles is the notion of a feminist ethics, again based on Deleuze: the pursuit of "joy", in the Spinozan sense of developing any interaction that expands our powers to think and understand the world. She seems to have in mind fairly concrete struggles going on in existing territories, especially the university and the state: in a particular example, the practice of extending feminist work across conventional subject boundaries.

PERVERSE SEXUALITY

Jervis (1999) takes the development of sexuality as a sociological topic, as a further form of embodied culture, indeed, as one of its major examples. Sexual preferences used to be strongly divided into normal and abnormal activities, and the adoption of an unusual preference would lead to exclusion, even imprisonment. Some still do, but there is a much greater awareness of and participation in sexual fantasy and its role in sexual activity: "sexual theatre", in one of Jervis's phrases. It is possible to partake in sexual activities in the pursuit of all sorts of symbolic and social pleasures, to locate one's self as either participant in sadomasochistic encounters, for example, or to simply be given pleasure by transgression and the acting out of power relations. Conversely, everyday life can be seen in fantasy terms. Jervis points out the irony in punishing the pleasures that masochists get from humiliation by subjecting them to a humiliating public trial. In a similar analysis, Anne McClintock points out the subversive possibilities in seeing the judge and jury as engaged in sexual theatre: the thought occurs that in real trials "Under his purple robes the judge has an erection" (McClintock 1993: 221).

As Ken Plummer once argued (1982), human beings are capable of sexualizing any encounter, and also of desexualizing any encounter as well. To take his examples, someone looking at a photograph of people playing football can find it sexually arousing while, conversely, both doctor and patient are capable of desexualizing a medical encounter involving actual intimate touching. People do not simply follow scripts provided for them, as in the classic Freudian analysis of perversions that sees them as an attempt to understand erotic feelings with infantile conceptions. People these days are perfectly capable of investing a shoe with an erotic charge, perhaps experimentally, with no compulsions, even if they have never had a perverse infantile encounter with one. People can find anything sexually arousing: recent reports (possibly apocryphal ones) describe men having sex with bicycles, venetian blinds or pavements. The activities that remain taboo – bestiality, for example – simply lack strong public advocates, Camille Paglia (1994) once suggested.

TOWARDS DEDIFFERENTIATION?

If we can generalize from these examples, it is possible to suggest that modernity has unleashed a particular dynamic that begins with the growing autonomy of culture from the conventional "social bonds": family, work, neighbourhood, religion. These social organizations no longer regulate, and experimentation, transgression and deviance become routine, at least in private and personal life.

Jean Baudrillard is famous for offering a particularly acute analysis. He translates the decline of conventional social bonds as the end of the real itself (e.g. in Baudrillard 1993). Incidentally, this is why we should forget Foucault, he says (Baudrillard 1987), whose description of a surveillance society with devilish machines for regulating people in tight detail involves a strong but redundant conception of social reality that has not described an actual social formation since Nazi Germany. Simulation becomes the norm, to such an extent that it becomes impossible to conclusively announce that one's views and practices are fitted to, or constrained by, "reality". One result is of special significance here in that our views of politics are hyperreal, saturated with commentary and refutations as spin doctors develop their art: politicians, celebrities and public figures issue statements that are promptly taken as evidence of a cover-up; these accusations are denied, which only deepens the suspicion of a cover-up; and so on.

It is not only the "real" that loses its validity and impact, but the "other" as well. Stephen Crook *et al.* (1992) explain that this arises from a momentum that pushes modernity over into postmodernity. The emergence of "differentiation" becomes so excessive that it produces an ironic "dedifferentiation", where there is so much social difference or otherness that it ceases to become remarkable or to have any particular political impact. Pressure groups for sexual minorities undergo further differentiation, or splitting. Everything becomes politicized, as more and more minorities emerge to claim their rights, until they become indistinguishable. All can seem very worthy. Sometimes they compete with each other.

For the egalitarian, it becomes impossible to know whether one should prioritize disabled wild swimmers, Welsh pagans or elderly bikers, and it is easy to experience "compassion fatigue" or "posture cramp" (Cohen 2004). There are discussions on prioritization, and we examine some in the Conclusion. In the earlier phases of modernity it might have been possible to appeal to some generally accepted form of rational ethics – utilitarianism, say – to arbitrate between the various claims or to invite expert judgement. However, in "second modernity" (*Journal of Consumer Culture* 2001), the legitimacy of experts, such as philosophers, scientists or social scientists, has been radically undermined. In such circumstances, an excessive individualism develops, but it is not an empowering one. Instead, individuals are left to find solutions basically from their own resources.

THE PERSONAL IS POLITICAL AND THE CHRIST IS ETHICAL!

It could be argued that feminist theologians want it all ways, that is to say, as feminists, we begin with the understanding that the personal is also political and, as theologians with a feminist stance, we claim that Christ is about ethics not about hypostatic unions. We are very interested in the kind of world that a belief in Christ seems to generate and, as has been seen in earlier sections, feminist theology has not always been delighted with the world that belief has, in the past, generated. Feminist theology is grounded in liberation theology and its overtly political stance towards the poor. This method, under the influence of feminist and postcolonial thought, has been expanded to critique many aspects of the systems under which we find ourselves. Liberation theology has, therefore, been struggling to rearticulate itself because it had originally placed a great deal of emphasis on the state and its ability to change (Petrella 2006: 2). Feminist theology has moved on and with the development of body theology and sexual theology it has been able to continue to address many of the urgent questions in society that often have economic underpinnings but are understood more broadly as political. Chapter 3 will have more on the changing method of classical liberation theology.

In terms of embodiment, feminist theologians have understood these matters of exclusion and even oppression as fundamentally Christological. If one central tenet of much feminist theology is that incarnation should be understood as an ongoing process in the human/divine then it goes without saying that each body should be considered in that light. In terms of race, while the early feminists such as Rosemary Radford Ruether and Heyward were active in the civil rights movement in the

USA, their theological reflections have laid the ground for a development in systematic theology. Ruether wished to take seriously the Jewish roots of Christian thinking and was not prepared to brush over Hebrew messianic thinking with a gloss of metaphysics. Central to Jewish messianic hope was political action, since for the Jews religious and political life was synonymous. Even when their ideas around the Kingdom became more transcendent, they never lost sight of the importance of politics. The Messianic Kingdom was one with its feet planted deeply in the earth; it was political and social. However, it appears that it was also deeply patriarchal and this is not entirely surprising given the patriarchal nature of much contemporary Judaism and the increased understanding of the Messiah as a warrior king. Ruether is insistent that this was a story that developed under pressure of circumstances and was not the entire Jewish heritage from which Christians could draw.

Further, Jesus did not appear to accept such a hierarchical scheme and evoke Davidic Kingly hopes; rather, he praised the lowly and outcasts for responding to his message while the reigning authorities stay encapsulated in their systems of power. Further, he did not envisage the Kingdom as otherworldly, nationalistic and elitist (Ruether 1983: 120). He saw it come on earth when basic needs were met and people could live in harmony. In this new community we would not simply be servants but brothers and sisters, thus replacing the old idea of patriarchal family with its inevitable inequalities (Matthew 10:37–38; Matthew 12:46–50; Luke 8:19–21). Jesus also declared that God was not speaking in the past but rather speaking now to challenge the law and its outdated, life-stifling interpretations (John 4:10; John 8:4–11; Matthew 9:10–13, 9:18–22; Mark 2:23–28). Ruether argues:

> Jesus, restores a sense of God's prophetic and redemptive activity taking place in the present-future, through people's experiences and the new possibilities disclosed through those possibilities. To encapsulate Jesus himself as God's "last word" and "once for all" disclosure of God, located in a remote past and institutionalised in a cast of Christian leaders is to repudiate the spirit of Jesus and to recapitulate the position against which he himself protests. (1983: 112)

While the battle against forms of exclusion such as racism are always central to the feminist theological agenda, the emphasis is on how this may be achieved through changing the religious roots of much of this thought. In short, the hierarchies of a dualistic theological way of thinking exclude all that is not like God, and God in this system is white, male, straight and master of all he surveys.

FROM EXPERIENCE TO SYSTEMATIC THEOLOGIES

Womanist theology has its roots in the historical suffering of black people in America. Their history, so embedded, in the inhumanity of slavery screams with pain, indignity, death and the stifling suffering of powerlessness. The emphasis in womanist theology on wholeness and life-affirming action presents problems for womanist theologians when they consider traditional models of atonement. The notion that Jesus died for us is not a healthy paradigm in a community in which coercion and suffering for the benefits of others has been a harsh and lived reality. Kelly Brown Douglas (1994: 95) is not alone in declaring that a new understanding of this central doctrine has to be sought. She is also fully aware that many within the black community actually find it strangely comforting to be able to identify with the suffering of Christ and to feel that he saw, and sees, theirs. However, Douglas reminds us that black people in slavery who declared that Jesus was their liberator knew nothing of Nicene creeds. Their declaration was firmly based in the reality of the here and now and not metaphysical theology. What they believed Jesus could do for them in the dire reality of everyday life was the crucial thing. This Christ was not one to be set aside for worship but was in the nitty-gritty of life and the transformative power of following his actions was emphasized. This has meant that womanists have developed an understanding of Christ that can never move far from the realities of the lives of ordinary black women (*ibid.*). While many womanists make a connection between Jesus's suffering and that of women they are also keen not to let his suffering obscure theirs. Alice Walker (1993: 274) places a plea in the mouth of one of her characters, Tashi, that the suffering of women should be the focus of sermons rather than the long-ago suffering of Jesus. Tashi asks, "Was woman herself not the tree of life? And was she not crucified? Not in some age no one remembers, but right now, daily, in many lands."

Of course, this requires a major shift in the Christian understanding of suffering. Delores Williams (1993: 169) challenges the notions of surrogacy and structural domination innate in traditional interpretations. Jesus is released to glory by his suffering while black women are imprisoned in theirs, yet encouraged to believe that suffering is somehow sacred. In identifying women with the tree of life, crucified womanists are careful not to glorify this identification. Rather, they look for the end of suffering and the full flourishing of their lives in this world. Christ, then, is the healer and the one who releases others into abundant life.

The re-examination of the cross and the place of suffering in Christian redemption has led some theologians such as Heyward and Dorothee Soelle (see Isherwood 2001: 89) to no longer see the cross as anything other than a political tool, the means by which many within the Roman Empire died in order to subdue the people; they go as far as to say it has no redemptive or atoning function beyond spurring us into action to stop the crucifixion of our fellow humans in the modern day in whatever form this may take. However, Rita Brock points out a potential danger since Christologies that are about submission, even if it is the Son of God who submits, "sanction child abuse on a cosmic scale" (1988: 63). By ritualizing the suffering of Jesus, kyriarchal power protects itself from those who may otherwise object to their own suffering. By making his death non-political, the status quo, be it ecclesiastical or governmental, can preserve itself. However, if we see his death as a callous political act and image the resurrection as the presence of Jesus "going before you to Galilee" (a place of political dissent), then the cross does not support kyriarchal power but actually undermines it (Isherwood 2001: 88). This is a profound change not just in theology but in society and one that comes from those who have through generations been seen as objects within white supremacist rhetoric. The theology that has emerged from the reflection of womanists on the double jeopardy of being black and female has implications way beyond their immediate sphere; it questions the ethics and politics of enforced suffering due to economic and other pressures from the powerful middle on those at the margins.

Disabled theology, like feminist theology before it, starts with the body and uses it as a positive place to begin theological reflection. Those who have been imaged as the modern-day "virtuous sufferers" have been swamped by Christian charity, which, however well meant, has acted in a disabling way. It springs from an able-bodied mindset, which assumes that those who are differently abled have to be "done unto". This kind of paternalism gives little respect to the abilities and ambitions of the disabled, but it attempts to make compliant children out of them so that we may all the more find some reason for their suffering. It becomes the suffering of the sweet innocent and is easily aligned with that of Jesus. By refusing to be limited by these stereotypes and engaging with the symbol of Christ the suffering servant, disabled theologians pose challenges for theology and for the "rituals of degradation" carried out by the "caring". These include avoidance of eye contact, speaking for or about a disabled person when in their company, and a strange fascination with the bodies of the disabled. All these modes of engagement are fuelled by basic Christian concepts such as virtuous suffering or segregational charity and not least the connection of sin and suffering. All these approaches will co-opt people with disabilities into their own oppression, that is, they help foster low self-esteem and dependency.

Nancy Eiesland urges "acting out", which she describes as a theological method that joins political action with resymbolization (1994: 62). It is the enactment of holding bodies together in societies filled with overt discrimination. The political action involves equal rights and access campaigning as well as face-to-face encounters with those who operate from the level of unthinking stereotypes. In short, acting out is the revolutionary work of resistance to acquiescence. Of course, this means coming to terms with bodies and their sometimes disagreeable aspects. This is not all celebration and can demand a huge price in terms of realistic engagement. Eiesland talks about "survive-able" bodies, which are those that refuse to be self-flagellating because they do not fit the standard norm but instead learn to live with the pain and pleasure of being who they are. She rightly points out that in a society that wants us to engage with the obsessive quest for perfect bodies, this act of self-worth and self-love is an act of resistance and liberation.

Elisabeth Stuart picks up on Eiesland's claim that "Jesus Christ the disabled God disorders the social-symbolic orders of what it means to be incarnate" (quoted in Stuart 2000: 171). Along with Graham Ward, she agrees that Jesus's body witnesses many displacements; that is, incarnation, circumcision, transfiguration and resurrection all profoundly destabilize our idea of what materiality really is. The Church as the body of Christ shares in a very unstable body, a body that calls all knowledge about bodies into question. Stuart suggests that this also calls into question notions of gender. In addition, according to Stuart, Christians live in a world that they believe is in the process of redemption so they have to live in critical connection with social constructions. Therefore, Christians will not only perform gender differently but will also have radical views about beauty and perfect embodiment. Stuart reflects on the experience of some disabled people, who have different ideas about body boundaries. Many who use wheelchairs claim there is an invisible boundary between them and the chair; the same is the case for those with artificial limbs. This body boundary fluidity is, according to Stuart, a good model for Christ, the one who knows no fixed rules of matter and dissolves boundaries. Christians have had at the heart of their symbolic world a broken, tortured and displaced body yet they have been slow to engage with this reality living as they have done in the ivory tower of dualistic metaphysics. Here we see that in the hands of those who claim their disability as part of their subjectivity a profound new understanding of traditional doctrine comes about: those who were simply objects of Christian charity and societal marginalization become those who are at the centre of a reworking of theology.

On the global stage, Christianity has, throughout history, often been exported along with an imperial agenda and, as we know, empire building is always done at great human cost to the indigenous people. In many of these countries women have reflected on their suffering and begun to imagine new ways of understanding it and indeed freeing themselves from it. Like other countries and peoples on the receiving end of colonialism and the imperial Christ, African Christians are very cautious about embracing a suffering Christ. On a continent where physical suffering seems endemic a suffering Christ is still a very attractive prospect for some because he could champion their cause. In this sense Christ's suffering is a midwife to the new, not a silencer of the oppressed (Oduyoye 2001: 25). The cross is political as well as religious because it is the focal point for radical change in society through the commitment of people.

As sociologists have pointed out, one of the new types of scapegoating is in relation to obese people, a category that in itself is constantly changing. While this is true for both genders it does seem to be particularly harsh in its treatment of women, who are even accused of wishing to kill their children through the way they feed them. This is if they manage to have any children, as the rhetoric tells them how difficult conceiving and labour may be for the large body; this is if the large woman can find a partner in the first place. This seems all the stranger because we appear to be at a time in history when medical advances have made it possible for us in the West to be more optimistic about the fact of embodiment, yet we fail to fully celebrate this new reality. Rather, we trivialize our new embodied possibilities through the "thinness religion which bankrupts us". It bankrupts us because it makes us despise our bodies because they are not perfect and not indestructible. In size, as in other matters that feminist theologians have turned their gaze to, it seems that we need to move towards a more generous, dignified and realistic way of living in the body:living in harmony with our flesh and not in a battle against it.

Certainly we can understand that the female body as a signifier of the state of the nation, the culture, the clan, which we now accept as one way in which it is seen, has to be controlled. It has to show that civilization is central to any particular group of people; this is why so many bodily behaviours that are not acceptable in women are tolerated in men, indeed, at times almost seen as part of "manly" behaviour. It is the female body that marks the boundaries of a decent society, which is why rape is so common in war; it breaks down the boundaries and insults and defiles the society, not just the woman, and as such those boundaries have to be policed by patriarchy. The interesting question for feminists today, then, is why it is the slender, almost anorexic, body that signals the edges of a decent society. The 1960s saw Twiggy introduce us to the girl/woman: the body that at 5 foot 7 inches weighed just 5 stone 7 pounds. We have to wonder how this body replaced Marilyn Monroe in her size 16 glory or, before her, the rounded bodies of a hundred years ago. It is curious though that this ideal body is in many ways not a female body at all. To be that slender means that all the female secondary sexual characteristics are suppressed. When a person weighs so little there is not much spare for hips, thighs and breasts. This is where plastic surgery comes in and we are given a strange creature: a body that does not have enough natural flesh to signal its femaleness with large false breasts attached, which declare its sexual attractiveness.

Kim Chernin (1983: 97) believes there is a direct correlation between the standards set for women's beauty and the desire to control and limit the development of women. She demonstrates this through a survey of the past forty years and the rise of feminist consciousness and the equal rights agenda. Starting in 1960 she reminds us that Marilyn Monroe was the icon of female beauty. This was the decade in which women protested Miss World because women paraded and were judged by the passive male gaze. It was also the same decade in which anorexia as we know it emerged and spread very rapidly among those who wished to work in what had been male preserves. In the 1970s bulimia began to be noticed and Weight Watchers opened its doors; it had been preceded by diet workshops as early as 1965. In the mid 1970s the "addict" status of being overweight was set in place through the opening of Overeaters Anonymous, which sits well with the psychopathological view of women and weight that was prevalent at that time. Chernin notes that these two very different movements competing for the minds and hearts of women, the women's movement and the diet industry, had very different languages for women, which she believes highlight social concerns beyond the body (*ibid.*: 100). The diet industry spoke of shrinking, contracting, losing, loss, lessening and lightweightness while the women's movement spoke of large, abundant, powerful, expansive, development, growth, acquiring weight, acquiring gravity and creating wider frames in relation to the lives of women. Interestingly, women who embraced either of these options were doing so in order to make sense of the world they inhabited yet the bodily permissions for them could not have been more different. While those entering the women's movement were aware that they entered a political struggle, those who joined diet groups had no idea that this was also what they were doing; this was the case because they entered the domain of the body, which was highly symbolically charged, and understood the body as something to be shaped according to the political ideals of wider society. Of course, this makes it appear that the worlds were divided along very clear lines but the truth may be more paradoxical. Most women are committed to the idea of their own growth and development while many are also concerned with the notion of full participation in society, whether they are feminists or not, and at the same time their bodies find it all too easy to be obedient to the conventional world. Chernin's focus on the emergence of the diet industry alongside the women's movement is very reminiscent of Daly's claim that the worst excesses of gynaecology emerged at the time of first-wave feminism. That too was a rhetoric of what would be best for women, how the real woman should be and a wider rhetoric about health concerns.

It was in the 1950s that the explicit link between size and religion raised its head and it was a Protestant phenomenon with all the trademarks one would expect. In 1957, Charlie Shedd (see Griffiths 2004: 166) wrote a book entitled *Pray Your Weight Away*, in which it is claimed that fatties are people who literally can weigh their sin. Fat, he argued, is the embodiment of disobedience to God since it prohibits the Holy Spirit from penetrating one's

heart. This has now become a multimillion dollar industry with such programmes as Gwen Shamblin's Weigh Down Diet. Shamblin hit the head-
lines with her bold assertion that fat people do not go to heaven because
grace does not go down to the pigpen (*ibid.*: 1). She entices people into
the programme with the promise of holy romance, telling the almost-all-
female audiences that God is a handsome and charming, loving and rich
husband; he is the hero they have all been dreaming of, who will give them
all they ever dreamed of. There is no questioning of social and economic
hierarchies and the accepted assumption is that women who become slender will have access to all these things, not just as a divine love affair, but
also in their lives. Griffiths is among the first to point out that beneath the
façade of the normal and natural beautiful body of the Christian diet industry lurk some very concerning assumptions about beauty itself. She writes
that Christian diet cultures have a central role in "the reproduction and
naturalization of a racialised ideal of whiteness purged of the excesses associated with non-white cultures" (*ibid.*: 225). The "otherness" of non-white
and also non-middle-class women was used to illustrate the elect nature
of those who could and should adopt the diet culture. It is spelt out very
clearly by Anne Ortlund in her book *Disciplines of the Beautiful Woman*.
In this classic work of white supremacy she states that "primitives" are not
expected to be slim; they are "plump and dark" and uncivilized, living as
they do, she claims, in mud huts. So the ideology of thinness carries with it
an agenda of race, ethnicity, civilization and breeding.

So, as Nelle Morton (1985) told us, the journey is home and, under the
cosh of a disempowering Christian diet rhetoric, this is a journey back to
our bodies, to a place of once again inhabiting this flesh that holds within
it the divine incarnate. What might a fleshy sensuous revolutionary Christ
bring to the world? Susie Orbach (1979) argues that bodies affect environments they are in, so a female body entering what had been an all-male
terrain had to become harder, more muscular and angular in order to pose
no threat to the system itself, let alone the males within it. The systems
that have been built on separation, independence and control cannot have
within them any hint of the maternal because the fear of the alternative
values this holds would be overwhelming. The maternal that is represented
by the large body is both the birth mother and, in this case, the divine
mother; the symbolic and not actual reality of this mother is of importance
here because both carry alternative, softer, more relational values. The
fear that the patriarchal order would crumble in the face of the devouring
maternal is a real one for those patriarchs who have built empires through
lives running from the intimacy with the mother that they felt was removed
and from which they have never recovered. Fat women have to be removed
from corporate life because they literally embody a set of conflicting values
that threaten. There is not only room, but an extreme need, for the presence
of the Fat Jesus and her sisters, then, in the public world of the patriarchs;

they need to carry their threat and their alternative life proudly on their broad shoulders and rolling Amazonian hips.

The fat body, rather like the grotesque body before it, represents multiplicity: a bulging, open body in the process of becoming that is completely out of keeping with a bounded theology and a bounded society. What appears to be emerging is an obscene Christ, one who challenges all the boundaries and opens up the whole divine process. Marcella Althaus-Reid has spoken of an obscene Christ. By this she means that obscenity uncovers what needs to be made visible. For example, she says that the black and feminist Christs are obscene because they uncover both racism and sexism inherent in Christology. Speaking of the necessity for the uncovering of Christ, Althaus-Reid says, "any uncovering of Christ needs to follow that pattern of obscenity ... at the same time, because Christ and his symbolic construction continue in our history, according to our own moment of historical consciousness" (2001: 111). For theologians, this consciousness had shifted and it is a matter of theological deceit and even falsehood if we continue to construct Christologies on the old knowledges. We too need to create an obscene Christ in matters of shape and size. We have seen the worlds that are created by fat phobia, fear of the maternal and the phallic world this gives birth to, and the glorying in the anorexic that is killing millions of women; all these worlds are in themselves a crime against the incarnational glory of individuals but they also play into larger systems of oppression. The Fat Jesus is obscene and asks profound questions that we need to answer in our skin. For followers of an incarnational religion, it is within that skin, that policed body, that their revolution lies since it is here that the God they claim to believe in situated the power to transform the world.

FEMINIST DISLOCATIONS OF THE OTHER

What these examples show is that those who have been seen as the "other" have, within feminist theology, become those whose experience actually helps to shape and recreate theology itself. In their marginality they become central to the process of change. However, as elsewhere mentioned, this does not actually mean that they wish their place to be centralized since this would render it useless in terms of challenge to traditional theology. There is always movement from margins to centre and back again; this is the nature of liberation theology and certainly of feminist theology. Those on the margins are a crucial voice but their voice must be heard in order that the margins do not remain the same and generations of people remain unheeded. However, what may be emerging here is what might be considered a weakness of liberation theology as a justice movement. After all, justice movements need victims and perpetrators in order to be effective.

What they are less good at is what Queer theory has helped theology be good at, and that is moving beyond boxes and boundaries, what might be called true transcendence, that is a crossing over from one social reality, one identity, to another. The value of Queer theory to Queer theology will be discussed in the next chapter but here it is worth mentioning that it has been a crucial addition to the liberation struggle in all its manifestations. It has, among other things, enabled a rethinking of the concept of transcendence that feminist theology has so vigorously held at bay in its combination with dualistic metaphysics in traditional theology. However, once we remove the idea of moving up and above and beyond and replace that with the notion of crossing over to new realities we have a space in which we can speak of the unfolding of God as a movement, not to a static and perfect space, but rather to engagement with dynamic encounter and transformation, which moves us in the here and now to new spaces of the here and now. It becomes a way of moving out of static immanence of repeating ways of being that do nothing but reproduce what is. The role of the other in this process appears to become changed from that of the abject to that of the essence of change itself and in this way not one that is to be eliminated but rather one that is to be the seed of the "I will become what I will become" of us all.

3. THE HERMENEUTICS OF OTHERNESS

Discussion of research methods in sociology has tended to become separated from other substantial themes, including theoretical ones, although there is still an approach that sees both as necessarily combined. In this older, and possibly more continental, tradition "methods" involve a theoretical struggle to clarify the proper objects of study. In British sociology, discussions of methods tend to be divorced from this wider context, but the broader approaches appear here too, in Adorno, and as we progress through feminism and get to theology.

In many cases of funded sociological research, particular methods are specified by the funder; they require quantitative data quite often, and sometimes even specify that there must be a survey, perhaps combined with some focus groups. Demands placed on sociology courses for vocational relevance quite often result in acquiring knowledge of methods that will suit commercial interests: opinion polls, surveys of customer responses, fairly simple feedback questionnaires, and, again, perhaps some focus groups. Methods tend to be taught in a separate module, and to be given a separate section in dissertations or theses, making the positivist assumption that adequate methods are the route to valid knowledge.

We are interested here in what assumptions are being made about otherness and how it might be studied systematically. It is clear, to begin with, that sometimes others are asked just to be a source of data for sociological purposes, sometimes they are modelled or typified in particular ways (as rational actors or typical schoolteachers, say), and sometimes they are allowed much more time and space to expound or demonstrate their worldviews in what is seen as their own words and actions. In this latter tradition, a sense of "surprise" is almost a working definition of an adequate grasp of others (Willis & Trondman 2000) although an "illusory co-presence" is also featured (Clough 1992).

SCIENTIFIC METHODS

Karl Popper expounded the view that there was only one kind of scientific approach, best developed in the natural sciences but equally applicable to the social sciences. Hypotheses will arise from processes of conjecture, but to be accepted as science they need to be subject to processes of refutation (Popper 1963). This is what distinguished science from other approaches that could not be refuted through empirical test, quite often because "ad hoc hypotheses" (see Magee 1974) were continually being brought forward in order to explain the lack of empirical success. The most famous targets of this critical approach were Marxism and Freudianism: in skilled hands they were impossible to refute because they offered explanations of the very intractability of empirical data that otherwise might have falsified them. It was the duty of scientists, on the other hand, to render their hypotheses in such a way that they could be falsified by empirical data. Ideally, the final decision would rely on agreed "basic statements" (*ibid.*: 36) such as whether something could be observed or not.

Considerable criticism greeted this argument. Of particular force was the offering by Thomas Kuhn (1970). In general, heroic exposure of one's own hypotheses to falsification was not typical; instead, most working scientists accepted the value of working within particular approaches, paradigms, which offered sets of theoretical and operational procedures to solve particularly characteristic problems. This was the way that science was taught as well. The result was that most "normal" science attempted to solve puzzles within paradigms rather than putting everything at risk by devising decisive tests. Popper and Kuhn finally met in public debate in 1965, with rather indecisive results at the time, although Kuhn's book went on to become a best-seller.

Steve Fuller (2003) saw the debate as a characteristically cautious event, with the major opponents carefully avoiding each other, and the subsequent "Kuhn/Popper debate" as a largely pedagogic construction of sociology and philosophy of science textbooks. He points out that the usually favourable citation of Kuhn in social science is curious to say the least, since Kuhn was advocating "business as usual" for science, including corporate science, and that he actually saw very little application of his ideas to social sciences. Popper's image as some conservative and elitist upholder of science as a superior form of cognition is equally unfortunate. Kuhn, ironically, became a flag-bearer for postmodern relativism, whereas it was Popper who argued for the constant need to judge scientific thought and policy in a sceptical and critically rational public arena.

Popper's radical credentials had been established earlier in another classically indirect debate with his critics, this time on the left: *The Positivist Dispute in German Sociology* (Adorno *et al.* 1976). In many ways, this can be seen to mirror many of the elements of feminist approaches, although it does not highlight gender and sexuality specifically. Popper's position paper, which sparked off the *Dispute*, argued for the objectivity of science, based on its full openness to criticism, and its independent evidence base; this stance, not at all the uncritical borrowing of the methods of the natural sciences, was the way forward. The concept of truth was also important, if only to aim to avoid error. For Popper, this involves a correspondence theory, the correspondence of hypotheses to facts, and it is this that prevents full relativism. Overall, rational discussion is possible, even in social sciences. We need to be aware of the limits of our efforts, but we should not retreat into nihilism. We cannot prove what we suggest, but we can falsify and make progress.

Perhaps the most fluent and prolific advocate of such a sceptical approach is the educational researcher Martyn Hammersley, who had caused controversy, for example, with his insistence that the common allegations of teacher racism needed critical testing: he had argued that despite their possible political value, many of the major studies displayed both logical flaws and evidential weaknesses. Foster (1993) summarizes the argument. Hammersley sparked a huge debate about the status of feminist methods (see e.g. Hammersley 1994), discussed below. He has written critical evaluations of all types of quantitative and qualitative enquiry, such as the very common use of case studies (Foster *et al.* 2000) and action research (Hammersley 2004), or the demand that educational research should always be "useful" (Hammersley 1997) and he is a famous iconoclast at the policy level, raising serious doubts about many of the cherished beliefs of teacher trainers; he sees problems in forming "communities of practice" (Hammersley 2005), for example. Educational researchers need to develop their own specialist roles, "concentrating on the task of producing knowledge and trying to ensure its validity" (*ibid.*: 18).

We can take Adorno's other contributions in the *Dispute* to explore further, although this simplifies the issues. Adorno insisted that even Popper's approach ignores the complex and contradictory nature of the social totality that is artificially simplified by the processes of abstraction required to pin down discrete factors, variables and their interactions in the laboratory: "One would fetishise science if one radically separated the immanent problems from the real ones which are weakly reflected in its formalisms" (Adorno *et al.* 1976: 109). As for empirical sociology, social events express "a field of tension of the possible and the real" (*ibid.*: 69), so there are "methodological" reasons for social theory to be critical: "methodological" being used here in its sense of being adequate to the object.

At a more detailed level, the categories in questionnaires often do relate closely to what people actually think about themselves, but the problem arises when these are seen as natural or final opinions; how they become natural is the real issue (*ibid.*: 75). It is necessary that sociology pursues a critique of illusions in this way, but positivist science forbids it: another way in which it maintains ideology. An adequate analysis would grasp wholes and parts and values, and pursue insights as well as following dedicated application of methods. Insight in this case arises not as a mere flash, but from attention to experience over a long period, the gradual recognition of its truth. Nor can an avowedly interpretive and subjectivist approach solve the problem; social life itself reduces humans to objects, and quantitative sociology's methods merely mimic this process. In this way they are actually more adequate than interpretive sociology! In particular, "opinions" are not to be despised in terms of some absolute concept of truth attainable only by scientists, but explained as the result of an untrue society. For Adorno, positivism is allied to political and social domination and bureaucratization, while value neutrality merely subordinates science to what is accepted as valid value systems (*ibid.*: 59).

Positivism promises absolute certainty, and thus relief from anxiety, but certainty is only possible through "identity thinking", a tendency to recognize connections between simplified concepts and equally simplified reality. It appeals especially to "new functionaries ... empty beings lacking experience" (*ibid.*). Positivism fits best the administered world. It was critical once but is now systematized. The systematization involves procedures that are no different from those of magic: mimicking reality in laboratories and models and hoping that successful intervention in the latter will lead to changes in the former; "the so called methodological purity of positivism really arises from the rationalisation of the process of research" (*ibid.*: 50).

Adorno argued that "The insight into society as a totality ... [means] that all the moments active in this totality ... [are not] reducible one to another, but must be incorporated in knowledge; it cannot permit itself to be terrorised by the academic division of labour" (*ibid.*: 120). The Institute for Social Research (the Frankfurt School) had always been interdisciplinary, and Adorno himself had collaborated in some empirical work on the "authoritarian personality", deploying insights from Marxism, Freudianism, psychology and sociology. More broadly, the underpinning concept of a totality meant that any attempt to classify social life or describe it in privileged concepts would be to reduce it: "The name of dialectics says no more, to begin with, than that objects do not go into their concepts without leaving a remainder" (Adorno 1973: 5). Adorno goes on to advocate an immersion into heterogeneity, an acknowledgement of the diversity of objects, rather than seeing them as "a mirror in which to re-read [oneself]" (*ibid.*: 13), an attempt to see individual and disciplinary perspectives as explicable given a "knowledge of the whole" (Adorno *et al.* 1976: 37), and the pursuit of negative dialectics as "an ensemble of analyses of thought models" (*ibid.*: 29). The whole project is quite similar to Deleuze's project, discussed in Chapter 5, although drawn from quite different philosophical resources, as Deleuze and Guattari note themselves (Deleuze & Guattari 1994: 99). It would be interesting to try out the criticisms of Adorno on Deleuze or on any version of an immanent totality, including any in feminist theology.

For defenders of Popper, such as Hans Albert (Adorno *et al.* 1976), negative dialectics clearly rests on the dogmatic and obscure foundation of "totality", prompted by a "decided reason ... namely ideological thought" (*ibid.*: 254n.). The dialectic is "an unrivalled instrument for mastery of complex connections even if the secret of how it functions remain concealed up till now" (*ibid.*: 257). Albert insists that totality is seen elusively and tactically, as *not* the sum of parts, and *not* just a more general concept, and this helps preserve it against the criticisms of the anti-holists, including Popper. Totality is *not* just a matter of formal logic either, which again avoids criticism and introduces arbitrariness. We are left with "metaphors rather than methods" (*ibid.*: 195). At crucial moments, totality is defended by a shift in ground, claiming that its main role is in political emancipation.

THE SOCIOLOGY OF DAY-TO-DAY SCIENCE

The underpinning role of non-specialist argument and social circumstances in the actual conduct of science has been studied in some detail since, by, among others, Bruno Latour and his associates. Latour (1987) argued that science in action could be seen best as the operation of a whole network of actors, or rather "actants". The network clearly included technicians, instrument-makers, funding bodies, and scientific entrepreneurs who mobilize resources in order to build laboratories. It is the size and power of these laboratories that really decide which theories get accepted, Latour argues, since they can amass so much support for their approach, in the form of subsidiary experiments, supportive research findings and so on, that it becomes impossible to criticize it. Latour is also notorious for arguing that scientific machines play such a decisive part in the formation and extension of networks and the transformation of data (into portable and widely applicable forms) that they deserve the title of "actant" as well as human beings, an additional twist to the usual French rejection of the humanist subject.

Other accounts (e.g. Latour *et al.* 1986) take us deeper into the controversial processes discussed above, where scientists are actually defining, measuring and operationalizing elements to turn them into "variables". Such accounts help open scientific findings to public discussion and counter reification and "scientism" (in the form of a belief that scientific methods just need to be followed in order to deliver the truth).

QUANTITATIVE WORK: AN EXAMPLE

There is space for only one example here, and an obvious one involves an attempt to acquire some quantitative data on spirituality, even if this is a choice that makes criticism easy. Kathleen Dillon and Jennifer Tait (2000) decided to research the claim often made by American sportspersons that "spirituality" is connected to better sports performance. Prayer before performance was of special interest. Dillon and Tait set out to operationalize and test this claim by employing two questionnaires that they devised themselves: the Spirituality in Sports Test (SIST) and the Zone Test (ZT) (as in feeling you are "in the zone" when performing well). SIST is a ten-item test, including items such as "I used spirituality or religiosity as a way to help me with the emotional roller-coaster of winning and losing". The ZT involves items such as "I have had the feeling of being able to move around, between, or through my opponents". Responses could then be collected together in an overall scale.

The problems of reducing large and possibly highly variable experiences to a range of options are clear, although defenders of the approach would say that at least there has been some attempt at clarification. However, the whole issue of what spirituality or being "in the zone" actually mean, and whether they mean the same thing to all participants, is being ducked by these instruments. In a classic manoeuvre, the authors compared their approach to similar ones developed by others to check their internal consistency: this is an agreed substitute for the much more vexed issue of validity (whether the answers indicate some meaningful response) in such studies. The authors claim that one test, with which SIST was compared, has been acknowledged to be reliable and valid (but we are not told how this other test was validated).

The authors administered their tests to sixty-two students who were involved in sports teams at a non-sectarian college, and processed the results. The ensuing data indicate statistical correlations between scores on the two tests: a correlation coefficient of 0.49, significant at the 0.001 level. The authors are conventionally cautious about any suggestion that spirituality causes presence in the zone, however. In another classic manoeuvre, residuals are suggested and more research recommended. No doubt studies like this could eventually become part of the coach's manual so that prayers before games become compulsory parts of warming-up, and then the clinching argument for positivist techniques might emerge; they yield useful knowledge that works. Critics could easily retort that one way in which such research "works" is in reproducing oppressive systems by taking their categories uncritically. However, at least the workings of the study are clear and transparent and open to criticism.

It is possible to see even this brief example as also telling us something about others (to address the specific issues of this book), to begin to see how important spirituality is to American team players. Of course, there is a need for caution in examining the results of quantitative studies, since those results were often produced in the form of summary statistics; average values are given, for example, and generalizations are based on them, which is a way of managing differences.

The medical journalist Ben Goldacre has done much to develop critical insights about the use of statistics in an accessible and public way in his columns in the *Guardian* newspaper, his blog and in Goldacre (2012). He has explained the need for random controlled trials, described how randomness and chance work, sometimes in ways that are counter-intuitive, and has done much to discuss various methodological biases in quantitative studies. The overall effect is to assist non-specialists in being able to discuss otherwise mystifying and apparently authoritative data – not rejecting positivism but taking it on, as it were. Perhaps the most startling example of a little-known influence is publication bias: the tendency for studies that produce interesting, "breakthrough" or majoritarian accounts to get published and read more often.

QUALITATIVE WORK: SOME EXAMPLES

The other main approach to understanding others, however, is to investigate their subjective opinions. This approach has been used with some success in understanding the reactions of particularly "deviant" groups such as drug-takers, extreme sports enthusiasts, people who administer tattoos to themselves or members of casual male homosexual groups, but also just minority groups such as professional boxers, immigrant street-traders and university students.

Actual research techniques to investigate the subjective can be generally called ethnographic, involving an attempt to see the world as others see it and then to write down an account, and the usual origin of the approach is located in anthropology, where intrepid researchers would go off and live with a variety of apparently exotic others in order to let the community socialize them into their particular worldview. Originally, this might have been done by launching particular expeditions to observe and to discuss, if possible, what was observed, but anthropologists soon "came off the balcony" in order to live with the people they were observing. The intention originally could be tied to the interests of colonial authorities in managing the peoples they were regulating, but, as with the studies of "deviants" above, later studies offered a more sympathetic view, helping to challenge stereotypes. E. E. Evans-Pritchard and Eva Gillies's (1976) classic study of the Azande showed that their system of witchcraft was complex and rational in its own terms, for example, while Frank Lutz (1988) was later able to return the compliment and show that the behaviour of some senior academics and university administrators displayed many of the characteristic beliefs and practices of witch-hunting among the Kuikuru.

Studies like these have made the other seem surprisingly normal, and normal conduct surprisingly variable, to paraphrase a common claim. Until Laud Humphries's famous study (1970), few people other than the participants knew of the complex practices of "normal", often married, men who visited particular public conveniences (known as "tearooms" in the relevant slang) for rapid, impersonal sex with other men. These men somehow negotiated successful silent interactions with each other, using all sorts of subtle signals and cues to decide what was appropriate, how to spot police officers and how to react to any innocent "normal" who might wander in. They would stop in on the way from work, and then go away to enjoy perfectly "normal" life with their families. Humphries's study is ingenious, and these days deemed highly unethical: finding a neutral role for himself as an observer, avoiding physical sexual contact, while posing as voyeur or lookout, and recording behaviour unobtrusively, then using contacts with the police to track car number plates to do some follow-up research on the "normal" sections of the men's lives.

"Autoethnography" is perhaps the technique most eager to break with all the tenets of positivism. Researchers confide their feelings to readers and sometimes to participants. Carolyn Ellis and Arthur Bochner (2006), for example, in an exchange about the value of the technique, say that they want to partake of the full emotional aspects of life. They are not ashamed of emotions; only male elitists try to avoid them (although it tends to be the nicer emotions that come through – any residual anger, jealousy or hatred are conventionally managed). They "want a feeling of community, and [we] have to admit that it would feel good to be validated by the academic community" (*ibid.*: 446–7). The authors say they are writing a story, and are not attempting to do "realist" description. They describe watching the victims of Hurricane Katrina on television, for example, and want to express solidarity with them: "He [A black man speaking to a reporter] speaks so poetically ... like the house he lost he is split in two" (*ibid.*: 430); and later "Art [Bochner] and I [Ellis] wipe tears. 'Those people feel all alone,' I say. 'Somebody's got to show them that we're all in this together'" (*ibid.*: 447). Norman Denzin, in a companion piece, agrees that the researcher needs to deploy "new writing practices ... autoethnography, fiction – stories, poetry, performance texts, polyvocal texts, reader's theatre, responsive readings, aphorisms, comedy and satire, visual presentations, allegory, conversation, layered accounts, writing stories and mixed genres" (2006: 420). We should be prepared to "write messy vulnerable texts that made you cry" (*ibid.*: 421).

Autoethnography and polyvocalism also display an interestingly limited form of poststructuralist argument, Susanne Gannon argues: a poststructuralist stance is sufficient to rebuke the scientist claims of other methodological approaches, but the conventional notion of the humanist subject is left intact, as a unified self "capable of self knowledge and self articulation" (2006: 474). The writing can slip into therapy as a response to "postmodern 'trauma culture'". It adopts "standpoint epistemologies ... identity politics and a politics of location" (*ibid.*: 476), assuming that there is some original experience to study which is somehow unconstructed and unconstituted.

It can come to rely on "the 'validity of tears'" (citing Lather 2000) and the "epistemology of emotion" (Gannon 2006: 476).

Ethnographic work has attracted a number of additional criticisms from poststructuralists and from one (possible) postmodernist. These criticisms can be seen as suggesting that otherness is subordinated to the same after all. Clough (1992) has pointed to the ways in which writing techniques create validity for the researcher and reader in transforming people's experiences into conventional and plausible stories. She points out that very similar techniques are used in more popular forms of writing such as in films or television programmes. These are all variants of realist techniques, where the idea is to create a plausible world with which it is easy to identify.

The possibly "postmodern" critique can be found in Baudrillard's (1993) work on simulation and the eclipse of the real. Ethnography seems to assume that people can be found who are not simulating a response, who are not aware of what research is trying to do, and who are not provided with a wealth of information, perspectives and opinions about the world but have to rely on their simple home-grown and authentic "beliefs" or "responses". Identical points have been made about questionnaires too. Clifford (1993) provides some famous examples in anthropology, including the controversy about the famous work of Margaret Mead on adolescents in Samoa: inspired by her own strong views about "natural" behaviour, Mead had to manage the responses of the Samoan girls she talked to. Clifford suggests the girls had already lived elsewhere, had knowledge of Westerners, but were content to conform to the stereotypes of Samoan girls.

Similar points are made by Bourdieu in his critique of Western scholasticism (2000). Anthropology (and sociology) works usually by imposing a model of the reflective subject. This seems entirely natural to scholasticism, which then has to reconstruct what is really practical logic as "spontaneous theories", as ethnomethodological "rules", or as "thick description" (*ibid.*: 52). In the latter example, Clifford Geertz's famous reconstruction of the Balinese cockfight and its symbolic significance involves creating "the Balinese with a hermeneutic and aesthetic gaze which is none other than [Geertz's] own" (*ibid.*). The subjects of research are assumed to be as interested in "pure" topics as scholars are, to go around interpreting every possible understanding, recreating their culture as scholars do. Actually, symbolic systems in particular are not just coherent grammars, but also have a practical dimension; they have to be "economical, easy to use and turned towards practical ends, towards the realization of wishes, desires, often vital ones, for the individual and above all for the group" (*ibid.*: 55).

Sociologists' own practice is even less frequently studied. Sociological language is only partly independent of ordinary language, which leads to particular confusions of translation. This is sometimes covered in sociology simply by assuming respondents can ask themselves sociological questions such as "Do you think social classes exist?" (*ibid.*: 59), or offering yes/no alternatives to scholastic questions. These are never normally posed and impossible to understand unless you adopt a scholastic perspective, which is often just assumed to be universal. The results are treated as serious data nonetheless, in what can only be described as using "symbolic violence", imposing scholastic interests while claiming to be neutral and universal. Bourdieu's own approach is to offer participants the chance to develop their own "self understanding and self knowledge" (*ibid.*: 60). The approach is best displayed in the massive collection of stories of "everyday suffering" preceded by more sociological commentary to help provide some sort of context (Bourdieu *et al.* 1999).

FEMINIST EMPIRICAL METHODS

It might be worth setting up themes for the next part of the discussion, by first spelling out some possible implications for feminist methods. At the risk of overgeneralization, feminist methods in sociology seem to have begun by offering a critique of positivism as inadequate to capture the totality of women's experience, and to continue the Adornovian suspicion of a link to political domination by suggesting that male interests and male logic lie behind what can look like neutral and universal techniques of investigation. At its simplest, this can involve a critique of the assumptions in commonly used definitions. To take some examples, "work" has often meant paid work, excluding women's unpaid domestic labour; "social mobility" has involved studies only of male earners and occupations (Stanworth 1984); "leisure" has implied a split between paid work and domestic life that is based on male experience and which is often literally incomprehensible to women in households (Deem 1986); "oppression" has focused too much on economic rather than domestic familial forms (Women's Study Group 1978; Kuhn & Wolpe 1978). Even when emotions are discussed, as in studies of adventure and escape, they are framed in terms of "male heroics" to display a strengthened conventional self (Beezer 1995), rather than the desire to experience "feminine jouissance", to disappear, lose oneself and become the other as in Fullagar (2002).

Ideas to develop more feminist ways to record such experiences have led to an interest in theoretically informed diaries, unstructured and unreconstructed life histories and autoethnography, as discussed above. Hierarchies between researcher and researched were to be abandoned in favour of "authentic" conversations between women (sometimes exclusively between women). Research adopted an open feminist standpoint, scorning the artificial neutrality of conventional social science and openly supporting feminist politics.

Hammersley (1992) inaugurated a controversy about feminist claims to have developed a suitable and separate empirical methodology: briefly, using subjective methods was not exclusively a feminist technique, while unstructured methods and partisan research invited challenges to validity. A lively debate ensued. Loraine Gelsthorpe (1992) suggested that the points Hammersley was making were actively discussed within a diverse range of feminist methods that did not cohere in the way he had suggested. Caroline Ramazanoglu (1992) argued that feminists had already shown that the tradition of research, with its criteria of adequacy and validity, and the institutions that supported it, were not abstract and neutral but were themselves deeply implicated in patriarchal power.

Hammersley's specific responses (1994) included suggesting that the same reliance on abstract reason and empirical evidence could be found in Ramazanoglu's retort, mixed with unsupported assertions, and that the distinction between politics and research, although problematic, should still be maintained, and was maintained at least in sections of Ramazanoglu's reply.

FEMINIST WRITING

The most general case to which the specific dispute refers can be seen in the controversy that arose over feminine writing among feminist French poststructuralist writers in the 1980s. Irigaray (1985) develops an argument that parallels Adorno's critique of positivism that we saw earlier. There is something broader and wider that escapes any attempts to pin it down, operationalize it, measure it and research it empirically, at least without leaving a considerable and crucial excess outside these efforts: "the feminine". The feminine eludes empirical research. It is fluid whereas empirical methods have to solidify before they can proceed. It is outside conventional representation, because the representational system is saturated with phallogocentrism. Conventional notions of the speaking subject will represent at best a frozen and reified version of the feminine subject. It follows that when femininity speaks, it does so in a fluid, diffuse, displaying "turbulent movements" (Irigaray 1985: 116) that resist male logic, and even male grammar and syntax. This can be misunderstood as "our restlessness, whims, pretences or lies" (*ibid.*: 215). The feminine is a multiplicity, a hybrid, heterogeneity, and it is possible to detect some similarities with Deleuze's terms here. This argument also reconceptualizes Otherness; as we saw in the previous chapter, women express the feminine corporeally or materially, and this reduces or structures as "instances" other (mundane) differences among them. But the same corporeal basis for sexual difference now makes women radically other, compared to men.

In answering questions about her work, both at a seminar, and in the formal setting of the defence of her thesis, Irigaray addresses methods directly:

> [I]sn't it the method, the path to knowledge, that has also always
> ... led us astray, by fraud and artifice, from woman's path? ... In
> order to reopen woman's path ... It was therefore necessary to
> note the way in which the method is never as simple as it pur-
> ports to be ... The method ... Is always a project, conscious or
> not, of turning away, of reduction and of reduction in the arti-
> fice of sameness. (*Ibid.*: 150)

Rather more aggressively, she responds to a question asking what a woman is by replying: "The question 'what is ...?' is the question – the metaphysical question – to which the feminine does not allow itself to submit" (*ibid.*: 122). This actually looks rather tactical, since she asks a "what is" question herself a couple of pages later, and responds "normally" to another one on another page. In response to the comment "I don't understand what 'masculine discourse' means", she replies, "Of course not, since there is no other" (*ibid.*: 140). She is asked how she can operate with standard language in her role as a lecturer and analyst, and replies:

> In order to [speak in conventional settings] it is true that I have
> to begin by using standard language, the dominant language ...
> [To] say something about your desire [as a woman] is scandal
> and repression. You're disturbing the peace ... You're shut out of
> the university. (*Ibid.*: 144–5)

Indeed, she was removed from her post at Vincennes soon after.

She also explains that, when doing her thesis, she engaged in a certain mimicry of conventional philosophy, in the role of "philosopher's wife", drawing attention to the absence of reflexivity and self-exploration, and narcissism, in a way that included deploying feminine charm to distract from excessive theoretical concerns. There is a clear implication that this is a common tactic among women when working with men or cooperating in their research projects.

This discussion illustrates perfectly the total entrapment of femininity for Irigaray. Conventional philosophy (and even more so social science) deploys categories that cannot grasp femininity and, indeed, help to freeze and marginalize it. It is so effective that people cannot even grasp alternatives to it. Those few feminist philosophers who have dared to explore the alternatives have been forced to choose between adopting an alienating marginal outsider position in universities, or be expelled for threatening the whole structure: "feminine pleasure signifies the greatest threat of all to masculine discourse, represents its irreducible 'exteriority' or 'extraterritoriality'" (*ibid.*: 157).

If empirical research can never examine femininity without first distorting it into a simple option within masculinity, a male other, how should femininity be expressed? Irigaray advocates building a feminist language based on the potentials of female bodies, which has led to some controversy about essentialism, which we discuss elsewhere: it will be a language based, for example, on the proximity of female lips, which indicates and actualizes a holism between women that breaks out of the compartments provided by the male imaginary. "You? I? That's still saying too much. Dividing too sharply between us: all" (*ibid.*: 218).

For sceptics, this is a suspiciously closed account that seems capable of defending itself against any criticism: "what is" questions are conveniently ruled out as inappropriate, at least on occasions; male logic happily does not apply; only women seem to be able to understand femininity, but in a rather mysterious way that cannot be subject to scrutiny. There is also a lingering elitism, since it is clear that most women themselves are trapped within phallogocentrism, except for a few philosophers. The sort of speech that Irigaray describes (and the sort of writing Hélène Cixous *et al.* [1976] described below) is the work of leisured elites with substantial cultural capital. Further, they depend for their force on substantial generalizations that are possibly empirical (if not, they are definitional or tautological), as in Cixous *et al.*'s views on the publishing industry (below). If these are empirical claims, they need to be researched.

Women have to speak, for Irigaray, but they have to write for Cixous *et al.* (1976), overcoming all the constraints of male language that threaten to silence them, overcoming their own doubts. Again they need to write in unconventional forms, if that is what suits them, whatever the consequences:

> Write, let no one hold you back, let nothing stop you: not man, not the imbecilic capitalist machinery in which publishing houses are the crafty, obsequious relayers of imperatives handed down by an economy that works against us and off our backs: and not *yourself*. Smug-faced readers, managing editors and big bosses don't like the true texts of women – female-sexed texts.
> (*Ibid.*: 877, original emphasis)

Irigaray's own writing might be taken as an example here, with its lyrical, poetic and what Deleuzians might call "delirious" pursuit of implications, themes and potential criticisms, seemingly as they occur. It is hard to illustrate this in a short commentary, but the controversial essay "When Our Lips Speak Together" provides an accessible example: "Wait. My blood is coming back. From their senses. It's warm inside us. Among us ... You mean ...? What? Nothing. Everything. Yes. Be patient. You'll say it all. Begin with what you feel, right here right now. Our all will come" (Irigaray 1985: 212).

Deleuze's interest in experimental writing (Deleuze 1995) and avant-garde filmmaking (Deleuze 1989) is also developed on the basis of similar critiques about conventional thinking and writing as "objectivist" or ideo-logical, as we shall see. Deleuze comes close to Irigaray in seeing writing as especially potent when it is minoritarian, depicting "the intolerable, that is a lived actuality that at the same time testifies to the impossibility of living in such conditions" (Smith 1997: xliii), and addressing a people to come. Such writing deploys unconventional language: "stuttering", "portmanteau words", abandoning grammar and syntax. Daniel Smith says the point is to develop a style that causes language to flow, all the way to its limits, as a process, a form of schizophrenia. Again, it is easy to detect elitism: Deleuze's first essay starts by announcing that "writing is inseparable from becoming" (1997: 1), but ends by saying "if we consider [this definition] there are very few who can call themselves writers" (*ibid.*: 6).

Bourdieu has offered a general form of critique, showing how sociologi-cal claims can be smuggled in behind literary forms in a way that fore-stalls criticism, although his barb was aimed specifically at Roland Barthes, whose work is:

> deliberately esoteric, flaunting all the external signs of scientifi-city, making liberal and often approximate borrowings from the combined lexicons of linguistics, psychoanalysis and anthropol-ogy ... Through a double break with the humility of the uni-versity "clergy" he sets himself up as a hermeneutic modernist, capable of unlocking the meaning of texts by applying the latest weapons of science, and ... through an interpretation itself insti-tuted as literary work ... [claims to be] situated beyond the true and the false.   (1988: 117)

Briefly again, the category of "woman" can also be seen as a performa-tive one (Butler 1990b). The "performative turn" sees all social life as a per-formance, not just the release of subjectivity but an attempt to orientate towards others (audiences). Social relations and understandings emerge from this interaction. This had the effect of avoiding any dubious essential-ism in research and politics, and then of avoiding some of the constraints of narrative theory, especially the apparent universality and unavoidability of narratives of the Oedipal scene and the incest taboo, both of which posi-tion women as powerless. Judith Butler extended the notion of gender per-formance to all sexual identities, ranging from "normal" heterosexual ones to "deviant" bisexual or "perverse" ones, including combinations of them. This avoided, for good or ill, the more partisan variants of lesbian and gay theory based on claims that lesbians and gays constitute the (only) "proper objects" of studies of sexuality (Butler 1994). It became possible to identity particular research traditions as becoming suitable, first those associated with analysing performances in popular culture, especially film (e.g. Butler 1999; Dyer 2002).

MODERN HERMENEUTICS

A prominent version of modern hermeneutics advocates a general approach that attempts to recover the subjective meanings in cultural products (books, say) by tracing the contextual effects of cultural traditions. There are several other inflections and perspectives, including a tradition of biblical interpretation, which seeks, roughly, to establish the parts of the Bible that are the word of God and those parts that are the specific interpretations of the human authors in their social contexts (Palmer 1969; Mueller-Volmer 1985). Cultural determinism is denied, but so is idealism, and the individual is accorded a genuine role in actively interpreting cultural traditions instead of just "bearing" the workings of a structural semiotic model.

Hans-Georg Gadamer's work specifically (e.g. Gadamer 2006) reinterpreted the explanatory strategies of the social sciences (and theology), including Freudianism, in terms that made hermeneutics the universal approach to action as well as to written texts: hermeneutics "becomes the foundation not just for theology but for all historically based humanistic disciplines" (*ibid.*: 35). In particular, the key notion in modern hermeneutics is the indispensability of preunderstanding in any form of communication. This has clear implications for the claims of positivist science to be able to work without presuppositions, but there are no easy answers for qualitative methods either. Actors do not always understand their own actions when they perform them, and to focus on personal meanings would risk "a subjectivist narrowing of the problem" (*ibid.*: 41). Nor is empathy much more than "an aesthetic drama" (*ibid.*: 42); it is asking too much of the empathizer, and it ignores the problems of "confronting his own horizon with the complex horizon of the past" (*ibid.*). Sociological models and typologies feature "a concealed dogmatic base" (*ibid.*: 37) in order to develop an apparently suppositionless method.

Ultimately, no method whatever can replace understanding, and no researcher can stand outside the processes of reciprocal understanding. Understanding only takes place "when one brings one's own presuppositions into play!" (*ibid.*: 45). The interpreter must have a productive role in understanding. The interpreter and the text each possesses his, her or its own horizon and every moment of understanding represents a "fusion of these horizons" (*ibid.*), involving a willingness to put one's own assumptions to the test.

The process of coming to interpretation with presuppositions, obtaining a limited understanding of the traditions of the other, then going back to modify one's own presuppositions before returning to find out more about the other, is the "hermeneutic circle". This endless circling is inconvenient, perhaps since it seems to defer understanding endlessly, but the alternative is worse: claiming to be able to impose some expert understanding of events, relations or processes is dogmatic and must exclude the other.

Another substantial debate followed Gadamer's claims, and, again, this can only be discussed very briefly here. One issue turned on whether or not there were various kinds of cultural universals that would assist or even explain the cultural traditions in question: interests in death, birth and sex, for example, or in life itself (see Thompson 1983). Others have focused on issues of more immediate interest to sociologists, such as the role of political and economic systems in shaping cultural traditions and the individual's reception of, and access to, them. Habermas, for example, has suggested a systematic role for "strategic" and "distorted" communication (in Habermas 1976): distorted forms get close to classic notions of ideology in that they represent particular interests as universal ones. Accompanying this analysis is a view that there is a genuine human interest in emancipation, later embodied in the critical potentials of ordinary language, which drives critique of cultural traditions, especially those that block potential emancipation.

John Thompson (1983) wants to reintroduce classic sociological concerns by suggesting that social institutions play a key part in mediating cultural traditions to individuals by translating general possibilities into "schemata" that are specific enough to guide action. At the same time, these institutions themselves are shaped by more general political and economic forces that "structurate" them. These processes proved an agenda for sociological investigation, clearly.

However, the methodological problem of the hermeneutic circle remains to raise doubts about the claimed objectivity of any such analysis. Gadamer (2006) argues that the emancipatory claims of ideology critique presuppose that the critic holds some special scientifically based knowledge in advance. Hermeneutics does not claim to know in advance what the case is, or, for example, that only distorted communication can take place. Nor does it claim to know what undistorted communication would look like. Hermeneutics is sceptical towards every system of knowledge, especially when it claims to deliver enlightenment, emancipation and the like. Specifically, hermeneutics argues that prejudgements are deeply rooted and not easily dissolved by reflection. Sociological endeavours must also answer the objections above about a dogmatic base and so on. Ultimately, in Gadamer's famous phrase, there is no "truth" and no "method".

It is worth noting for this book especially that the same problems must apply to theology. For example, Gadamer (2006) says that Rudolf Bultmann attempted to see theological hermeneutics as a matter of demythologizing, a term that implies both a critique of historically flawed notions of understanding, and some universal understanding. However, such a universal understanding was itself "a construction absolutely full of presuppositions based in the modern Enlightenment" (*ibid.*: 38).

In another example, Ward (2004) notes that cultural assumptions must inform readings of the Bible and understandings of God and gives several examples of how this has led to misunderstandings of human bodies and of sexuality. He then faces the problem of the hermeneutic circle: that Queer or embodied theology might equally reflect the cultural assumptions of the theologians he supports. His solution is to develop a transcendental or immanent turn, actually rather a similar one to Deleuze (Chapter 5), and argue that God is, or lies behind, all of these more specific and culturally contaminated interpretations. God is everywhere, so relativism is misguided. As with all such arguments, however, there is a claim to special knowledge of the non-empirical, gained reliably and without presupposition. Knowledge of God, or the virtual, must claim to break out of the hermeneutic circle.

It is worth noting that, for Deleuze at least, there is another solution. There can be no guarantees in consensus, and no fixed or agreed ultimate grounds upon which to found such a knowledge of the virtual: we encounter eventually the deep and groundless contingency of the "eternal return", and connecting "the individual, [this] ground and thought" (Deleuze 2004: 191) ends in madness or melancholy. It amounts in the end to a matter of philosophical taste: "it is certainly not for 'rational or reasonable' reasons [sic] that a particular concept is created" (Deleuze & Guattari 1994: 78). This "faculty of taste ... is ... instinctive" (ibid.: 79). Rather than developing knowledge or truth, "it is categories like Interesting, Remarkable, or Important that determine success or failure ... Only [mere] teachers can write 'false' in the margins, perhaps" (Deleuze & Guattari 1994: 82).

However, with Deleuze and Guattari, and with other forms of radical philosophizing, a turn towards politics offers another way forwards. We might accept the abstract point that no knowledge can be presuppositionless, and listen to the voices urging us to investigate our own presuppositions, but that does not stop us from following a more limited project to identify the harmful presuppositions in particular politico-philosophical traditions.

Overall, it is quite a while since sociologists confidently claimed that they could provide useful and completely accurate knowledge of others. Ritualistic faith in the ability of particular research methods to deliver such knowledge still persists in some subdisciplines, but a pragmatic approach tends to be more common where one does what one can to deploy suitable methods, often in combination, and remain alert to the more obvious kinds of threats to validity. Serious challenges tend to be sidelined in this pragmatic approach; after all, some sort of empirical work is usually demanded by credentializing or funding bodies. Ethics policies offer some sort of minimal safeguards for participants while not preventing the necessary symbolic violence inherent in most conventional sociological procedures.

Social science will never deliver a presuppositionless science. If we compare it to the powerful techniques of natural science, and the technologies it can deliver to supplement or even replace its methodological dilemmas, it will always seem insufficient. It is unlikely that sociology will ever regain its position as a kind of research wing for government. Perhaps that is the wrong comparison though, and we should look instead at some of the rival claims to knowledge, including knowledge of others. If sociological samples, research instruments and data handling techniques are suspect, how much more so are the bases for the confident pronouncements of politicians, journalists and spokesperson of various kinds? Such people also assume that unified subjects are the source of knowledge, and they operate with a false universalism that simply ignores the serious limits and implications. Has sociological analysis led to a better understanding of others and otherness than before?

FEMINIST THEOLOGY AND METHODOLATRY

As we have seen, secular feminists have had their issues with sociological methods and it is fair to say that feminist theology, while employing certain "takes" of its own, has a sceptical eye on what Daly calls "methodolatry". For Daly, people get lost in methods and she insists that most methods have been developed by men in order to shield themselves from realities of real lives and situations (Daly 1981). This holds the feminist theologian to account and suggests caution in any method used. Further, unlike sociologists, we are not researchers, but are rather engaged in processes of co-redemption and co-creation. This means we are less concerned with describing the world than in changing it, but this also involves having some idea of how the systems in place actually work and how to offer alternatives both within and through feminist theology. Classical feminist theology used four starting-points: process thought, liberation theology, women's experience as norm and Elisabeth Fiorenza's hermeneutics of suspicion in relation to texts. Process thought enables the use of experience as central in creation of any theology; it emphasizes mutual becoming and relationality as well as questioning the narrow specializations used by most disciplines. In encouraging an interdisciplinary approach, which has been central to feminist theology, it also lays open the way for imagination as a method. This is taken up in the hermeneutic of suspicion in which Fiorenza (1983) urges what she calls creative actualization as the fourth part of that process. As the name of the approach suggests, Fiorenza scrutinizes each text with a suspicious eye looking for androcentrism. She then encourages a proclamation of the absence of women or their thoughts, a remembrance of women who are absent and then a creative actualization that involves putting women back in the picture. This involves a multidisciplinary approach, since women cannot simply be inserted into texts without a real understanding of how life may have been and what clues there may be in

91

the absences for where women may have been. A very good example of this is the discovery of the Corinthian women prophets, a search that began with Paul's command for women to stay silent in church. Rather than assuming he meant do not gossip, the question was asked about what they may be saying and this led to an interdisciplinary investigation of women in the period and what their concerns may have been, as well as searching Christian documents of the time to look for other gaps that may shed light on women's lives, which in turn led to a wonderful creative actualization of the lives of these women prophets. Fiorenza is not willing to abandon the power potential that lies in women remembering our heritage. She argues that to abandon our history, particularly our authentic history within biblical religion, is to give in to oppression, since it is oppression that deprives people of their history (*ibid.*: xix).

One of the tasks of contemporary feminist scholarship is to extract the "content" of the message from its patriarchal "form". This requires a critique of the prevailing patriarchal culture as much as it requires textual analysis. Women have suffered under patriarchy and because of this are asking if the texts that would perpetuate such suffering can really be "divine absolutes". This question is translated by feminist biblical scholars into research that shows the texts not as absolutes, but as faith responses, therefore not as archetype but as prototype. This is a major shift in scholarship because it opens up the possibility that scripture can be transformed, thereby effecting its models of faith and community (*ibid.*: 33). Feminist biblical scholarship enables us not only to "find the women" in Christian beginnings but to locate the power struggles behind the texts. They were struggles that women lost but looking and finding them can be an empowering experience for contemporary women.

Women of colour have also been recovering their own history both as historical fact and as biblical narrative, which has led to very challenging readings. For example, women of colour who sit with the Syro-Phoenician woman understand Jesus to be exhibiting sexism and racism; the references to dogs can be less easily spiritualized when such words of abuse are part of one's everyday life. Hagar has also been claimed as a woman who highlights the myth of global sisterhood; she is doubly abused both as a surrogate and as a scapegoat and the story highlights that Sarah is not her ally.

The constant questioning of received truth and wisdom is a project that is not that of feminism alone. Postmodernism has just such a task as its lifeblood. However, many feminist theologians warn that while it would be foolish for feminist theology to attempt to overlook the postmodern discourse, it may be equally foolish to embrace it wholeheartedly. Beverly Harrison (1999) is cautious; she is concerned that the political edge is lost when we are required to accept all truth claims as equal. For her, feminism is more than one truth claim among others; it is a political agenda set against the worst excesses of the patriarchal mindset and actions and as such she feels it cannot be overlooked by mainstream theology and particularly its fundamentalist wing.

I AM WOMAN?

The emphasis on women's experience has often been the place in which critics of the method have attacked feminist theology. Obviously, for the traditionalist, God has laid down all that is needed so the application of anyone's experience to dogma and doctrine is seen as a no-go area. Of course, what is overlooked in this approach is that dogma and doctrine themselves are only fossilized versions of someone's original experience and reflection upon it; these were men, so women asking that their experience be brought to bear is not quite as strange as traditionalists like to believe. Old norms were based on external authority, which meant calls to conform according to set religious and societal patterns. The leap of faith that feminist theology is willing to take is the opposite; it places authority firmly within the individual's own experience; it is internal authority that guides one to truly moral action. Networking has always been at the heart of this form of method since simply ending at personal experience was never envisaged; giving a voice to women meant to all women. Naturally, this immediately strained and even broke the notion of global sisterhood because it quickly became apparent that "woman" is a broad category that encompasses many forms of experience, some of which are in tension with each other. However, networking remains a particularly important method and one that women have always engaged in when they support one another in unofficial groups. Networking is a method of working on the same level with each other, of engaging in activities beyond hierarchical structures, of developing one's talents not in the field of competition but in solidarity with other women and men sharing the same goal. Through networking women promote goals by creative nonconformity. This is also a space in which the complexity of what is understood by women can be explored.

Butler suggested that woman is in process and so not a finally defined other who can be placed outside; she is a body becoming; this is a language of its own, a language of materiality (Butler 1990a: 30). And Braidotti speaks of figurations that are politically informed accounts of alternative subjectivity: the living "as if", which is "a technique of strategic re-location in order to rescue what we need of the past in order to trace paths of transformations of our lives here and now". She continues, "'as if' is affirmation of fluid boundaries, practice of the intervals" which sees nothing as an end in itself (Braidotti 1994: 6) – not even the Symbolic Order, one suspects! While she does acknowledge that we as women have no mother tongue we do have linguistic sites from which we both see and fail to see. For this reason, we need to be nomads, taking no position or identity as permanent but rather trespassing and transgressing, making coalitions and interconnections beyond boxes. No language, but we do have bodies, bodies that have been "the basic stratum on which the multilayered institution of Phallocentric subjectivity is erected [she] is the primary matter and the foundational stone, whose silent presence installs the master in his monologic mode" (*ibid.*: 119). These same bodies can be radically subverting of culture when they find their voice beyond the fixed language and meaning of the masters' discourses. However, this does not require us to be static or defined by male definitions because, as she tells us, it is the feminine that is a "typically masculine attitude which turns male disorders into feminine values" (*ibid.*: 124) and not the female body – this is free to roam and to express itself, to find new ways of being by thinking through the body.

Critics of feminist theologies often cite this open space, this embrace of endless possibility, as the weakness of the discipline. Surely we need to fix something in order to have a discipline related to anything at all; surely we need women to have feminist theology! But has it not been the simple definitions that have led over the centuries to the exclusions? Butler (2004) declares that multiplicity is not the thing that makes agency impossible but is rather the very nature of agency, precisely the condition in which agency flourishes. Further, she suggests that it is in the fear of the questions posed by multiplicity that we find the creation of the rhetoric of morals as a defence of politics (*ibid.*: 180). She illustrates her point by considering how the Catholic Church deals with issues of gender and sexual difference. The Curia has called for the United Nations to eliminate the language of gender from its platforms to do with the status of women, declaring that the word is simply a cover for homosexuality, which they condemn and do not see as having a place in a rights agenda. They insisted on a return to the word "sex" and their rhetoric attempted to indisputably link sex with maternal and feminine, reflecting, as they saw it, the divinely ordained "natural goodness" of things. To those observing, the agenda was very clear: it was an attempt to reverse many of the gains that women had made in relation to human rights, and it was a narrow defining that could be once again placed at the service of containment and control. Butler puts it as follows: "the Vatican fears the separation of sexuality from sex, for that introduces a notion of sexual practice that is not constrained by putatively natural reproductive ends" (*ibid.*: 191). It is no surprise to her that the Vatican considers the inclusion of lesbian rights in United Nations legislation as "anti-human". In order that all humans may be recognized, it seems that "the human must become strange to itself" (*ibid.*).

Butler goes on to say that this new human "will have no ultimate form but it will be one that is constantly negotiating sexual difference in a way that has no natural or necessary consequences for the social organisation of sexuality" (*ibid.*). Butler reminds us that the body is the site on which language falters (*ibid.*: 198) and the signifiers of the body remain for the most part largely unconscious, which in itself is a language, but one ever unfolding and of many tongues. Performativity is a whole-body engagement, just as incarnation is, and both resist the deadening claws of narrow and controlling definitions of personhood; both expand the edges of where it is we think we inhabit.

Ettinger gives us another slant on what it may be to say we are woman and how this statement speaks of subjectivity in a new way. It appears to move us beyond the creation of the other as the essential reality of the very core of our being. As has been said, Lacan postulates the Phallic symbolic and in so doing creates the space in which we develop a sense of self or as women we become the other, this is found in Freud in relation to loss of the penis and taken up even by people such as Melanie Klein, who mention expulsion from the womb as the reality in which the other is created. Ettinger wants to move behind the notion of phallic castration model to a place where she believes we begin to form a sense of self in subjectivity. She draws us into the borderspace, where she believes there is the potential for a shared threshold, a creative partnership of encounter: where we share without fusion and are different without opposition (Condren 2010: 231). Ettinger does not want the womb to replace the phallus, as this would simply make it a new phallic symbolic; rather, she wants the relation to replace the organ and she sees mother and baby as co-emerging subjects in process and relationship. She suggests that we come into being in the presence of An/other rather than in an absence and that subjectivity is found in relationship not in opposition or loss. She is non-Oedipal, sub-symbolic and non-phallic and in this way suggests that one does not need to displace the other in order to be (*ibid.*: 241). Ettinger is rethinking desire and the Unconscious by reference to a transgressive encounter between an I and a non-I grounded in the maternal. Of course, this is a co-emerging, so the mother is also emerging in this process; she is not the already formed, against which the child would be the incomplete other. There lingers, she suggests, a knowledge of being born together that is not cognitive. To be able to live in this memory space enables us to be constantly renewed and transformed and to achieve compassionate hospitality to the other. This matrixal prenatal borderspace is where we know the co-affecting other, where we are transformed by co-eventing with a radical other, radical in the sense that it is not human but humanizing (Ettinger 2006: 166). Both others are partial and co-emerging; they are the unthought known to one another, the trace of which may be remembered through life. After birth, Ettinger says, the mother and child become phallic objects to each other but a trace remains that gives us glimpses of the known in the unknown and refers to the irreducible strangeness that cannot be utterly other. Ettinger believes the matrix speaks to the strangeness in me, which is where both the political and ethical lie. It is this that makes me aware of the co-existence I share with a stranger, a non-I who cannot be left alone in otherness. The stranger can come close with no fear of oblivion. So the creation of subjectivity is an ongoing ethical and political process as much the outcome of choices as of any gendered psychic inheritance (Condren 2010: 243).

It is the repression of maternal origins that leads to many creations of culture and religion that replace the mother's body with that of the male and place mastery at the centre of reality. Christianity has been particularly good at these stories and rituals and one can also say in its insistence on monotheism it has sacrificed the co-emerging of the multiple in order to ensure the mono-authority of the male God. It seems that the importance of the mother's body and the co-emerging that is envisaged here can be understood as central to the creation of radical otherness if we do not fall into the cultural psychic defence mechanisms developed over generations by the male in order to overcome insecurity and fear. This may appear essentialist but this is not the sense in which Ettinger develops it, since it is not the womb as a physical organ that Ettinger emphasizes, but rather the co-emerging relationship, and this is something that can be carried on between people throughout life. If we are to take Ettinger as a starting-point, it would seem that what we have laboured under with Freud and Lacan has simply been a male defence, this time in psychology, against maternal materiality, which has led to a social symbolic that excludes and damages.

LIBERATING WOMEN

Feminist theology grew out of liberation theology when it was realized very early on that even poverty, a central concern of liberation theology, looked and felt quite different if one was a woman. Feminist theology found much to underpin its own becoming in the work of liberation theologians: women as the doubly or even triply oppressed under current economic systems could be the focus of theological investigation; the violence done to women could be seen as unacceptable, not simply as the outcome of the fallen nature of humans; and the "doing" of theology by the people enabled women to network and actually "do" theology together, focusing on matters that concerned them within both Church and society. Of course, what also happened was a naming of women as other in an attempt to overcome woman as other; as with the poor in liberation theology a group was overtly named in order to overcome the injustices performed on the group. This overt naming was perhaps the first necessary step towards change.

Like other forms of liberation theology, feminist theology has been asked a fundamental question with the dramatic shift of economic reality since the fall of the Berlin Wall. Althaus-Reid is among those who ask if an economy of solidarity between people can replace debt models of economics (more of this in Chapter 4). The Peruvian economy of Tenderness is one in which people help each other; the gift of love is supported by the whole community because even those who cannot physically help still turn up to show that the community is behind the action, making it a spirituality of reciprocity on behalf of the whole community. A fiesta marks the end of the help and what is celebrated is a spirituality based in minimizing the inequalities in the community. It may be, then, that once again liberation theologies need to turn to indigenous models for a way ahead. Others suggest that the basics of the liberation model still offer an economic alternative, no longer the Marxist model but the very basic humanity of people. Pedro Trigo suggests that a new social imaginary should be based on common humanity. He says that individuals and relationships should be secondary and what should be central to a new economics is the violation of common humanity carried out by advanced capitalist systems (Petrella 2006: 6). He suggests that rather than revolutionary movements being the focus, it is the everyday life of the poor and their rituals of community life that becomes the place for resistance. This is not unlike the move that feminist theology has already made in terms of the individual lives of women becoming places for the critique of the wider social order. In privileging the wider social order, Trigo is moving classical liberation theology a step closer to feminist theology. He says networking is crucial if civil society is to flourish, a place he sees as offering alternatives rather than state power, which he, like many others, sees as having diminished. He understands capitalism as idolatrous because it is willing to sacrifice people to its greed. This is irrational because, through the destruction of nature and the exclusion of large numbers of people, the market will eventually collapse. Feminist theology offers its notion of international networking and the way in which this is based in local groups making their situation and needs known to the larger community and world as an alternative to this choking excuse for democracy under which we currently labour. It is in this way that imaginative and people-friendly alternatives to current capitalism may also emerge, by and through the needs and abilities of the people becoming known. What seems to be on offer here is a way in which the other becomes the radical other in the sense that, while not becoming me, or indeed not even arguing to be the same, the needs and abilities of others play a full and democratic part in changing the systems that have, until now, made them the excluded other, the exploited other and even the invisible other.

QUEERING METHODOLOGY

A relatively new method that has extended the reach of feminist theology is that of Queer theology, which understands its aim as transcending boundaries and crossing over to a new standpoint or identity, often in defiance of Church dogma and politics. This is understood as a breaking towards and a bursting open rather than a destruction, so in theological terms it is opening to greater understanding of the incarnational religion Christians proclaim. So Queer theology takes seriously the Queer project of deconstructing heterosexual epistemology and presuppositions in theology, but also unveiling the different, the suppressed face of God amid it. Queering theology is therefore a deep questioning or an exercise of multiple and diverse hermeneutical suspicions aimed at unveiling the extensive influence not just of heterosexuality but of heteronormativity in even radical theology such as feminist theology. In theology, the question is how the politics of heteronormal identities (political and divine) are deeply embedded in our representation of God and the key themes of Christianity.

Queer theory has three characteristics: the emphasis on the construction of sexuality, the element of plurality, which needs to be present in any reflection, and the idea of ambivalence or the fluidity of sexual identities. But theology has been organized around a givenness, a monotheism, and an exercise of the authority of the metanarratives of heteronormativity. Therefore, Queer theory works as a new "mediator science" in radical theologies. If we were to mention some common characteristics in the process of doing Queer theology, we shall need to consider issues concerning theology as a genre, how people write theology and the focus of reflection of this theology. As a genre, Queer theology partakes of the irony, humour and self-disclosure of the camp genre. This means that it is an "*I*" theology. The theologian does not hide in a grammatical essentialism: for instance, to use a "we", which presumes the authority of an academic body. In this way, Queer theology is a form of autobiography because it implies an engagement and a disclosure of experiences that have been traditionally silenced in theology. Those who wish to incorporate this method in their theological work and particularly those who wish to use it in feminist theology are not without their critics, not least because there appears to be an essential contradiction in using both methods together. Queer theology insists there are no categories and, of course, feminist theology needs a category! However, this paradox does seem to work.

Sheila Jeffreys is at the forefront of those who ask where women go if we transform the discourse from feminism to Queer. If gender is nothing more than a performance that can be adopted at will then, she argues, the edge is taken off feminist politics (Jeffreys 2003: 33). Another of Jeffreys's concerns is that, in considering gender as a performance, we are still stuck within binary opposites when looking for ways to perform. She is, therefore, not at all convinced that anything is challenged but rather the categories male and female are reinforced. She is not alone in her concerns. Liberation theologians are worried that Queer politics has no interest in analysing capitalism, viewing the main issue as one of access and not the system itself. While not overlooking these concerns, most feminist liberation theologians remain aware of the dangers but also of the possibilities when they apply all three methods to their work.

One such example of this is Althaus-Reid who develops the image of a Bi-Christ, a figure who is not bi in the sense of sexual preference but rather in terms of thought and life. This Christ she sees as fluid and full of contradictions: a gospel-based picture, in fact. She argues that the gospels present us with the Prince of Peace and the one who whips the traders from the temple, the one who talked to the women at the well and could not change the impurity laws regarding menstruation. Far from wishing to harmonize these points of tension, Althaus-Reid wants us to embrace them as the fluid movements of Christology (Althaus-Reid 2003: 112). As a theological category the Bi-Christ erases the establishment of hierarchy and power, and overcomes mono-relations; this has an impact in sexuality and beyond, even into economics. She notes the hetero-Christ even defines sexual relations that are not heterosexual: the gay man is seen as effeminate and the lesbian as either butch or femme. These are heterosexually developed categories that prohibit the naming of the diverse range of sexual identities (*ibid.*: 116) that are actually operational within people's lives. It is a stabilizing of categories, a colonizing of experience in order to keep some control. The second example is of how mono-relations also give us economic oppression. Using the colonization of Africa as an example and the way in which the Africans were "civilized through Christ", Althaus-Reid points out that the relationship all under one heavenly Father was indeed under the Father. It was patriarchal and therefore hierarchical in nature, with the African never quite being equal but rather submissive in a mono-relationship (*ibid.*: 119). Here we see that even with an exploration of a sexual category it is possible to also explore the economic system.

We can see how Queer theology offers exciting possibilities in systematic theology in terms of understanding the other but it has also enabled new readings in the history of women in the Church and opened new understandings of what our fore-sisters may have been attempting in terms of overcoming their status as other. What we find in many of the stories are women who defy physical boundaries and so question social sexual roles by their actions. For example, Thecla is an interesting character. To modern eyes and ways of understanding is she a transvestite, is she transgendered or is she transsexual, or is this motif used to tell us something of significance about the relationship with their environment of people who become Christian? Cross-dressing is an ingenious tool because it does not fit categories of sex or gender alone and as such exposes both, so in this way is a form of gender iconography, making visible the spaces of possibility, which are closed off by dichotomous conceptualization.

It seems entirely possible that these stories of gender-bending were written by and for women who wished to subvert the social order, which they obviously saw as part of living the new reality promised by the message of

Christ. Women like Thecla offer a gap in an otherwise assumed "heteronormative history". Of course, we might also note that perhaps they simply played within existing gender categories but we have no way of knowing because we have no details of how they performed.

Queer theology has given many ways to enter into history, scripture and doctrine to find new outcomes and has indeed acted in a creative way as a new mediator science for theology. Coupled with feminist Christological work that insists that the idea of Christ is one of endless possibilities, it has offered a deeper ability to examine notions of the other, placing it, as it does, in a vertical relationship rather than horizontal as traditional theology has done. The other is simply "over there", not out there below the norm or as an alien; the other becomes one that the many displacements of Queer theology makes it easy to be with. The Christian is spoken of as a stranger in a strange land and perhaps the queerer the Christian becomes, the more at home they are, not as an insider or an outsider but rather as the process of incarnational living.

4. CONSUMING OTHERS

> Our enormously productive economy ... demands that we make
> consumption our way of life, that we convert the buying and use
> of goods into rituals, that we seek our spiritual satisfaction, our
> ego satisfaction in consumption ... We need things consumed,
> burned up, worn out, replaced and discarded at an ever increas-
> ing rate.   (Lebov, quoted in Taylor & Tillford 2000: 42)

Capitalism works. It has turned things into rituals, consumption into spirituality, even using the language of religion to sell its goods, and has created
within us a compulsion to consume in order to mark our place in the world
and declare our personhood to ourselves and others. It is reported that,
when asked what it is to be American, many teenage Americans said it was
the freedom to buy goods, echoing Scott Fitzgerald, perhaps, who declared
the difference between rich and poor to be that the rich have longer shopping lists and are happier for it. Given the devastating consequences of this
wholehearted consumerism for the planet and many of the people on it, we
wonder how religion ever gave ground and how theology has failed to find
a usable response. Perhaps it is because there is something very comforting
in consumption and many people do believe, and indeed experience, that
they buy their way to happiness, especially when objects are endowed with
almost spiritual significance. However, perhaps like indulgences before it,
the buying culture of happiness, based as it has been in debt, is about to
reveal that heaven is not for sale. Weber (1985) argued as long ago as 1905
that the Protestant Reformation was geared towards denying the holiness of "things" in its attempt to get back to a book-based holiness and the
result was that meaning was also removed, leaving a large gap to be filled.
The marketplace stepped up to fill this gap in meaning and applied it to
secular products, thereby enchanting objects with what was once religious
holiness. Similar human cravings existed but were fulfilled by vastly different objects found in the cathedrals of consumerism, shopping malls, and

the theologian is left floundering for a language of symbolic exchange that can overcome the advertising gurus and their seductive language.

When thinking about otherness and capitalism/globalization we made the deliberate decision to view the question through the lens of desire because this gives us a different trajectory into the issue and perhaps allows a way to understand something more about the desire for meaning through the consumption of "things". For the feminist theologian it allows an eye on the issue that has been lacking in traditional theology and for the sociologist it leads to issues of choice and determinism, incorporation into capitalism and resistance to it.

We wish to argue a number of things in this chapter, one of which is that the link between the once and for all saviour of mankind and globalization lies in total disregard for the body and the notion that suffering brings us closer to heaven. Under such a scheme we should not be at all surprised that Victorian Christian factory owners had no regard for the working conditions of their employees. They did, however, insist that the workers attend church. If people are of no consequence then the earth itself is even less valuable. There are many reasons for this but, broadly speaking, they fall into two categories: hierarchy and eschatology. The male God of dualism has a strict hierarchy with matter right at the bottom, while the Christian saviour will come again at the end of time and all will be renewed for the faithful. With these parameters firmly in place there is no call for anything but belief and use of the world's resources. Indeed, President Reagan's environmental advisor, who was a Mormon, counselled him that it was our duty to strip the earth of its resources since this was the best way of discharging our stewardship responsibilities. The same hierarchical view lent itself extremely well to the Christ the Conqueror theology, which encouraged "superior righteous Christians" to enslave and exploit most of the world's population and resources (for more on this, see Isherwood 1999). The understanding was that they had a duty to do so.

This history has led to Christians having two quite diverse views about markets and economics. On the one hand, there are those who see the control of markets as a gift of God. These people do not, on the whole, enquire too closely into the effect on workers and the environment. On the other hand, there are those who, setting the scene against a colonial and exploitative background, see the market as almost demonic. In the middle sits the Catholic Church, which wants to see controlled markets in order to protect the poor. Two strong themes emerge from these perspectives: stewardship and justice. Both could guarantee a positive way ahead but neither has to. Stewardship in this context means control of the resources in order to generate capital, but with a "responsible hand", while justice can also mean not stamping too hard on people. We are being too harsh in our judgement, and deliberately so, in order to attempt to highlight that these concepts, while sounding good, are also open to abuse, especially when rooted in certain kinds of biblical theology. It is true to say that much work in traditional theology and capitalism tends to sit between these two poles. Good work is produced but theology itself is rarely interrogated for its part in the problem. God is the focus, as if there were no problem there either. If humans are mentioned it is in terms of their lack of justice/stewardship with little investigation as to why. Even many of those who claim to use a Marxist approach in theology often fail to push home the point that Christianity, with its focus on the abstract and fear of the body, is an ideal home for the development of fetishized consumer capitalism under which products become commodities; that is, they are ascribed financial and symbolic value way beyond what is intrinsic. In theology and economics there is an assumption of a superior value underlying both as a benchmark grounding both in an exchange system.

We should not be surprised that many Christians, far from attempting to find ways to counter the secular value system of consumer capitalism, have actually bought into the idea that a worthy Christian is also a rich one. The prosperity gospel has mass appeal in certain parts of the world where disenfranchisement meets a spirituality that equates the wealth of the Christian message with the wealth of the believer. It emerged in the 1960s within charismatic, fundamentalist and Pentecostal groups and was spread by evangelists. Simon Coleman, quoted in Grau (2004), believes it is no accident that the prosperity gospel arose at the same time as a resurgence in global capitalism, since both display expansionist tendencies and, in fact, in his view, aid one another in that task. Likewise, he says there was no accident that prosperity theology arose in Latin America in the 1980s when the countries were under pressure from the International Monetary Fund (IMF) and World Trade Organization (WTO) to adopt neoliberal economic policies. Christian theology needs to take a long look at itself!

As well as work in theology there have been a number of attempts (e.g. Goody 2007) to create spirituality robust enough to hold back the tide of global capitalism, or at least convert it to more socially just ways of operating, and in the main these have been based on the notion that if we can change the hearts of people then we can, in time, change the world we live in. Unsurprisingly, these spiritualities have taken root in the parts of the world most exploited by the system we have and the question that the West has attempted to face is how to root creative and liberating spirituality within the souls of those who actually benefit from the globalization agenda. There is a slow dawning of realization that the markets do not actually care for anyone, even those who may be said to benefit, because this benefit also has a cost. People in the West are realizing that they work harder in more competitive and demanding places of work without the benefit of union representation and, while this may not compare to the destitution that globalization inflicts on other parts of the world, it is some level of wake-up call for some people in Europe. This desire for a spirituality that addresses the pressures of globalization has led to a new market: that of books in the spirituality of work! While many are attempting to create more justice-seeking practices for workers, others are claiming that spirituality at work will lead to greater productivity and output, which is well documented by Jeremy Carrette and Richard Young (2005). There are some good outcomes from this move to spirituality at work but this is not enough to address the spread of globalization; it merely makes it more humane in places. It seems that some of the theological reflections that wish to strike at the construction of this narrative, rather than its consequences, may be worth consideration in the next decades.

Many became quite excited that just such a theological reflection was to be found in the work of Daniel Bell Jr (2001). Despite declaring the end of history in much the same way as Francis Fukiyama, Bell made a rallying call for theology to deal once and for all with capitalism and globalization. A larger part of Bell's argument deals with desire and the fact that he believes it has been captured by the forces of capitalism. What we need then is a "therapy of desire", which he believes lies in forgiveness. Through returning God's gift of forgiveness for us to others, we are liberated from the hold of capitalism. God did not demand what was due to him; rather, he forgave us and gave up on the terror of justice, as Bell sees it. Bell states, "the claim that forgiveness more faithfully characterises the way God overcomes sin than does the liberationists' account of justice rests upon an interpretation of the atonement" (*ibid.*: 146). This interpretation is that of substitution atonement, which has certain problems attached to it. We may not have paid but an innocent did, an interpretation that sits well with savage capitalism, since Christ's sacrifice is interpreted as belonging to an economy of credit and exchange that is reimaged as a gift of love, a point that Bell seems to entirely overlook. Bell sees those events as Jesus returning the gift of love and obedience to God (*ibid.*: 150); the fact is that there was a crucifixion and this should not be overlooked, even in the light of a resurrection, in the world in which we live today. In fact, Bell does not overlook it, but states that crucified people are bearers of salvation in the world (*ibid.*: 168): that is, as long as they do not complain about their crucifixion and their communities remain open and hospitable to those who have oppressed and crucified their compatriots. Bell finds it amazing that, despite the fact that the blood and tears of the poor make capitalism grind on, they do not lash out but forgive, open their doors and share what they have. This is a very sentimentalized view, the kind that allows us to place the blood and pain within a greater scheme that has the effect of neutralizing it through an argument about greater goods. It is not based in much reality either since in the countries Bell speaks about there has historically been resistance that has been met with US-backed defeat; America has not been slow to bomb countries that do not fall into line, train torturers of regimes that hold the people in bondage and provide money to governments that fulfil its global aspirations. As we see, if we transfer his argument to the Middle East there are outcomes other than forgiveness. Bell is, however, insistent that forgiveness is the first step and that once people receive that grace they will change their ways. He boldly states that capitalism cannot handle forgiveness.

This is the male theology that feminists have been critiquing for decades. It is the kind that valorizes suffering, seeing it as a way to ontologically change reality. Children continue to die and women who have never previously done so sell their bodies in war-torn countries to feed their dying children, but if these are aligned with the suffering and obedience of Christ, all will ultimately be well. This seems to be a green light for savage capitalism, which does not have to worry about suffering but can console itself that it gives people the opportunity to be noble, heroic and salvific for themselves and others under its crushing weight. As feminist liberation theologians have endlessly pointed out, this is a narrative that works only in theory. When placed against the lived experience of women and men, new stories emerge that are less reassuring to the supporters of this slightly warped theology. Suffering and oppression take their toll in the lives of people who do not necessarily become ennobled by it, but simply become reduced and worn down, dehumanized and marginalized.

Bell, however, is relentless when he says reparation is never possible so for liberation theology to look for it is futile; unjust suffering is not overcome by looking for justice but by being borne, and it is the refusal to cease suffering that is the great act of hope in God that is the only solution to savage capitalism. At the heart of this theology is crucified power, the community of the crucified gathering together, where God empowers them and delivers them from being disempowered victims (Bell 2001: 192). These are extraordinary claims from an author who, early in his work, called for religion and politics to be closer bedfellows and criticized even liberation theology for not being radical enough.

Bell argues for the urgent recovery of desire, understanding, as he does, Deleuze and Guattari's (1984) claim that capitalism does not exert power just by extracting labour and production but by capturing and distorting the fundamental human power of desire. Mary Grey (1989) has reminded us that this reclaiming of desire is also a language game because the language of desire, once the domain of theologians, has been taken over by the high priests of the market. While we continue to long and yearn for the new car, the new house and all the goods that shine so brightly, in them we silence God. She is right but we would also wish to point out that the traditional language of theology also sounds like that of the market: in other words, the market did not totally distort it, there were traces there of capitalist exchange in the beginning! The Christian God and the salvation he offers have always had hints of an exchange economy; this exchange economy is evident in some of the more bloody notions of substitution atonement, where the exchange is seen as fair and the sacrifice sufficient in order that the gift of salvation may be bestowed. The price has been paid and the wages of sin satisfied. It is no accident, therefore, that it tends to be fundamentalist Protestants who make the links between financial prosperity and salvation, totally encompassing the suffering of others into their blessed life.

Bell overlooks this glaring problem and prefers to profess that our desire is restless in consumerism, which consumerism encourages, because its true end is found in God. This is not a new suggestion but has a new twist when Bell suggests that to achieve this fulfilment of desire we should examine the world of the twelfth-century monastery. Bell asserts that we are constituted by desire for God, a desire that has been corrupted through sin, which bends desire towards unnatural ends. Capitalism is one such sin that disciplines and enslaves desire, and Christianity "is a therapy, a way of life that releases desire from its bondage" (2001: 3) in order that desire may flow again.

Relying heavily on Deleuze and Foucault, Bell argues that the subject is an assemblage of desires in varying intensities captured, as it is, by particular regimes. The state and also capitalism include a host of what Foucault calls technologies of the self (*ibid.*: 19) but, says Bell, so does Christianity. It works with technologies of desire and this is its great strength in overcoming capitalism (*ibid.*: 2). Liberation theology, with its appeal to justice, has failed precisely because it does not work at this level of desire; it does not have a therapy for desire. Of course, the big assumption that Bell is making here, that we wish to challenge, is that desire for justice is itself misguided and so not real and correctly aimed desire. Bell seems unable to understand God as justice, a concept that is biblical in origin, so he is able to relegate the desire for justice to some second-rate position. It is also necessary to understand human desire as distorted if he is to do this. Feminist liberation theologies certainly have what Bell would wish to call a therapy for desire and it is Christological in nature, understanding our very passions and desires, our *dunamis*, to be the very stuff of Christ. The therapy for desire, in this case, is to embrace and develop the passion that draws us into mutuality with one another and not just with an abstract God. What is called for is an engagement with all that makes us human – passion, desire and relationality – in order to be grounded more fully in who we are rather than uprooted still further through a "therapy" that assumes some innate dysfunction that can be put right only through rooting in an external divine.

The splitting-off from desires and, in so doing, splitting from what makes us fundamentally human, so favoured in much traditional theology, has a strange effect in the world of capitalism; through denying ourselves the right to truly nurture our deepest desires we render ourselves vulnerable to the capitalist treadmill, where what is on offer is quick, short-lived fixes that satisfy manipulated desire. In addition, bodies that do not nurture themselves well are willing to labour for what is in the future, delayed gratification being both a fundamental of Christian eschatology and advanced capitalism.

There is a gendered dimension to the matter of desire. While Christianity has encouraged both men and women to subdue desire, it has also given the power to men to subdue women's desire and in so doing set in place a world of woman-excluding systems. Male domination and, with it, the denial of desire in women works through the hegemony of impersonal organization and both the bodies of women and society at large have been impersonally organized by aesthetics and rationality, two aspects better suited to Greek metaphysics than the sensual engagement of the divine with the world through the materiality of incarnation. Benjamin is very persuasive when she gives us some insight into how this works through the organization of gender. Like many before her she acknowledges that masculinity and femininity are based on very different assumed principles and experiences and not just biological difference. Boys, she argues, lay the basis for the supremacy of the cold, impersonal nature of rationality from birth. They are not their mother and so their maleness is defined by discontinuity, which leads them to objectify her as an object, instrument of pleasure but not an independent person. This she sees as the very base of the lack of equality within the hetero system, which she understands as sexual but also political. Erotic domination, she says, is male anxiety about the relation to the mother, which manifests in power over women and denigration (Benjamin 1983: 77). In this association of women with desexualized mother-object, the woman is stripped of agency in desire and viewed as empty, that is, of having no autonomy or meaning beyond that which will be found when she is penetrated by the phallus, which is the counterbalance to the fear of being engulfed and devoured by the maternal. The phallus becomes the instrument of autonomy for men, the representation of freedom from the dependency on the powerful mother. However, it must not connect them with an object that they cannot control since this may call into question the autonomy that is so crucial to their sense of self. For women, this is entirely different; all the while they have no object with which to overcome this phallic monopoly (*ibid.*: 88).

This is why it is so important that women do not further cripple themselves through a removal from the reality of their bodies. If we are to create new ways of being then we have to learn to tell the truth about our desires, which enable us to embody powerful ways of being female in the world. Benjamin says an understanding of desire as a need for recognition changes our view of the erotic experience, "it enables us to describe a mode of representing desire unique to intersubjectivity which, in turn, offers a new perspective on women's desire" (*ibid.*: 126). For her this intersubjectivity is spatial; it gives women room to grow, to be, and is not confined. Following Donald Winnicott's insights, she argues that the relationship between the self and others is spatial; it is a space that holds and a space that allows us

107

to create (*ibid.*: 128). It is this space that is denied women through the rigid boundaries of hetero reality but it is the space that is crucial for the emergence of our interior self.

Benjamin examines how this initial arrangement is worked out in society through the separation of the public and private spheres. This she sees as the public face of the split between the father of autonomy and the mother of dependency with the separation intensifying under the inevitable weight of rationality from the public sphere. Rationality is all that saves men from their fear of being swallowed by the maternal; it also, inevitably, leads to the destruction of maternal values. It is depersonalized, abstract and calculable and neatly replaces any interaction involving personal relationships and traditional authority and belief. Benjamin points out that it makes a wonderful partner for bureaucratic systems – just like advanced capitalism! The denial of dependency is crucial for the bourgeois idea of individual freedom which carries with it the illusion of choice so central to the perpetuation of the multiple myths of capitalism.

There is interesting research that links women's desire for power, and to have their desires recognized within society, with capitalism: women, desiring to be recognized – go shopping! Polly Young-Eisendrath believes that women's will for power does not simply go away in the face of patriarchal reality but rather moulds itself to what is possible within society. Male dominance and the psychology we have just examined mean that men have the power to dictate even the body size they prefer. Women, then, can aspire to share the dignity of man if she can become his object but she can never share his power because she has nothing to give in this way that the world would receive (Young-Eisendrath 1999: 43). In order to achieve the status of object of desire, many women in this world take heed of the media bombardment of their psyches and begin to reshape their bodies. It is the case that very few people are grossly overweight and, as we have seen, the medical evidence that links all kinds of dire consequences with weight is questionable, but nevertheless women submit to the diet culture. Gradually the ideal women emerges, which has to be kept in place through an eating disorder because the female body is not meant to be devoid of fat and angular. Two rather contradictory things then happen for women: they have transformed into objects of desire and at the same time they believe they have control. The realities of the world demonstrate that they do not actually have power so the sense of control does not lead to the fulfilment of one basic need, as it may have been hoped it would; rather, it leads to shame, guilt, self-consciousness and a need to be reassured that the image is still in place (*ibid.*: 42).

Young-Eisendrath tells us that research shows that for women who are denied connection with their desire, shopping has a crucial role. In a world where men are the subjects and women the objects in a power game played on the skin, women do not simply give up a will to power or subjectivity;

they simply have to gain it through diverse means. Women shoppers are seduced into an atmosphere that promises them power of choice; they can be subjects of their own desires. Further, the "stuff" and the means of selling it play into the female feelings of lack of worth, she is told that "she is worth it" and buying a certain brand will demonstrate this worth for all to see. Consuming "stuff" is a means of escape from the resentment of having given personal control to others but still does not wholly overcome the dilemma women are in. That is to say, while exerting subjectivity through consumer-object choice, women are often buying those things that make them more desirable as objects of the male gaze (*ibid.*: 40). Retailers seduce us into buying freedom when it is not really available and, even if it were, we live in a throwaway society. In order to be fully human we need to understand our desires and we have to face them, acceptable or not, because only when we know can we really choose to live an intentional life, one that is reclaimed from patriarchy, one that recovers the erotic unmoulded woman within each woman. This deep knowing depends on dialogues in community and women often find they are given manipulative dialogical partners who are patriarchal in one form or another. It becomes difficult to find authentic desire under those circumstances and thus within the frame of the present chapter we see how easy it becomes for the commodities on offer to offer temporary relief.

While this chapter has looked at the way in which Christian doctrine has made us vulnerable to markets through a damaging of desire and a disembodied theology, it would be remiss not to mention that at the very heart of its theology lies a debt economy that is intimately linked with desire. The one who died for us, who places us in eternal debt due to the sacrifice which can never be paid off, is also the one we are to desire above all else. We are placed in an economy of redemption that many theologians are now beginning to see is having damaging effects. Traditional theologies see the incarnation as simply a bill of exchange and Grau (2004) has demonstrated how in the West the notion of salvation for the few rather than abundant life for all has been at the heart of political and economic systems. It is a scarcity model of salvation that leads to the same in economic theory and ultimately to the savage form of capitalism we have, where people grab for as much as possible because there is not enough to go round.

Althaus-Reid (2007) reflects upon the lunchtime crucifixions that people undergo in the squares of Buenos Aires as a protest against the crushing realities of globalization in their lives. They stand tied to crosses for hours in the public spaces of their cities with their names and the social problems they are experiencing tied to the cross. This is the twenty-first-century Golgotha, the real crucifixions of people at the hands of the markets, the consequence of eternal debt and disregard for the lives of people. Althaus-Reid wishes to strike at the heart of this debt economy by going against the grain of the Christian doctrine of redemption (from the Latin *emptio* meaning to purchase or buy back). She wishes to rethink redemption as an economic metaphor for salvation, as this lays the foundations in society for a commercial culture of oppression. How could it be otherwise with God the supreme good and giver of life versus humanity subjected to a violent ontological debt? Althaus-Reid wonders if this was an early Christian attempt to sacralize a patriarchal economic order based on debt. Even if we say the debt has been paid, it is in blood, and demands the same from humanity. Those in poor countries are indeed paying in blood and human sacrifice; they are sacrificed to the global markets and their genocidal systems and as such are the tortured God on a cross (Althaus-Reid 2007: 294). Althaus-Reid demands that Christianity rethink this notion of redemption as an economic metaphor for salvation, since in her view it is the basis of a commercial culture of oppression that extends around the globe. Christianity had helped to promote the idea that being in debt is normal and has ontologically engrained it in a Christian understanding of relationship. She claims it is more fundamental in Christianity in real terms than love, which is spoken of a great deal but seems lacking in a debt understanding of redemption.

Althaus-Reid asks how different the economy would be if it were based in gift and love. This is not such a strange idea because we are told that God gave himself to the world in the form of Jesus as an act of love, while many contemporary theologians understand the planet itself to be the body of God, which gives generously and graciously to all that inhabit it. Unless it is thought that what we have here are modern fanciful ideas about theology, we can demonstrate that the foundations of Christianity did celebrate this central notion of love, gift and beauty. Rita Brock and Rebecca Parker (2008) spend some time examining the Eucharistic practices of the early Church, which their thesis suggests did not take place within a theological frame of blood sacrifice. In order to ensure that no connection was made with blood sacrifice, they suggest that meat and wine were both excluded from the communal table and the people brought offerings that represented the resources of the community and signalled their wealth in God. So while all meat was banned, fruits and other products of the harvest were accepted, with wine being replaced with milk or water. This signalled the generous outpouring of the earth coupled with the work and care of the labourers, which resulted in a communal act of thanks and appreciation. The beautiful feast of all that the earth could give was seen as awakening the senses to beauty and joy, through which an encounter with the divine that infuses all life was believed to take place. The beauty of the world opened the heart to the holy presence and enabled humanity to be in "present paradise". The purpose of the Eucharist was to awaken the senses and celebrate the community life shared by those gathered and not to emulate a final sacrifice. Macrina (328–384 CE), who was the sister and teacher of Basil of Caesarea, spoke of the dynamic, fluid and diverse created world, one of universal harmony, that was made known in the Eucharist and offered the communicant an experience of transcendence in which the self was renewed and expanded through this connection with the things of the earth, which emphasized the brilliance of the divine presence. This experience could bring about life-changing knowledge in which divinity is restored to humanity and the world is returned to the beauty in which it was first made. The emphasis on transforming people's original divine beauty and harmony was understood to be not connected in any way with blood sacrifice but rather with the beauty and gift of nature and human labour.

Brock and Parker note that the mosaics surrounding the worshippers in their place of worship were of the beauty of creation and not of crucifixion because it was believed the heart should not be offered images that may bring to life the evil that brought about the crucifixion. No images that could harden the heart or numb the senses were used and the crucifixion was understood to be one such image. Images of the bounty of the world reminded communicants that they too were the bounty and blessing of the world and were here to live in paradise in the present. The Church today may not be able to imagine an economy based in the gift and love framework, owing to its emphasis on the redemptive death of Jesus, but there are countries that are still able to, for example Rwanda and Peru, where an economy of love and gift replaces one of redemption and debt, as mentioned in Chapter 3. Lunchtime crucifixions denounce the debt economy but can Christ survive without redemption theology based on the indebtedness of sinful believers? This theologian believes so and will attempt to demonstrate how in the next chapter. For now it is the turn of the sociologist to examine this question of consumerism and desire.

SOCIOLOGICAL APPROACHES

Many of the themes in the account so far are clearly recognizable in sociological debates about desire and consumerism, most clearly where Lacan, Foucault or Deleuze and Guattari are detectable. These theorists have influenced sociology too, although they are all difficult to "apply" to actual cases. There are earlier sources of critique in Marxist accounts as well, and here too feminism has played a major part in getting sociologists to take seriously women's activities such as shopping or watching particular kinds of television programmes. Sociological debate about consumerism is obviously less concerned with the development of a properly spiritual consciousness and how it gets threatened, and more concerned with the theme of political liberation through variants of cultural politics.

One tradition in the sociological commentary on consumerism sees it as the way in which capitalism enforces ideology at the individual level. Consumerism binds us to capital by offering to satisfy all our needs as long as we conform. The binding mechanisms include the manipulation of desire and of the very notion of the subject in an unprecedentedly deep and powerful way, through the specific mechanisms of advertising especially. However, there is a much less condemnatory discussion of consumerism too. Here, conscious and active subjects use consumer goods in a kind of popular aesthetic to develop their own projects, declare their own preferences and celebrate their own otherness. As with the discussion above, the problem is to see whether such consumerist identity politics can provide any sort of critical insight or whether it is easily recuperated as a kind of capitalist market choice.

The pessimistic tradition was probably the first to develop. A number of home-grown British commentators were worried about the impact of the Second World War and the contact with American society, as Alan Tomlinson suggests (Tomlinson 1990: "Introduction"). Consumerism was seen as the worst aspect of such contact, encouraging young people to seek immediate gratification in the collection of consumer goods in ways that would only encourage irresponsible personal debt and ruin the whole "moral economy" of deferred gratification, the discipline of saving for things and only buying things that you really needed.

A major early influence was the work of the critical theorists Adorno and Horkheimer, who, in exile from Nazism had been horrified by the consumer society of Los Angeles. They had a series of conversations about the problem, typically posed at an extremely abstract level – the ambiguous legacy of the Enlightenment – and the heroic Frau Adorno took notes. The result was the classic *Dialectic of the Enlightenment* (Adorno & Horkheimer 1979). The conversation was clearly wide ranging, and touched on the work of Homer and de Sade as early theorists of consumerism, as well as discussing anti-Semitism, and the culture industry.

THE CULTURE INDUSTRY

The pair insisted that what passed for popular culture was very different from the earlier traditional folk cultures, and was produced for commercial gain by a definite industry, which had cunningly used customer research to deliver a "circle of manipulation and retroactive need in which the unity of the system grows stronger" (Adorno & Horkheimer 1979: 121). The industry produces a hierarchical range of products to meet different types of consumers in the sort of "individualization" or "customizing" that is completely familiar today. All this is organized rationally, using statistics and a set of quantification techniques "so that ... none may escape" (*ibid.*: 123). This calculating commercialism really explains, for example, the emergence of different marketing categories such as genres in films or literature. Consumers are required to be "active" in one sense, to be quick and perceptive and to be able to "read" products such as films without thinking.

Occasionally, the industry requires novelty – so directors such as Orson Welles are allowed to experiment with the conventions of film – but this only confirms the naturalness of the conventional categories. The industry seems to permit deviance and even dissidence, but this is easily incorporated into the overall structure, becoming the kind of novelty that assists business: "Realistic dissidence is the trademark of anyone who has a new idea in business" (*ibid*.: 132). Nothing is exempt, not even cartoons. The subversive Chaplinesque qualities of the first Mickey Mouse film are quickly replaced by more conformist characterizations: "Donald Duck in the cartoons, and the unfortunate in real life get their thrashing so the audience can learn to take their own punishment" (*ibid*.: 138). Amusement is needed not just to "recreate" docile workers but for social integration more generally.

A pseudo-individuality is encouraged, a matter of "individualized" additional detail, which does not prevent absorption into the generality, and a major role is played by advertising. For Adorno and Horkheimer, "Culture is a paradoxical commodity. So completely is it subject to the law of exchange that it is no longer exchanged; it is so blindly consumed in use that it can no longer be used. Therefore it amalgamates with advertising" (*ibid*.: 161). Art and advertising collapse into each other: effects, effectiveness and artistic techniques are the same in both. Simple significations only are permitted. Fashionable words are repeated in the service of magic (*ibid*.: 166), to stave off fear of the unknown, make the world familiar and predictable. Layers of experience long connected with words are now removed: words act now only as triggers for conditioned behaviour; they are no longer understood but simply stand for something desirable but unintelligible (*ibid*.). Finally, the culture industry triumphs in the end because "the consumers feel compelled to buy and use its products even though they see through them" (*ibid*.: 167).

ADVERTISING

The pessimism, and many of the same themes, continued as consumer culture developed. There have been many critical studies of advertising, for example, including pieces by Judith Williamson (1978). Williamson offered a classic analysis of the seductive power of advertisements in suggesting we can find all sorts of associations, suggested usually through images (it would have been forbidden to refer to these associations in writing, especially as restrictions developed in various advertising codes). Thus the classic technique of showing a product associated with the celebrity – Chanel No. 5 with Catherine Deneuve – for example, clearly implies that anyone using Chanel No. 5 will be able to transfer some of the marvellous personal qualities of Deneuve to themselves. Stated explicitly, anyone could see the absurdity of this claim, but at the level of fantasy the work becomes more effective. The viewer of the advertisement does this work as her own contribution, so to speak.

Perhaps the most sinister advertisements draw in the viewer in this way. In an example discussed by Barthes (1973), an advertisement for margarine started by openly acknowledging the hostile views that the customer might have of the product: basically that it was inferior to butter in every respect. Having dealt these views, however, the narrator then goes on to say that you can still produce marvellous cooking with margarine. It looks as if the narrator has considered all the negative views and yet still is prepared to endorse the product. Barthes calls this strategy "apology". In an analysis of televangelism, Peter McLaren and Richard Smith (1989) were able to identify a similar strategy, which they call offering "prime knowledge". The televangelists began by acknowledging the awful crises and problems in modern societies, which included the rejection of God. They claim to fully understand this position but still, at the end of the day, announce that their personal convictions are as strong as ever: they know all about the difficulties, but they still possess some infallible knowledge that God is love. There is almost a critique of naive positivism in the early stage!

Robert Goldman and Stephen Papson (1998) continue with the same theme, and their analysis is of one of the most extraordinary consumer durables of recent times: Nike trainers. Nike advertising began with associational devices, where celebrities and sports stars were seen in the same picture as the product. Nike then began to develop much subtler campaigns with the attempt first to substitute the slogan and the logo for the actual product, and then to associate the slogan ("Just Do It") with all sorts of aspirational subcultures, including those of the urban black youth, or female athletes. According to Michelle Helstein (2003), Lacan can be used to explain how "female athletes … [are] summoned, disciplined, produced, and regulated" in Nike advertising, and how it works within "psychoanalytic understandings of fantasy and desire" (*ibid.*: 277). It all turns on notions of excellence and emancipation and how they are reconciled within "the discourse of Nike". Basically, these notions have to be stripped of any particular local meanings, filled with neo-conservative meanings and then articulated together in a way that enables viewers to construct their own fantasies and desire: "we only know the female athlete, or emancipation, or excellence in reference to their relation within the symbolic and the imaginary" (*ibid.*: 287). The Nike discourse links female aspirations with more political themes: for example, encouragement of excellence enables capitalism to accommodate itself to feminism, and picks up on the neo-conservative "nostalgic liberal" themes that stress free will and the pleasures of distinguishing oneself from unproductive others, or that explain social problems as a result of individual inadequacies. Nike discourse offers us no respite or resolution since we can always see a way to improve on what we are: in Lacanian terms, our ideal self "is the embodiment of desire constructed by fantasy at the level of the signified" (*ibid.*: 288). Advertisements let us fantasize that we may eventually become a hero even though we do not realize it ourselves at the moment. This also avoids explicit politics, relating to the chances of actual social mobility.

Nike also moved to incorporate some of the obvious criticisms of these campaigns; for example, in one advertisement a black athlete specifically denied that he wanted to be seen as a role model. He thought the customers were far too knowing to fall for that argument, and reiterated that parents are the most suitable role models. For Goldman and Papson (1998), that seems to be abandoning the commercial agenda but is really developing another one, building a flattering personal relationship with a sophisticated consumer, credited with insight.

Josée Johnston and Judith Taylor (2008) make similar points about the recent campaigns by Dove skincare products to use apparently feminist critiques of the idealized female body to promote their products. Just as with Nike, Dove's campaigns utilized an interactive website and the company worked with groups to raise the self-esteem of young women. Nevertheless, the company still subscribed to the view that attaining beauty was a major goal for women, usually mediated through a male gaze, although they broadened the definitions slightly, to develop attention and brand loyalty, the authors suspect. Thus Dove provides a classic example of "feminist consumerism, a corporate strategy that employs feminist themes of empowerment to market products to women" (*ibid.*: 955). The study contrasts this domesticated kind of feminism with that embraced by a feminist activist consumer group, PPPO (Pretty, Porky and Pissed Off), who offered "dissonant images of beauty" (*ibid.*: 957), not dependent on male approval. They also listed examples of the damage caused by conventional conceptions of beauty on normal women.

THE RESISTING CONSUMER

It was not until the 1970s and 1980s that alternative conceptions of consumerism finally emerged, rather guiltily at first. Consumerism gave pleasure, not only to deluded youth, but to respectable academics. To deny this pleasure was to render ordinary people as "cultural dopes", completely taken in, again and again, by an all-powerful cultural industry. Much of the consumerism that women did especially could be seen as skilled and insightful work, despite the disdain of male academics for activities such as "shopping". Shoppers were seen as well informed and skilful.

When women watched film or television programmes, they were perfectly capable of seeing through patriarchal ideology and ironically inverting it or ignoring it altogether. Thus Ien Ang (1985) invited women viewers of the television soap opera *Dallas* to write in explaining what they saw in the programme: many seem to take an ironic delight in seeing the female characters as parodies, as female impersonators. Geraghty (1991) saw redemptive readings even in the most commercialized melodramas: they centred and explored structures of feeling and thus revalued female abilities to read emotions. Romances actually offered a kind of female triumph and utopia, as the wayward male heroes were softened and feminized. bell hooks (1999), addressing a famous analysis by Laura Mulvey (1975) on the passivity of the female spectator in the cinema, argued that black women in particular had always had cultural resources to prevent any easy identification with the white heroines who spend so much time being dominated by the male gaze.

Perhaps the biggest discovery was the critical potential of youth culture (discussed in Chapter 2). The most spectacular street cultures clearly offered a challenge to conventional bourgeois conceptions of respectable behaviour, and perhaps the best and last example, punk, included open challenges to conventional female sexuality, with the challenging flaunting of fetishized underwear worn on the outside (Hebdige 1988). Less spectacularly, some of the most degraded and reviled youth activities – arcade video games – became seen in an entirely new light. John Fiske (1989) saw these as offering a chance for youth to engage in the construction of meaning, no less: to play with the signifiers as they adopted different characters, roles and scenarios. He also saw another degraded form, the rock video, as offering considerable potential to experiment with identities and meanings; almost inevitably, he chose Madonna videos as an example, and showed how the fans had been encouraged to experiment with sexual identity almost as much as the star had.

This is clearly an unusually positive view of videos and video games, compared to most of the public discussion, which turns on matters such as their effects in encouraging violence or exploitative sexuality. Such effects have been the subject of perhaps the most extensive empirical studies of consumerism. However, all such studies encounter formidable methodological difficulties, as would any empirical study in the whole field. What would be an adequate sample? How could we agree to measure effects such as heightened aggression? A brief discussion might show the problems.

One of the best studies of the possible effects of video games on violent behaviour, according to the American Psychological Association at least, was undertaken by Craig Anderson and Karen Dill (2000). Anderson is a prolific researcher in this area, and has recently produced a meta-review of the field too. Before we get to that, the earlier study is worth examining for its scrupulous methodology: positivism at its best (or worst). To be brief, the authors attempt to pin down terms such as "aggressive behaviour" in observable and measurable terms and then to conduct two careful studies – one in the field and one in the laboratory – on samples of volunteers (with about 200 people in each case). They suggest that combinations of personality traits and playing violent games can produce "a behavioural script", prompting people over how to respond to aggression, or other ways to psychologically access "aggressive cognitions" in particular situations. Basically, the argument is that violent video games help people:

> rehearse aggressive scripts that teach and reinforce vigilance for enemies ... increase hostile perception, develop aggressive action against others, expectations that others will behave aggressively, positive attitudes towards use of violence, and beliefs that violent solutions are effective and appropriate.   (*Ibid.*: 778)

The field-based study involved giving people a self-report questionnaire so as to record data on individual differences, aggressive behaviour, delinquency and worldview, gauged, for example, by asking how unsafe and crime-ridden the USA is perceived to be. Then members of the sample were given another questionnaire about their video-game habits. People were asked to name their five favourite games, and then rate them, reflecting how often they played the game and how "violent the content and graphics of the game were" (*ibid.*: 785). A great deal of careful work was then undertaken to validate scales and compare other studies, and results from the two questionnaires were correlated.

In the laboratory study, aggressive thought, affect (emotions) and behaviour were measured, and the effects of gender and aggressive personality (only one measure of aggressive personality, in fact, using a scale of "irritability") were assessed. Participants were allowed to play the game three times, measuring different variables each time. To facilitate these comparisons, participants were selected who were particularly low and particularly high in irritability. The precise arrangements of the laboratory studies were designed to minimize the effects of the presence of the researcher or differences in terms of instructions. To prevent participants guessing the point of the experiment, they were given a cover story about learning in developing skills. Another play session ensued, then participants were tested for aggressive thinking by showing them particular words, including aggressive words (e.g. murder) and "anxiety words ... escape words ... and control words" (*ibid.*: 798), and measuring how quickly people were able to read them. After a pause of a week participants came to play again, and aggressive behaviour was tested by measuring "competitive reaction time", involving a competition to press a button faster than an opponent can, and punishing the loser by operating a blast of noise: "Aggressive behaviour is operationally defined as the intensity and duration of noise blasts the participant chooses to deliver to the opponent" (*ibid.*: 799).

Overall, "Aggressive delinquent behaviour was positively related to both [personality] trait aggressiveness and exposure to video-game violence" (*ibid.*: 788), and measures of the strength of these correlations are given as 0.36, and 0.46, respectively. Similar but lower correlations were established between trait aggressiveness and exposure to video-game violence and non-aggressive delinquent behaviour, and between exposure to video-game violence and aggressive personality. Gender was strongly related to several of the variables, especially "perceived safety ... video-game violence ... and time spent playing video games" (*ibid.*: 789). In the strongest test of the relationship between the terms, Anderson and Dill pursued what they call "destructive testing", which involves establishing a link between video-game violence and aggression, and then attempting to introduce more and more variables until the link disappears (this also has methodological problems, including making sure you have all the relevant variables and that the order of testing them has no effects of its own). Subsequently, video-game violence exposure persisted as a predictor of aggressive behaviour.

Anderson and Dill then depart from technical caution and difficulty and draw a controversial conclusion: "Thus, the link between video-game violence and aggressive behaviour is quite strong indeed" (*ibid.*: 790). Clearly, much will depend on how the reader interprets these suddenly vague terms such as "quite strong", and responds to the textual modifier "indeed". The authors promptly return to a more cautious summary: "Violent video game play and aggressive personality separately and jointly accounted for major portions of both aggressive behaviour and non-aggressive delinquency" (*ibid.*: 793). Further:

> concern about the deleterious effects of violent video games on delinquent behaviour, aggressive and non-aggressive is legitimate. Playing violent video games often may well cause increases in delinquent behaviours, both aggressive and non-aggressive. However, the correlational nature [of this first study] ... means that causal statements are risky at best. It could be that the obtained video-game violence links to aggressive and non-aggressive delinquency are wholly due to the fact that highly aggressive individuals are especially attracted to violent video games. Longitudinal work ... would be very informative.
>
> (*Ibid.*: 794)

Anderson's (2003) meta-review is summarized briefly on the American Psychological Association's website, and he vigorously defends his position against subsequent critics. However, another meta-review insists that there is considerable publication bias in this area and that when this is removed, "There is no support for the hypothesis that violent video game playing is associated with higher aggression" (Ferguson 2007: 309). Christopher

Ferguson is particularly critical of Anderson and Dill's study, mostly on the grounds of their using non-standardized tests (including the sound-blast one) and assuming too much (statistical) confidence in the size of their effects. He also says that exposure to family violence is a variable of such importance that it outweighs any effects of playing violent video games. If such dissent still arises, after more than forty years of frequent research, it is surely impossible to think that empirical research could prove decisive in any other of the debates about popular cultural activities. As with the debate about the politics of otherness in an earlier chapter, it seems impossible to remove personal preferences, experience and taste.

CONNOISSEURS AND BOYCOTTERS

Whichever side of the debate one chooses, it is obvious that there is a considerable range of consuming going on. Some consumers will be connoisseurs, well informed and with the ability to resist pressure and sales techniques. Some of these will be collectors, for example, pursuing a hobby as a kind of complex leisure (Kjølsrød 2003). Some groups have been engaged in a form of political activity, organizing consumer groups to boycott goods and services from aggressive capitalist companies, ranging from early campaigns against the apartheid regime of United Fruit in the USA to recurrent campaigns against Starbucks coffee company (Simon 2011). Bryant Simon suggest that the boycott is "one of the most dynamic forms of political expression today" (*ibid.*: 148), countering the usual picture of individual absorption, political apathy and non-involvement, and exploiting the company's apparent responsibility and openness to its customers. Boycotts have achieved some success, for example in urging Fair Trade policies on Starbucks, but Simon ends by reminding us these are still limited.

At the other extreme, there may well be consumer pathologies of various kinds: "shopaholics", youths who will literally kill in order to acquire a pair of trainers, addicts, people who take on unmanageable burdens of debt in order to consume. Other types have also been identified, for example in a study designed to test whether "postmodern" malls were cunningly designed to disorient consumers in order to make them more susceptible (Woodward *et al.* 2000). Earlier work suggested four basic types of shopper: the economic, the personalizing, the ethical and the apathetic shopper. Shoppers were asked to compare themselves to the different vignettes, enabling them to be classified on a four-point scale ranging from not enjoying shopping to loving shopping. There was a gender difference here, with women opting for the more enjoyable and social kinds. Overall, the study, based on an admittedly small sample, seems to support the idea of active and pragmatic visitors, and suggest that "the influence of architecture is eroded over time and consequently the fatalistic vision of the mall by scholars and

119

post-modern architectural theorists is misplaced" (*ibid.*: 350). Those fatalistic visions lead to an overemphasis on structural accounts rather than
practical action: "Indeed, it is the intellectual, not the shopper, who constitutes the ideal typical *flâneur* of contemporary postmodern spaces" (*ibid.*:
351). The usual fears about malls arise from "academic-cum-touristic activity" (*ibid.*), not the routine way of finding strategies that enable participants
to navigate. This perspective seems not to have led to particular "methodological and theoretical reflexivity", but to a self-confirming theoretical perspective: "the analyst's own lack of practical mastery is projected back into
their social theory and forwards on to the people and places they study"
(*ibid.*: 352).

The design of malls introduces another example of the black arts for the
critics, in this case the development of the design industry. The study above
hints that shopping malls are sometimes seen as designed to confuse shoppers and prevent their escape. They can offer a whole combination of experiences – banks, restaurants, cinemas, travel agents – and can be designed
to create the illusion that one is on holiday, or visiting the future or the
past. They are "cathedrals of consumption" for Ritzer (1999). They show
how consuming can take on additional social or even spiritual values. There
are some additional studies that indicate that some of this is reinterpreted
by mall visitors, however, who make their own use of the weatherproof
facilities and attend the mall just to people-watch (Lehtonen & Mäenpää
1997) and to meet friends or family (Morris 1993). This sort of cheerful
pragmatism to offset the Helsinki winter or the Australian summer, respectively, stands in contrast to the semiotic immersion described by Mark
Gottdeiner (1995) or Ian Buchanan (2006), who see the shopping mall as a
postmodern reductive parody of a city, complete with its soulless visitors.

For Ritzer (1999), designers do much to conceal the rationalized production and cynical commercialism of modern society: they help to "re-
enchant" the world. Ritzer draws deliberately on Weber's views of the
increasing rationalization and "disenchantment" of the world. In one case
study, Ritzer and Todd Stillman (2001) discuss modern baseball and note
that there was a definite trend to demolish the old stadia and replace them
with more rationalized examples: regular-sized pitches, protection from
the vagaries of the weather, modern seating for the fans and so on. But this
also removed all the "enchanted" elements of the game for the fans, including destroying the places where they had seen their teams perform mira-
cles, where they sat with their parents in more innocent days, and so on.
Attendance at games dropped until some bright designers introduced new
attractions to bring about "re-enchantment", including heritage displays of
the great days, team shops, competitions to involve fans and live television
coverage of events on the pitch.

There are, however, several indications that consumerism, despite
its deployment of advanced cultural and semiotic skills, is not infallible.

Ritzer suggests that re-enchantment can never be adequate, though, since enchantment comes from participants as well as designers, and companies are doomed to have to repeat attempts at re-enchantment, quite possibly with diminishing returns. The social world itself is the source of the values we enjoy, despite attempts to "add them" to or incorporate them in manufactured goods or services in versions of "the experience economy" (Pine & Gilmour 1999). Michel de Certeau (1984) makes the same point about the limited impacts of themed environments in city gentrification programmes; unlike the tourists, locals walk around their own cities following their personal maps and narratives. Without invoking Deleuzian notions of Desire, the point is to suggest that everyday life itself is able to resist colonization by commercial semioticians. For Michael Gardiner, quoting de Certeau:

> Although the cultural activity of the non-producers of culture is largely "unsigned, unreadable, and unsymbolised" because it is not governed by formalized logic and escapes the gaze of official power, it is nonetheless present [and indicates] the "ruses of other interests and desires that are neither determined nor captured by the systems in which they develop".
>
> (2000: 170, quoting de Certeau 1984: xviii)

The reference to everyday knowledge and practice leads to a final point. The topic of the effects of consumerism has been a very popular one to research, with major studies on many of the major global capitalist companies, Disney, Mattel, McDonald's and Sony in particular (see Harris 2004). Much of the work is speculative, assuming that the researchers' reactions will be the same as the consumers'. Where there are empirical studies, these are necessarily limited by sample size, and there is a wide range of methodological devices in use, from the sort of psychological testing discussed above to the use of consumer diaries (Chin 2007). In nearly every case, there is a combination of pessimistic and optimistic views, with gloomy diagnoses of the wicked machinations of desire matched by studies of lively and insightful consumers subverting the companies' intentions by imposing meanings of their own, and, often, later evidence of commercial recuperation of these apparent forms of resistance, with, no doubt, further consumer resistance to come.

One consequence has been described as a persistent sense of "banality" (Morris 1988), where studies of consumerism become familiar to the point of predictability. Banality also implies that the customers themselves are well aware of the debates, remain unsurprised by any theoretical analyses, and learn to cope with the "good" and "bad" sides of consumerism in the practical "unsigned" manner suggested by de Certeau. A similar approach is suggested by Alan Warde (2005), who suggests we study consumerism in the future as a part of routine practices, rather than as some specially central behaviour. Whether this represents a resigned acceptance of the inevitability of the limits of capitalist desire, or a potential reservoir of resistance to it, is the issue.

5. OTHERNESS AS A METATHEORETICAL/ PHYSICAL PROBLEM: BACKGROUNDING THE FOREGROUND

No other civilisation [than the Western] ... seems to make the principle of sexual difference so crystal clear; between the sexes there is a cleavage, an abyss, which is marked by their different relationship to the law [religious and political] and which is the very condition of their alliance. Monotheistic unity is sustained by a radical separation of the sexes, indeed this separation is its prerequisite. ...

On the other hand and simultaneously monotheism represents the paternal function: patrilinear descent with transmission of the Father's name centralises eroticism in the single goal of procreation in the grip of an abstract symbolic authority ...

The economy of this mechanism requires that women be excluded from the single true and legislating principle ...

One betrays one's naiveté if one considers our modern societies to be simply patrilinear ... or capitalist-monopolist and ignores the fact that they are at the same time ... governed by ... monotheism.   (Kristeva 1974: 19–22)

As the opening quotations illustrate, it is the intention of this chapter to demonstrate that Christian monotheism has sprung from a particular take on metaphysics and lends itself to mono-logic within religion, economics and politics, which has and continues to have violent and abusive outcomes. Sadly, the incarnational message of Christianity used Greek metaphysics as its interpretative tool with which to interact with the cultures around it. This proved to be a sound political move in its early days of formation, as did the embedding of this hierarchy through the traditional patriarchal family, but it may be argued that it also numbed and even killed much of the original potential of such an extraordinary message as that of incarnation. However, while we may concede the occasional advantage over the centuries, the unfortunate combination of state power and dualistic metaphysics laid the foundations for a metaphysical space never envisaged in an incarnational religion, one that led to control, denial of the body and hierarchical systems rather than opening of the luminal space of possibilities of which incarnation sings.

We should not at this stage lose sight of the way in which the nomadic Jewish tribes had used monotheism, that is as an identity statement amid the cultures and religions in which they wandered. However, it is also true to say that scholars also believe that it was never a strict monotheism in that it did acknowledge the existence of other gods but rather wished to state the superior power of their own one God. There are additional issues, such as does that God have power outside the land in which he wishes his people to dwell? This is shown when the Psalmist asks, "how shall we sing the Lord's song in a strange land?" What we are hoping to highlight is not that monotheism as a concept is wholly negative; we see that, for the nomadic Jewish tribes, it grew up from their experience and enabled them to remain within a meaningful identity. Of course, it was not an exclusive identity, since we note throughout the Hebrew scriptures how inter-marriage took place and how cultures met, not always in an antagonistic manner. There appeared to be room for integration into the Jewish identity and, conversely, scholars are now showing that with such integrations came change. It is when these boundaries become fixed and impermeable that, Laurel Schneider and others argue, monotheism becomes the tyrant it appears to have been for centuries. When under the influence of state power, culture and philosophy, the story of God becomes the story of totality, of a closed system, of the One that excludes the "other" and becomes a rigid and impenetrable story of ONE (Schneider 2008: 3). Monotheism came to signal civilization and advancement and it is in this capacity that it became a central component of empire in the hands of a variety of European states. Jürgen Moltmann (quoted in *ibid.*: 20) has argued that this is inevitable because monotheism sits best with theocracy. The logic of the One suggests that we are able to distinguish between the truth and falsehood, which is ideal if one wishes to set up a theocratic society. It is also very useful if, like Aquinas, you wish to set down a substantial theology, influenced by the writings of Aristotle, which demonstrates that the world itself reveals the unchanging One, the Unmoved First Mover, the One that relegates all other knowing to fiction and myth in its supreme presence. Sameness becomes the basis for establishing what is real from what is unreal and Christian ontology becomes reductive with the result that "the other" is lost, given no existence or demonized (*ibid.*: 88). Stasis becomes the nature of the divine, the same yesterday, today and tomorrow, sustaining a world that is the same yesterday, today and tomorrow.

This is, we have to acknowledge, very appealing to many people who understand safety as the ultimate purpose of religion; they live in a world that does not change with a God who does not change and what they have to do is live by the rules that do not change. However, it takes very little investigation to realize that none of the aforementioned is true: the world changes; the rules, both theological and ethical, change; and one assumes that this implies the divine may change, although this has been masked by dualistic metaphysics. We may also wish to challenge the notion that religion is the ultimate security blanket because such an understanding excludes more than it can allow in. For Bob Goss (2002: 85) an ethic of what he terms "communal survivability" is not Christian. It was not an ethic that Jesus held dear when he went to Jerusalem and disrupted the temple. Goss suggests that the motivations of Jesus were love and solidarity with the marginalized, which far outweigh safety and survivability.

The Christian story is based in dramatic change, which involves risk and challenge. The God from above becomes impregnated in a young girl living under political tyranny. In this moment the divine is embedded in a world of object relations, mutual becoming and co-emergence, as we have seen in the work of Ettinger (Chapter 3). This is not a place of absolute unchanging divinity but one of radical transformations from divinity to flesh and blood, to bread and wine and spirit, all products of time and space and context.

Even in the gospel narratives themselves it can be argued that what Schneider calls "monotheistic eschatologies that fantasize the end of all difference in the truth of God" (2008: 170) are being challenged. For example, in the temptation stories we see that the incarnate Jesus refuses the Almighty power over things in favour of a life of experience and struggle with the people. Schneider goes on to say his life and death were his own, which is the scandal for those who prefer to believe in a Big God, the ONE already there rather than the God who is occurring (*ibid.*: 174). As Irigaray (1985) has pointed out, bodies tend to disrupt the perfect logic of the ONE as they signal only too graphically the presence of "others" in this perfect picture. The Church Fathers, too, realized that bodies are untidy, even the body of Jesus, so they turned him into the body of Christ (Isherwood 1999), a body that could exactly reflect the ONE, the ideal type who could control and regulate all other bodies throughout history. The divine/human incarnation disappeared in the hands of the early theologians and instead became a bill of exchange; in so doing Jesus was delivered into the systems he appeared to reject (Schneider 2008: 175). If we are to take seriously incarnation then we have to lessen our grip on absolute monotheism and give space for bodies and lives to be narrative realities in our creation of theology: to be more uncertain than we have previously dared to be.

Schneider reminds us that without incarnation there can be no Christianity yet with the logic of the ONE there can be no incarnation (*ibid.*: 192). So again, for her, the choice is clear: do we settle for the world of categories and abstractions that the ONE presents us with or do we embrace what she calls the multiplicity, which is the diverse nature of embodiment? This embodiment refuses categories because bodies do not tend to come as general, despite what fashion, medicine and the like try to tell us. Schneider points out that a fundamental gospel principle of love and peace cannot be satisfied under the regime of the ONE. In accordance with other feminist theologians, she suggests that love needs another, it cannot be without encounter and it cannot be ethical unless it recognizes the presence of others as they are. Heyward (1989) spoke powerfully of this, saying that it was the desire to love and be loved that drew the divine from the heavens and into relation through incarnation.

We do not see here any hint that a wayward people needed the incarnation of the once-and-for-all son of God in order to die for them and thus offer redemption to the few. It was God's desire to love and be loved that brought about the outpouring of the divine into flesh and for Heyward (*ibid.*) it is this continued desire that means the divine will never retreat to the heavens and the place of absolute oneness, since in such a move all relation is lost, all possibility of loving and being loved. In short, this is quite the reverse of what the gospels declare: that the greatest thing is love.

For Schneider (2008: 206), incarnation that signals love is a willingness to show up and fully risk; nothing less will do. The ONE brings safety, as we have seen, but incarnation changes things. Schneider speaks plainly when she says: "to follow God who became flesh is to make room for more than One, it is a posture of openness to the world as it comes to us, of loving the discordant, plentipotential worlds more than the desire to overcome, to colonise or even to 'same' them" (*ibid.*: 217). Thinking beyond the One makes room for difference, for the stranger and for strangeness. This requires that we face imaginatively the ONENESS erected in our own minds, cultures, religious systems and environments and overcome it through the power of intimate connection with the multiplicity of difference we see and experience all around us and within us.

This is, as can be seen, not an argument for an evolutionary view of Christ such as we find in Teilhard de Chardin's *Hymn of the Universe* (1970), with his concept of the Omega Point. Although his idea allows for movement, it fails to take the ultimate step in the direction of risk by falling short of saying there is no fixed endpoint: that what we face is an open future. This process is never finished and is always fragile and partial, which is why the temptation to run to the safety of metaphysics and already-created ideal worlds is always there. It is important to stress that the whole of creation is involved in this process of risky Christic becoming so no human hierarchy can be set in place.

Within Christian theology, the issue of monotheism also throws into relief the issue of transcendence. There have been many Christian theologians who have addressed the issue of transcendence and all cannot be mentioned here, but one who must be, if only briefly, is Soelle (see Heyward 2003), whose work will never allow the divine to escape to the outer reaches of reality and who always understood theological questions to be deeply embedded in the personal sense of identity, which is always political. It is self-evident that her work was dedicated to creating a new social order and this she did through political action but also through theological creation, a task she understood as crucial to counter dispassionate Church dogma and individualistic theology, which she saw as a component of patriarchal theology and "capitalist spirituality". As her work progressed, we see the God of transcendence becoming a spirit of transformation among us, one who enables us to transcend the places we find ourselves in to move to another way of liberative being. In *The Silent Cry* (2001), Soelle "is planting theological seeds ... for a Christian life that transcends popular understandings of both 'spirituality' and 'politics' – and that transcends most Christian understandings of both divine and human life" (Heyward 2003: 236). Here we see how a reworking of theology can indeed offer new ways to at once challenge the existing order of patriarchy with its divisions of gender, class, race and its feeding of capitalism and sustain the individual in that struggle through an empowering understanding of transcendence rather than a system that feeds other metanarratives.

In Soelle's work, traditional views of transcendence are seen as just as dangerous as the metanarrative of monotheism, since it supplies a crucial component in that narrative: distance! If we are to keep the concept and think theologically then we must, she insists, see it as moving among us, a notion that Heyward has more recently taken up. For Heyward, transcendence is here and now in the lived reality of our lives as we move beyond limited and destructive ways of thinking into new ways. It is important to realize that there is no fixed and pre-ordered place to which we move but it is rather the ability to move, to change, to incorporate that is the vital part for theological thinking that is meant to change the world: the ability to use imagination and love to create new spaces free of the logic of the ONE; the imagination and willingness to break into what we cannot yet see, to spiral in search of what is not yet but lies beyond all boundaries, to seek, one may argue, for the stranger we have not yet met. Heyward does acknowledge that this breaking free of categories and identities does make social justice a more difficult task but, for her, this may be the beauty of spiralling, which can bring us back again to more fixed points if patriarchal politics need to be specifically challenged.

Not everyone sees things quite in the same way as Soelle and Heyward and, indeed, some would suggest that there is awkwardness in the relationship between feminism and transcendence (Howie & Jobling 2009). This is highlighted in Europe by the emphasis on psychoanalytic theory in feminist theory whereby the feminine is either unsayable or excessive within any system (*ibid.*: 3). It is within this tightly controlled system that transcendence can play a useful part for the feminine since it allows the moving beyond boundaries that the feminine marks within these bounded systems. This is not a moving above but a moving beyond and this distinction is an important one; Gillian Howie and J'annine Jobling claim that in this way we avoid the dualism of transcendence and immanence, infinite and finite and no longer understand these terms as oppositional (*ibid.*: 4). Further, they claim that the divine is emerging in feminist theology as a category of critical thought and that this, too, has to grapple with the idea of transcendence, but they suggest that we see emerging a vertical and horizontal transcendence. The former points to another world and the latter suggests an experience of an incomplete present that may also remain incomplete in the future. Through shifting between both meanings, they claim, the notion of the divine is able to act as a catalyst for re-examining ideas of love, truth, grace and the spiritual without running the risk of reasserting hierarchical and gendered categories (*ibid.*: 2).

In this way they are not unlike Irigaray, who, as we saw, argues that the sensible transcendent allows women an expanded horizon for female becoming. For her this would be a horizontal transcendence, since the vertical kind plays once again into the sameness of the divine. It is interesting that Howie, Jobling and Irigaray do not mention a re-examination of globalization in these new categories but it could be seen to be possible through the new shifting notion of transcendence as beyond into an open future. What they are saying does not entirely resonate with Soelle, who would understand the political as inherent in any new world we may imagine, although she too understands something of the notion of transcendence to be in the realm of moving across boundaries. Heyward may wish to challenge them on the notion of the incomplete present, since within her thought each moment or mode of being does hold completeness even in its dysfunction, and moving beyond would not have to be linked to the idea of incomplete presents since that notion also holds within it an idea of ideals of the "mono" kind.

A relatively new voice in the transcendence debate is that of Mayra Rivera (2007), who approaches it through a postcolonial theology of God although she, like Howie and Jobling, speaks of the touch of transcendence. Right from the start she makes her position plain: God is beyond our grasp but not beyond our touch, just as we find that in human touch we touch, but can never fully grasp, the other, creating what she suggests is an "intimacy of transcendence" (*ibid.*: 2). Situating her argument in postcolonial theology, she demonstrates how the dominant imperial theology of the West has never acknowledged anything beyond itself. While using the disembodied nature of the ONE God to set in place the Western masculinist symbolic, at the same time it stops the world, both physical and symbolic, at its own narrow vistas. Rivera is also aware that falling into the untouchable, vertical transcendence that usually follows on is no place to go for those who sit beyond the vista of the Western mind, those who have not been seen or acknowledged as inhabiting land and ways of life that fall beyond. It is precisely because of this that she sees the need for a form of transcendent theology that breaks down the Western stranglehold. For her there is nothing abstract about transcendence because in the hands of the powerful it even controls the creation of time and our spatial perceptions. Her argument is that Western industrialism needed to move beyond the rhythms of natural time and impose a universal time in order to maximize the profits it wished to extract and to disconnect people from their land and their natural ways of being. This also separated the public and private sphere, with the private time being seen as feminized and trivial while public time was of the greatest importance, the masculinized time of uninhibited production and detached transcendence (Rivera 2007). She argues that horizontal transcendence has divided space itself, with what is north being understood as closer to God while the south is nearer the depths of stagnation and even depravity. In accordance with Jacques Derrida, she believes that such overarching systems of knowledge produce, rather than discover, all-encompassing foundations; they create the illusion of totality and suppress anything that is at odds or, as Rivera sees it, anything that is beyond.

It is this view of the world she wishes to challenge and she states her hope in:

> the ineffable affinity that links all creatures in open relations of mutual transformation which may help us to envision the beyond in the world without losing sight of the transcending character of all creation. This world is indeed more than it appears, calling us to apophatic alertness. God, the creatures and even we exceed all our representations. (*Ibid.*: 38)

Along with Gutierrez and others, Rivera is happy to declare that the profane no longer exists but, contrary to how this has been understood, it is not an elimination of transcendence but rather a refusal to understand it as identifying God with the status quo. Transcendence is understood to be in history because if we see God as external then the liberation claim that salvation lies in a remaking of history, undoing injustice and replacing it with inclusive and just systems in the here and now, is a false hope and an empty theology. It is the possibilities lying in the living of history in the material body that allow for the great hope of human kind; things may happen that have never happened before, "newness is not just discovered as being already present in nature, nor is it externally imposed upon reality. Genuinely new things come into existence from the actualisation of possibilities through collective choice" (*ibid.*: 43). Rivera claims that this notion of historical transcendence found in the work of Ignacio Ellacuría is dynamic, allowing for contextual structural difference without implying dualism, and for intrinsic unity without strict identity categories being imposed.

Jesus can be said to be the supreme form of historical transcendence because he is present in material form as the dynamic outpouring of God, signalling that divine transcendence is not distance and absence but actual material presence. It could be said that in the material existence of Jesus what Christians are claiming is that God is touching the very limits of its own divinity in and through the untouchables and outcasts that Jesus interacted with. If this is indeed what is claimed then Christian theology has a long way to go before it actually allows itself to be changed by the experiences its God is said to have had.

As Rivera says, we should "aspire to a love that overcomes its consuming impulses and opens itself to be touched by the other" (*ibid.*: 140). This seems to us to be a call to theology as much as to individuals. Theology should be touched by what transcends it and thus be transformed; it should live in the "symphony unceasingly played by the infinite creativity of *life*", as Ivone Gebara (1999: 167) puts it and always reach not beyond but deeper and wider. Derrida and Gayatri Spivak (cited in Rivera 2007: 90) refer to "hauntings", by which they mean encounters with those who are not present, those who are dead or not yet born, as places where we are called beyond ourselves and asked to embrace possibilities for the future. Ethics, politics and theology all seem to need such haunting in order to understand what is missing from our great schemes and metanarratives, who is not present and what difference consideration of them would make.

While the historical understanding of transcendence is a great deal better than the traditional, and the notion of the touch of transcendence and the intimacy thereof is very appealing, both suggestive of breaking through totality into a face-to-face encounter that changes systems, there is something about the language that remains disquieting. For so many centuries it has carried a distant meaning and feeling, making it very easy to slip back to these engrained habits of use. Certainly there is a strong argument for words meaning what we wish them to, but there is also the caution that enfleshed habits of use can be hard to shift. We must always look beyond, dream dreams and have visions as the Bible writers encouraged, but we are not sure that old language brings new insights.

In the approaches to transcendence mentioned there is no challenge to monotheism as such, although the location of that divine does change the face of monotheism. That is to say, if God is between and among us then we do have to think rather differently than if that God is above, beyond and untouchable and completely unknowable. However, returning to the central question of monotheism, it is the argument of Maaike de Haardt (2010) that monotheism itself is the root cause of many of our ways of thinking and being and as such is a threat to our global relationality. Just as Fukiyama was signalling the grip of savage capitalism when he declared that history has ended, there is not space for development but only repetition and the spread of one ideology, so de Haardt (2010) argues that it is the singularity of the creator and creation that has set in place very destructive mono- thinking in the Western world. We become locked into what she sees as a unilateral relationality, where the power is all on one side and does not reside in us as subjects. For de Haardt this is clearly demonstrated in the story of the sacrifice of Isaac, which has become foundational for Western culture through the Judaeo-Christian heritage. It is a story that in itself is damaging enough in terms of societal underpinnings but when we realize that it is still, within theology, referred to as prefiguring the "ultimate" sacrifice of Christ, we begin to understand where de Haardt's objections lie. For her the core problem is this unconditional absolute obedience to God as the only authentic way to express faith that sets in place a psychology of abuse: a psychology that does not question the hierarchy of obedience and suffering – one, in short, that can live with the consequences of the worst international excesses of globalization. The hierarchy of obedience to, and suffering for, that is inherent in Christianity has been pointed out many times in the history of feminist theology (e.g. Ruether 1983; Grey 1989; Hampson 1996; Soelle 1996) but, as already stated, has not always led to questioning the ethical implications of continuing with monotheism itself (Korte & de Haardt 2009). What has been more usual is the notion of co-creation and co-creativity within a process model of the relation between the divine and humans. However, for de Haardt this also falls short because it is, she claims, a largely male-centred model that fails to move from the inherent problems of a mono-generativity. She believes there remains an unequal notion at the heart of even the process model that leads to at least a devaluing of the female and at worst a system that actually takes for granted that hierarchy and therefore service and suffering are inevitable.

It is in the work of Catherine Keller (2003) that de Haardt sees some way ahead from the mono-generativity of Western monotheism through an engagement with the Deep or the multiplicity of difference in relation that God is thought to be. However, de Haardt still remains uncomfortable because she feels even these theologies that she admires are attempting to find models that fit at the same time as attempting to overcome models that have dominance and power at their heart. It is here that she makes her main point, which is that perhaps we need new practices that change the still-dominant, imperialistic, abusive, unilateral relations, language and reality under which we live: practices because she is not sure to what extent ideas, concepts and theologies impact on social reality but she acknowledges that they do. The challenge to monotheism that she offers is to a way of living that stems from deeply rooted notions that are so deep that they have largely been forgotten but still impact on the way society and international relations and economics are shaped. Of course, we shall reflect and think but it seems that the way ahead is to "live" ourselves to a new space, a new shape of being, that challenges globalization and offers more relational ways of being together on the planet. As Keller puts it, "becoming what we never dared for the first time and forever" (2008: 176).

BACKGROUNDING THE FOREGROUND: OTHERING THE PLANET THAT GREW US

> I did not know the background and so I have often missed the meaning of the foreground. (Hoffman 1998: 90)

In this section we shall take up de Haardt's suggestion that Keller enables us to move from monotheism through an investigation of the Deep, which is the very ground of who we are but, as we shall see, is no fixed identity relying on the ONE. It is a deep situated in the cosmos itself that gives the lie to *creatio ex nihilo* and opens before us the God who is of intimate/infinite entanglements (Keller 2012): the God who is the all in all of Corinthians – not beyond, not distant but entangled. Keller visits Paul's writings on the body of Christ in 1 Corinthians and reminds us that in the Greek *energeia* is used in 12:4–6 when he tells us that there are differences, but it is the same God who is in all. For Keller, this disables any theology of distance and separation; God is not above, nor is the divine simply androcentric but rather the very Bible itself declares God to be eco-centric, all in all. Energy is not something we have but something we are (*ibid.*: 12) and it is the same energy that gives life to all; it is the stuff of entanglement. She writes, "feeling the pulsations of our bodies in our planet and the pulsations of the planet in its universe our earthly interactions are rendered simultaneously intimate and virtually infinite" (*ibid.*: 13). This is the energy of eternal delight that comes from the free flow of these energies uninhibited by repression, exploitation and denial: and uninhibited, one may add, by a desire to see distinctions between it and God. Just as Heyward before her accused theology of making us less than we are by dampening and denying desire within us, so Keller suggests that exploitation and denial of entanglement block energy, which leads to depression and lack of meaning. The mono-God who has dragged us from our cosmic home in order to find salvation has done us no favours. As Keller puts it, "God in heaven who we create without a body to do work for us and who in the name of religion represses the rhythms of the human body and pulsations of desire" (*ibid.*: 15) leaves us adrift. And what happens to all that Christian theology has placed in heaven? Well the answer is that heaven is the earth's becoming and all energy is eternal and the human and divine act reciprocally. This puts any notions of the other, even the divine other, in a very different light.

So what does Keller's approach offer us in terms of overcoming the mono-God? We are moved away from a search for perfect origins and back to beginnings from where we are grown and nurtured, not judged and cast out. Beginnings give the Christian theologian the chance to decolonize this space of origins in creation and the inevitable creator who sits apart and to challenge, as Keller puts it, "the great supernatural surge of father power, a world appearing zap out of the void and mankind ruling the world in our manly creator's image" (2003: 6). We are thrown back to cosmic beginnings, to void and chaos, to understand who we are and who we might be from *tohu vabohu*, the depth veiled in darkness. Once we give agency to void and chaos there can be no creation out of nothing as our power laden dualistic origin. Creation ceases to be a unilateral act and the divine speech in the pages of Genesis is no longer understood as a command uttered by the lord and warrior king who rules over creation, but, as Keller tells us, "let there be" is a whisper of desire and what comes forth emanates from all there is rather than appearing from above and beyond. In this shift we also see the possibility for incarnation to be understood as the rule rather than exception of creation because the whisper desires enfleshment (*ibid.*: 56). Keller certainly moves us significantly from creation out of nothing to a place where the divine is more humble and entices ever-unfolding acts of becoming grounded in the chaos at the heart of the cosmos. However, she perhaps still leaves that gap between the divine and material order.

It is this gap that secular theorists have no difficulty challenging. Eco-philosopher Val Plumwood (2002) is among those who insist that it is this gap that continues to harm both us and the planet. While we understand ourselves as something other than the rest of the created order we shall inevitably see that as "better" or "higher", and this false consciousness leads to alienation and destruction. She is quick to point out to us the logical absurdity of such a position; monological relationships will eventually weaken the provider and we need to move to dialogue between mutually recognizing and supporting agents and come to realize we live in a communion of subjects rather than a collection of objects. Plumwood argues that removing agency from the cosmos, a technique we have so often used in our colonial history in relation to the discovery of "new lands", makes it and all that lives in it an empty space, one that can be used for profit through the maximization of its development potential. She reminds us of the knock-on effect of this way of thinking. Nature is no longer viewed as a creator of our environment and the land and those who depend most directly on it are relegated to the realm of Other.

Plumwood argues for a return to what she calls the "heart of stone" in order to overcome the "sado-dispassionate" rationalism of scientific reduction. This involves a re-enchantment of the realm designated as material, the rematerialization of spirit as speaking matter. She warns that this project should not slide into the world of the romantic and in order to guard against this it needs to be ever mindful of the spirit/matter dualism and resist it at every turn. By journeying to the heart of stone we have to move stone (the material world of nature) from the background of consciousness to the

133

foreground, from silent to speaking, and from the ordinary to the extraordinary, to the wonderful and even to the sacred. This move is needed in order to challenge the false consciousness of the Western world, so rooted in our Christian heritage, which tells us we no longer live in nature but in culture. Plumwood claims moving to the heart of stone opens the door to a wide range of interspecies dialogues, drama and projects that would otherwise be unimaginable, which free us to rewrite the earth as sacred, earth exploration as pilgrimage and earth knowledge as revelation. The political and economic implications of this are quite clear. What impact would such thinking have on logging companies, chemical companies and the bodies of those who labour to make £2.50 T-shirts? Not just the people but the environment are moved from the silent place of other to a place of influencing how we all relate.

But can Christian theologians truly address the intentionality and re-enchantment of nature in their story? After all, we have a story of speaking snakes and beckoning trees as a cautionary tale in our beginnings, so we shall require a rethink of beginnings and, flowing from that, a reimagining of what we understand by redemptive activity. Grey (1989) has understood that redemption as at-one-ment brings us into a new and exciting world of co-creation and becoming. She argues that if relationality is at the heart of reality then it is at the heart of the creative redemptive process, so entering more deeply into this reality is the kind of "redemptive spirituality" needed to transform the world. Isherwood (1999) prefers radical incarnation, that is, taking incarnation seriously without the comfort of metaphysics, delayed parousias and absolute godheads, as the key to our living this profound reality. This is an understanding of incarnation based in empowerment and the shared heritage of *dunamis*, that raw energy which is our birthright, the energy that attracts us to the world and those in it. This is the concept spoken of by Jesus in the gospels when he rejects "authority over" and urges those who come after him to claim their empowerment to live in vulnerability, mutuality and relationality. In naming those who were around him as friends he was declaring that this *dunamis* lived in all and increased in the free sharing between equals. The raw dynamic energy that exists between and within us is, according to a feminist reading of Mark's Gospel, the power of incarnation; it can also be seen as the cosmic explosion that still resonates through the universe, that raw dynamism that empowers all that lives. In calling it divine we have perhaps enabled ourselves to shape our understanding of who we are and how we should live but we also run the risk of disempowering its wild and challenging core by attempting to capture it in systems and dogmas. It is, perhaps, engagement with this wild and empowering core that moves us closer to an understanding of radical otherness that includes not just all that is inanimate but also the heart of stone.

If we have the possibility of a Christology that enables us to live in the world rather than imagining that our true home is elsewhere, then we have to keep asking what it means to be alive and embedded in the cosmic story. We are creatures made from the stuff of the universe, our brains carry remnants of ancient mammalian structures, every fibre of our being is related to ancient bacteria and our ancestors are the stars. We are members of a symbiotic universe in which nothing stands alone so, in short, we are creatures of belonging and relationality. Our alienation from this process is entirely a fiction. But what kind of belonging is this? It is belonging to creatively interacting systems, a network of interplay that moves always towards novelty woven from instability and an ever-moving universe. It is not the kind of belonging that Christian theology has been used to, with its alpha and omega point, the unchanging God who requires followers to mirror his image and his alone.

The Christian story tells us that we are people of promise. What can that mean if our privileged position in creation is not that promise and we no longer may see creatures and inanimate objects as others? Diarmuid O'Murchu (2004: 29) believes promise should be understood as that which we give to honour and promote creation's own wishes, which are to enable a meaningful future to all creatures, to remove them from the background of otherness and relate with them as fellow unfolders of divine reality. This relationality will also impact on millions of women whose relationship with nature is direct and harsh. Our industrialized world has widened the gap between rich and poor and women bear the brunt of this because they and their children make up the largest number of the poor. It has highlighted for us how economic growth has become another form of colonialism that drains the resources from those who need them the most. Many women are actually being removed from the means of growing food through such activities as cash-cropping. This simply highlights how productivity for survival is very different from productivity for the capitalist market. In our change of gaze from the one absolute God to the foregrounding of the environment, we are propelled into ongoing political struggles for economic justice based in land and those who rely on it.

The cosmos did not emerge from Platonic forms but rather from tehomic chaos; there was no blueprint but rather glorious outpourings of surprise and novelty. Christian theology with its mono emphasis has preferred the Platonic model because this enables the "ins" and the "outs" to be more easily identified. It also offers stability to these categories with constant repetition at its heart. However, while the unformed future is made up of repetition, from early in cosmic development this repetition always added something new. In every repetition there is a transgression. Our bodies and that of the cosmos are in constant flux and as they regenerate they change; they are, in essence, transgressive. The reality of our cosmogenesis is one of change, a place from which it is very difficult, if not impossible, to create and maintain "the other" as a fixed category. Further, embedding ourselves in the universe as spiritual home is pitching our tent on earthquakes and seismic shifts. Cosmology shows us that new reality emerges from "explosively vola-tile exuberance" (O'Murchu 2004: 85), which offers us big dreams/futures as well as dangers and risks. What it does not offer is one fixed identity as a creative and healthy place to situate ourselves. There are some who suggest that as the universe is unravelling so too is the truth of the ONE God, but this is kidnapping scientific theory to bolster an ever-wavering set of theological principles. New discoveries in science do not see the universe as unravelling to a fixed point; rather, it is now being suggested that the universe is more cyclical than at first thought and that dark matter will itself reach a point of decay, thus slowing expansion and, indeed, moving all to a big crunch from which comes a big bang, which starts the whole cycle of new galaxies, stars, planets and the new life forms they hold (Rubenstein 2012: 40). There are, in short, endless possibilities and the energy in this is the energy "all in all", the same that creates such amazing diversity.

It does seem as though theology has within it a number of ways in which to destabilize the mono-God who, it has been suggested, creates the many and various forms of the Other that have been less than helpful in human history. What forever militates against a full embrace of such theology seems to be psychological more than theological or intellectual: the desire for the father protector even if he hurts us seems to be deep in the human psyche.

SOCIOLOGICAL APPROACHES

The struggle between the ONE and definite Otherness at the theoretical level echoes the struggles in conventional sociological theory, over the exist-ence and functioning of transcendent structures of various kinds. Oddly, these structures are usually seen as operating "beneath" empirical reality rather than above it, serving as a "base" to describe a complex empirical "surface". Various "post-" positions aimed to undermine this "base/surface" metaphor, as we shall see, seen at its height, perhaps, in postmodernism. In France, it seems, there were three sources of structuralism that came under particular attack – Marxism, Freudianism and linguistic structuralism, including the unholy alliance forged between the last two by Lacanians reading the Freudian Unconscious "as language". These approaches domi-nated the French university system in directly material ways, so that most poststructuralist critics, including Foucault, were initially marginalized in career terms. Bourdieu (1988) tells us that this was one of the factors in the discontent that led to the events of 1968.

In the UK, Althusserian "structural" Marxism appeared in various guises, especially influencing the analyses of institutions such as schools acting as "ideological State apparatuses" (Althusser 1977b). Structural Marxism of this kind was locked in combat for a while with other variants, especially more activist Gramscian Marxism, as we shall see below. Louis Althusser also saw an early connection with the work of Lacan on the development of subjectivity to endorse his notion of individual subjectivity as at the centre of "ideology in general", and this synthesis also played a part in film studies, as in Colin MacCabe's (1981) analysis of "realism" as a "knowledge effect" produced in the viewing subject.

Freudian accounts appeared in analyses of film and literature in various ways. Elsaesser (1985) saw cinema as featuring the characteristics of dreams for Freud. More common was attempting to "read" film or novels in Freudian terms, as examples of neurotic thinking (Smith [1997] has some examples) or as incorporating key aspects of the pleasures of scopophilia, as in the work of Mulvey (1975) discussed earlier: this work combined psychoanalytic with structural linguistic analyses to form "positioning theory".

Saussurian linguistics formed the basis of a powerful "semiotic" approach to understanding film (and English literature, but this was initially fiercely resisted), and applications of this approach can be seen in such classics as Umberto Eco's (1981) analysis of the Bond novel as a series of binary terms (such as Bond versus M, Bond versus the villain, villain versus the main woman) and game-like "moves" (M moves and gives a task to Bond, the villain moves and appears to Bond, the main woman moves and shows herself to Bond). This admirably parsimonious structure enabled some progress to be made at last with interminable discussions of the "Bond formula".

There was some admiration for the "structural anthropology" of Claude Lévi-Strauss, especially for his demonstration of the structures of kinship that lay behind actual complex patterns: all patterns could be explained in terms of various basic binary terms and their emotional modalities. According to Lévi-Strauss there are four basic terms:

> (brother, sister, father, and son), which are linked by two pairs of correlated oppositions in such a way that in each of the two generations there is always a positive relationship and a negative one ... [This is] the most elementary form of kinship that can exist. It is, properly speaking, *the unit of kinship*. (1977: 46)

This is so logically, since there must always be three types of family relations in any kinship system – "a relation of consanguinity, a relation of affinity, and a relation of descent – in other words, a relation between siblings, a relation between spouses, and a relation between parent and child" (*ibid.*). This piece also reasserts the notorious conception of the incest taboo as universal, and as driven by the deliberate swapping of women by men in order to achieve this balanced structure between and across generations.

Each of these structural approaches was to attract criticism, mostly on the grounds that the structures they proposed were normative, even ideological, as well as technical. Powerful aspects of the critique were developed by feminists, as we saw. More neutrally, free will is connected to mundane otherness, since it permits choice, and we have followed the options in the specific debates about consumerism in Chapter 4, and in discussions of body politics in Chapter 2.

The debate with Marxism can be seen as exemplary, partly because there were traditionally strong boundaries between sociology, psychology (how Freudianism was read) and anthropology, but weak ones between sociology, Marxism and cultural studies. General interest in Marxism dates from when the "humanist" early works of Marx was translated into English in the 1960s (*New Left Review* 1975). These became popular as a way of rescuing Marx from all the unpleasant associations of state socialism, iron laws of history driven by economic factors, political dictatorship, and the need to join the Communist Party (which had always been small, if influential, in British academic circles). The work of Althusser (1966) caused problems, however, in arguing that marxism (Althusser pioneered the small "m" so as to emphasize the collective nature of the effort) actually contained works that broke with that humanist tradition and hinted at a new scientific conception. It was to be scientific in the French structural sense, however, offering a universal underlying model of the social formation (with semi-autonomous economic, political and ideological/cultural sectors, all bound within and limited by a problematic supplied by the economy), which could be realized in various specific social formations. The work was especially unpopular in the UK for its apparent insistence on the need for Communist Party intellectuals to play the key role in penetrating capitalist ideology (which centred on the very notion of the autonomous individual) and for leading political activism. British activism took a very different form, outside the Party and involving "free" intellectuals and militant workers (including white-collar ones): the "events" in France in the 1960s were the preferred model, and the French Communist Party had found itself outmanoeuvred by, and critical of, those events.

Much debate ensued, for example a gripping debate about the notion of "value" in Marxism between Hegelians and Althusserians (Elson 1979). There was close interrogation of the structuralist claims of Althusserian work by Hirst (1977), focusing on the exact nature of the economic problematic in both underpinning and limiting activity in the relatively autonomous sectors. If we reject economic determinism, we have no theory to link political agents with economic ones as in classic class analyses. Indeed, if we grant any kind of autonomy, even relative autonomy, to political forces a "[logically] necessary non-correspondence" is implied (*ibid.*: 130) between political forces and economic classes. If concrete political or ideological/cultural activities are to be analysed, they need to be theorized, but this is half-hearted in Althusserian approaches; they are only defined negatively as "relatively autonomous" from the economic. Some theorists introduced sociological analysis subsequently to explain the specifics of these activities and institutions, and their reproduction, but this can only be related back to Marxist notions of class and class politics formally (by definition). Hirst's work became one the first major applications of post-Althusseriansm, which in turn ushered in "poststructuralism" in general (Crook 1991) and then postmodernism, with its "scepticism towards all attempts to discover privileged foundations" for specific analyses and to operate with metanarratives.

The work of Gramsci seemed useful in restoring a Marxism for the modern British social formation, although, technically, his approach was as foundational and incoherent as any other. The approach emphasized the importance of educational, political and cultural elements in struggles for hegemony and gave these elements more autonomy (Harris 1992). Since Gramsci's work was clearly incomplete, given that much of his work was undertaken in prison, certain partial fusions with Althusserian approaches were attempted (especially in the work of Hall *et al.* 1978). The growing threat of relativism from discourse theorists and, eventually, postmodernism was initially countered with systematic investigations of neglected Marxist linguists (including Bakhtin/Volosinov). Eventually, it seemed as though Gramsci could be integrated to some extent with Foucault, controversially, to found a Marxism compatible with discourse theory, where knowledge was inextricably linked to power and linguistic discourses to institutions and practices.

To take one approach in more detail, Jules Townshend (2004) has written a critical account of the subsequent trajectory of the work of Ernesto Laclau and Chantal Mouffe. They began with the once fashionable rejection of essentialism, foundationalism and grand narratives in Marxism. Discourses were seen as the result of hegemonic struggles, but class antagonisms were not central. Psychological mechanisms were as important as economic ones, including "the individual's desire for 'fullness', the result of a primordial 'lack' of a satisfyingly stable identity [based on Lacan]" (Townshend 2004: 271). This leads to a necessary and universal antagonism with the Other (including other objects as well as other people), who blocks this fullness. However, tactical alliances can be made with others based on various discourses of equivalence and difference, and hegemonic struggle involves the mobilization of political force in order to get support for particular definitions, "such as 'freedom' and 'equality'" (*ibid.*).

However, the whole project was to corrode their own efforts to establish their own work as central (only in the academic context, since no actual political movements seemed keen): operating at the general, formal, abstract level simply misses the differences between scientific discourses about truth and those "such as aesthetics/imaginative or certain political discourses that have a clear symbolic dimension and do not require, or aspire to, agreed methods to demonstrate proof" (*ibid.*: 274). Laclau and Mouffe do not seem to recognize that some interests can be mobilized around "mistaken beliefs ... the result of ignorance and/or superstition" (*ibid.*). Just because discourses exist, that is no reason to support them politically. Townshend says that Laclau prefers "to dissolve structures into discourses" (*ibid.*: 279), which leaves out the role of institutions in promoting or limiting discourses. This leads him into "some form of utopianism" in the case of his own radicalism.

Mouffe, even more curiously, "derived her notion of 'the political' from the Conservative/Nazi Carl Schmitt", who had developed some underlying philosophical anthropology based on "passion-driven human conflict" (*ibid.*). These conflicts had to be transformed into peaceful politics, based around the "'paradox of democracy' – the impossible promise to eliminate conflicts, especially between the 'logics' of equality and liberty" (*ibid.*). The democratic appeal of these logics led to a constant challenge to all forms of subordination, as witnessed by the new social movements. However, in practice, Mouffe is left expressing a mere preference for liberal democracy. Her insistence on pluralism also means she cannot simply support political movements that claim to be true, as do the new social movements, despite their potential to develop radical democracy. Critical intellectuals of whatever stripe seem to be unreliable allies in actual political fights!

SOCIAL CONSTRUCTIVISM

Despite the difficulties, this kind of theoretical amalgam of discourse theory and political radicalism helped to underpin the recently widespread support for "social constructivism", often based on a possibly too literal and non-contextual reading of the work of one of those quietly rehabilitated Marxist linguists, Lev Vygotsky (see Hua Liu and Matthews 2005). This was grafted on to other radical traditions, including feminist ones, to emphasize the politics of the personal and its qualitative methodologies, which enabled the oppressed to speak unhindered by any positivist constraints. It might be worth revisiting the point about sameness and otherness here. It is clear that despite its attempt to de-reify orthodoxy as "socially constructed", there is still a danger that others might be incorporated in limited ways; their views are also merely socially constructed. A general relativism beckons, which can be avoided only by incoherence again (see Morss 2002).

Eventually, as the next chapter shows, a new revived interest in the real promised to ground analysis and radical politics in a more compellingly logical and well-theorized fashion. The best-known current example is the work of Deleuze and his associates.

DELEUZIAN APPROACHES

Deleuze's work had been noted, indeed translated, by feminists (Goulimari 1999), but sociologists probably were more accustomed to Foucault with his institutional analysis. It was probably only when Foucault (1970) announced that "Perhaps one day this century will be known as Deleuzian" (1970), that Deleuze emerged as of interest for social theory too. Deleuze commented to a critic that "his little remark's a joke meant to make people who like us laugh and make everyone else livid" (Deleuze 1995: 4), but Foucault's remark has often been quoted.

Foucault's 1970 article went on to celebrate the creative thinking in two major Deleuzian works of the period: *Difference and Repetition* (1968; Deleuze 2004) and *The Logic of Sense* (1969; Deleuze 1990). Foucault identified some radical new thinking in *The Logic of Sense* about Plato and the metaphysics of essences and judgement; new concepts of "the event", which reintroduced movement to an otherwise static analysis; and a new revalidation of the Freudian notions of the phantasm as an embryonic form of sense-making involving both linguistic capability and the influence of biological processes. *Difference and Repetition* offered a way to both break decisively with common-sense and good-sense assumptions that had underpinned philosophy so far and to liberate a proper concept of "difference" from that which merely repeated "the same". The philosophical approach that was most susceptible to this new thinking was dialectics. Deleuze's concept of difference was based on a radical mechanism of the conjunction of heterogeneous elements, especially in concrete "actual" objects.

Beneath these more specific processes lay a radicalized notion of Being. While other philosophers had seen Being as a single substance, Deleuze saw it as displaying a groundless process that endlessly produces differences. Being was a real substance, but operating at the virtual or immanent level, not a hierarchical transcendental conception.

It is already possible to see how these notions have heavily influenced conceptions such as the virtual in feminist thinking, and the dethronement of a single judgemental god in feminist and Queer theology: Deleuze's position "does not tolerate the subsistence of God as an original individuality, nor the self as the Person, nor the world as an element of the self and as God's product" (1990: 176), and later "Philosophy merges with ontology, but ontology merges with the univocity of Being (analogy has always been a theological vision, not a philosophical one, adapted to the forms of God, the world, and the self)" (*ibid.*: 179).

Perhaps the greatest impact on sociological thinking was seriously to challenge social constructivism, as we suggested above. For Deleuze, there is indeed a reality that exceeds human activity and thinking, and which has long preceded it. The chaotic cosmos has produced divergent and convergent trends, some of which have come together and been actualized, and some of which have been frozen in reality and in thought. Some of our most cherished conceptions reveal this frozen thinking: taking snapshots of actualizations and taking them to be the only reality that exists; ignoring the virtual as the source of all actualizations, including some that do not yet exist, but which could exist equally easily. Even our cherished notion of ourselves as unified individual subjects representing or even "constructing" the world is a result really of a habit, and of socially supported common sense. For Deleuze, individuation does not mean "individuals constituted in experience, but that which acts in them as a transcendental principle: as a plastic, anarchic and nomadic principle ... No less capable of dissolving and destroying individuals than of constituting them temporarily" (2004: 47).

Again we can see traces of these arguments in some feminist thinking, such as that of Grosz (Kontturi & Tiainen 2007), suggesting a primary grounding of sexual difference in a long evolutionary development. Ettinger (2010) develops a notion of pre-linguistic communication in the matrixial, in the form of "vibrations". Deleuze and Guattari say that sensations are as much an aspect of brains as our concepts, and arise with excitation itself, with vibrations from stimulants. Sensations preserve these vibrations and can resonate. When contracted, these vibrations "become quality, variety" (1994: 211). Deleuze (2000) repeated this idea of a non-human basis for "affects", objective forces experienced as sensations, when discussing how cinema seems to sidestep representation altogether and communicate directly with our brains. Ettinger (2010) also embraces the immanent rather than the transcendental when she discusses the horizontal relationship between I and non-I, and we have seen a similar turn in feminist theology behind the conception of incarnation as a continuous process.

Deleuze himself often offers only a "compressed" account of these ontological issues, one that "assumes so much on the part of the reader, that it is bound to be misinterpreted" (DeLanda 2002: 5). Mercifully we have Manuel DeLanda's own reconstruction of the main argument, using more modern terminology. For Deleuze, there is a virtual reality (in the sense of offering potentials or immanence), and it is populated by multiplicities, bundles of vectors and attractors, operating with quite different conceptions of time (or "speed") and interconnections. This virtual world is chaotic (although some attractors might lead to equilibrium), but intersected by "planes of immanence", which permit aspects of multiplicities to generate singularities that can take actualized forms, and appear as the familiar states of affairs in the normal empirical world. DeLanda argues that Deleuze's realist ontology describes "a relatively undifferentiated and continuous topological space undergoing discontinuous transitions and progressively acquiring detail until it condenses into the measurable and divisible metric space which we inhabit" (*ibid.*: 56). The key characteristic of a multiplicity is its display of "symmetry-breaking bifurcations, together with the distribution of attractors which define each of its embedded levels" (*ibid.*: 30).

The connections between the virtual and the empirical cannot be simply asserted or deduced but must be explained in a particularly rigorous way using "concrete empirico-ideal notions, not abstract categories" (*ibid.*: 86). We know that the "empirico-ideal notion" is what is meant by a concept, which not only describes or categorizes, but alludes to the virtual and to the pre-conceptual as well (Deleuze & Guattari 1994). Whether DeLanda's hyphen conceals an incoherent relation between the components is discussed in the Conclusion.

Deleuze's reciprocally complimentary reading of Foucault in *Foucault* (1986; Deleuze 1999) shows some implications for sociologists as well. The essay on *Discipline and Punish* (Foucault 1977) solved a problem in arguing that the empirical mixtures of institutional power and discursive knowledge found in particular institutions was not the source of an annoying incoherence, but rather Foucault suggesting that a multiplicity (described as an abstract machine in this case) could be deduced from these mixtures. Institutions themselves were best seen as actualized structures holding together heterogeneous themes and elements, keeping out the outside, the chaotic universe. In this way, sociological analysis of institutions seemed entirely misplaced, especially the emphasis on social reproduction; the point instead is to see how institutions were constantly being produced, and then dissolved, by the cosmos actualizing itself. Sociologists, in other words, were operating at the wrong level, as if actual objects and processes were self-sufficient, the only ones that existed. It might be possible to exempt social theorists operating with two-level transcendental realities, such as Giddens and Roy Bhaskar, as we have suggested earlier, and DeLanda's (2006) critique of sociology agrees that these two approaches were on the same lines as Deleuze, although they still operate with a transcendental rather than an immanent structure.

STOICISM OR ANARCHISM?

For Alain Badiou (2000) in particular, the "chaosmos" producing actualized empirical products left no real space for human activity to change anything. The chaosmos produced singularities and actualizations that were "quite indifferent to the individual and collective, the personal and the impersonal, the particular and the general ... Singularity is neutral" (Deleuze 1990: 52).

Deleuze's stance in *The Logic of Sense*, then, was explicitly a stoical one: to accept fate and to deal with whatever arose without resentment. The only consolation for the philosopher was to grasp the connection between empirical events and the movements of the virtual, in "counteractualization" to see the big picture, as it were. Badiou comments that this is not a stance that is available to everybody.

It then becomes a problem to explain the apparently more active revolutionary texts that Deleuze wrote with Guattari, especially *Anti Oedipus* (1972; Deleuze & Guattari 1984) and *A Thousand Plateaus* (1980; Deleuze & Guattari 2004). These texts are perhaps the most popular of their joint works, with their notion of a pulsating and endlessly creative Desire driving revolutionary attempts to escape from institutions, pursue lines of flight, discover rhizomes beneath trees, develop nomadicity, and pursue programmes of becoming. There are also much debated terms such as "the body without organs", and powerful critiques of Freud and, by implication, Lacan as domesticating Desire by imposing on it an Oedipal or Symbolic framework. Deleuze and Guattari urge us to listen to schizophrenics instead, who are much more in touch with the endless flow beneath. In those works they also develop their own delirious style, where *délire* is defined as "exactly to go off the rails" (Deleuze & Parnet 1987: 40).

These terms have also inspired much additional comment in feminist and theological work, as is readily apparent from earlier chapters. They have also inspired some educational radicals such as Warren Sellers and Noel Gough (2010), and the Italian autonomists Sylvere Lotringer and Christian Marrazi (1980).

What of other people? Deleuze seems to deny the ordinary conceptions of subjectivity, as we have seen, and replaces them with the idea of the subject as a heterogeneous conjunction of sub-persons and pre-individuals. Others are as heterogeneous as selves, and appear to us as "other structures", as we have seen. However, there is a liberating side to these conceptions as well, several commentators have noticed, because they help us move away from any idea that the "normal subject", especially the white and racist, male and dominating, liberal or pro-capitalist entrepreneurial subject, is grounded ontologically. Both Guattari (1995) and Ettinger (2010) have seen the therapeutic implications of persuading their patients to relinquish this fixed subjectivity and to begin to interact instead as sub-persons encountering other sub-persons. For Guattari, this would be a way to establish non-psychotic relations with "alterity", while for Ettinger it would generate new ethical relations of responsibility and respect, and the dissolution of old fixed conceptions, for example of the "devouring mother".

For Slavoj Žižek (2004), revolutionary politics came along just at the right moment to rescue Deleuze from the stoical dead end of the earlier works. For Badiou (2000), the earlier emphasis on Being represents the "real" Deleuze, and this is just detectable in the apparently anarchic writings. Badiou cites in particular the continued reference to machinic conceptions of Desire in the later work, which is not at all compatible with more anarchist readings implying autonomous human subjects. Eric Alliez (2006) insists that Guattari fostered Deleuze's interest in moving away from abstract philosophy, to "physicalize" the concept: to ground Desire in machinic operations or in the body (without organs).

In support of this view, it might be possible to cite the work on "becoming". Deleuze and Guattari might mean this to mean far more than taking on another role or losing an old repressive one, because it seems to be grounded in the ontology developed in Deleuze's earlier work: becoming alludes to multiplicity. Freud's Little Hans is not a neurotic made anxious about horses by fear of his father, but wants to become-horse:

> Is there an as yet unknown assemblage that would be neither Hans' nor the horse's but that of the becoming-horse for Hans? An assemblage, for example, in which the horse would bare its teeth and Hans might show something else, his feet, his legs, his peepee maker, whatever?   (Deleuze & Guattari 1984: 284–5)

We can only wish Deleuze and Guattari had clarified their arguments as well as physicalizing them. There are endless difficulties in reading the work, partly due to the deliberate avoidance of conventional writing in order to develop a style that alludes to what it is depicting. Foucault's "Introduction" to *Anti-Oedipus* (*ibid.*) says this is a way of avoiding "fascism", but it also produces reader incomprehension when confronted with an elite and private language. The problems arise for experienced readers as well as tyros. We have seen some of the disputes between major Deleuzian scholars, and even Buchanan admits, "We are still a long way from being able to say what a Deleuzian analysis ... might, much less should look like ... not one of [the dozens of books on Deleuze and Guattari] can tell you how to read a text in a manner that is recognisably Deleuzian' (2006: 147–8). Without precision, Deleuze's conceptual toolbox is useless, Buchanan says. It is not enough to refuse "interpretation" in the master's name, since Deleuze himself says that we must return to actual problems. Many readers of Deleuze want to refuse attempts to find any kind of analytic programme of action, in order to be anarchic (or "pragmatic") but Deleuze himself said "that he wanted to create a practical, useful form of philosophy. This is what he meant when he said *Anti Oedipus* is an experiment in writing pop philosophy" (*ibid.*: 148).

THE RETURN OF THE EMPIRICAL?

Whatever Deleuze wishes, there is no easy way to develop empirical analysis, or an empirical politics for that matter. We have seen that Irigaray argued that "becoming woman" as an abstract concept simply ignores all the empirical political forms that prevent actual women from developing sufficiently as a political subject to pursue becoming. This criticism can easily be generalized to other aspects of the politics. Deleuze and Guattari tend to take political structures as abstract ones only, and therefore to miss the empirical detail that is so crucial to launching a concrete political strategy.

Stratification in organizations is discussed by Deleuze and Guattari (2004), for example, as an inevitable result of failing to pursue critical thinking. It is a kind of sedimentation, rather like the way in which personal selves develop as a result of habit, driven as much by the tendencies of language systems to stratify as by any particular political action by a social class. In another example, the only form of organizational politics that seems to be theorized is the constant contrast of the concrete organization with its virtual counterpart, to theorize a necessary "trembling" and insufficiency in organizational routines (Thanem & Linstead 2006). The political activist here is an individual, probably an academic, seeking refuge from bureaucracy in a philosophy of difference.

This oscillation between actual and virtual is a severely limited way of conceptualizing relationships and collective efforts to change. We see it in the discussion of Otherness too, where the only stances towards other people are naturalistic and commonsensical or philosophical and ontological. One obvious omission is the research stance taken by sociologists and others, moving beyond the naturalistic but also resisting what might be seen as ontological reductionism and abstraction.

Deleuze's own cautiousness in recommending even this individualized kind of artistic experimentation and philosophical journeying has also been noted. For every section urging us to leave aside convention and habit, there is a dark warning about the dangers of madness, melancholy or alcoholism. Again, we might be entitled to ask what comes next. Do we just endlessly oscillate between these two abstract possibilities or try to establish some kind of political trade-off: is it worth risking alcoholism to develop a militant oppositional stance to, say, recent educational reforms? How likely is the danger of reinstalling fascism if we join or establish disciplined political organizations? We suggest in the Conclusion that there are similar problems in the proposal that we pursue "joy" as a working ethic.

If these analyses and recommendations are not to be grounded in concrete analyses of political situations, they surely remain as little more than bourgeois injunctions to try to be as creative as possible and to live a full life.

The whole debate shows the dangers of excessive theorizing, so to speak. Poststructuralist commentaries are corrosive and difficult to contain, undermining not only the positions of fascist enemies but also those of potential allies as well. The same approach leads both to deep insight and cracking up. Revolutionary potentials escape recuperation only by remaining in thought. We discuss further implications in the Conclusion.

CONCLUSION

Organizing a dialogue between the two authors of this book has replicated and focused the problems of otherness that we have been discussing throughout. Although we are both academics, and we have been colleagues, the academic traditions we represent and draw upon feature a common pattern of similarity and difference. At the most basic level, both sociology and theology are clearly centrally interested in relations with and between other people, and in the relations with what might be called the non-human, including the divine and the social. Both are committed to understanding the subjective reactions of other people, and also in making their theoretical work related in some way to those reactions, most obviously as a kind of therapy or politics.

That the two disciplines have shared an intellectual heritage that persists has been argued in a number of ways. William Keenan (2003) represents one of the more recent commentaries, drawing on earlier work, especially that of David Martin, a sociologist and an Anglican priest. There are residual and unreflected theological influences on sociology that have influenced a number of theoretical debates. Unfortunately, they include a narrow puritanism, Keenan argues, which has informed a defensiveness, an interest in strong subject boundaries. Technicism has added to this conceptual isolation. Sociology must reawaken its interest in the sacramental, Keenan suggests, not only to acquire new ideas and new resources with which to criticize advanced modernity and its meaninglessness, but also to put it in touch with everyday thinking, which remains religious, in a good sense that cannot be reduced to ideology or neurosis.

Of course, these are cognitive arguments, which do not consider any deeper personal commitments on either side. Sociology operates with a view that the world is awash with subjective and cultural meanings, that everything has a sociology. The preparation and consumption of food is not just a necessary act to preserve life, but is also a way of representing ideas about nature and culture, about civilized behaviour and the growth of manners, about relations between the genders and the generations (Mennell 1985). We also know, from Chapter 1, of the Christian significance of meals and of eating as a spiritual practice. Where there might be disagreement is in whether we see one of these meanings as divinely privileged.

This is not to say, as we argued, that sociology can operate without presuppositions, faiths and beliefs of its own. There are no purely rational agreed grounds to prioritize the social as a level of analysis or as a concept. There is a mixture of theoretical and political, including micropolitical commitments instead.

The discussions we have launched show the rich theological resources available to mount the kind of "sacramental" critique of modernity that Keenan has in mind. There is some dispute about the actual connections with the sacramental, however; the divine is found in prosperity, in the market economy and in the medieval monastery for some writers, while for feminist theologians, these are false gods.

Some specific academic work is shared by both traditions, since sociological work has been used as a critical resource in order to displace and disconcert conventional phallocratic theology (argued in Althaus-Reid & Isherwood 2004: "Introduction"). Neither discipline can be seen entirely according to the purposes of the other one, however: to any theological readers of this book, the examples of sociological work might seem unhelpfully descriptive, technical and politically uncommitted, while theological examples might seem to the converse sociological readership as over-committed and over-generalized.

Other critical work has been used by both sociological and theological approaches, notably Marxism and, more recently, poststructuralism. The currently fashionable work of Deleuze and Deleuze and Guattari has a particularly lively critical relation to the most relevant aspects of both the traditions where they explore Otherness.

At the same time, it would be misleading to regard the development of both traditions as being driven entirely by theoretical controversies. As professional university activities, there are tendencies towards specialization, as we have suggested above. Both disciplines have found themselves concerned with relations with those others specifically found in universities: students, but also colleagues and administrators. Here, an organizational micropolitics has developed, sometimes involving a struggle for institutional survival, and certainly involving the usual professional academic concerns for resources, academic careers, the development of research programmes and so on. The desire to be funded, published and included in the periodic government reviews of research output and impact shapes academic interests in a major way, and in the direction of separation. Apart from anything else, it becomes difficult to find the time to even read work in another discipline, let alone engage in any sort of critical debate with it: non-specialists finds themselves precisely in the cognitively disoriented position of "the stranger" discussed in Chapter 1.

Feminist and then Queer theorizing seems to have thoroughly over-hauled both disciplines, pointing to significant omissions and falsely universal working assumptions, to the adoption of unacknowledged dominant masculinist interests and categories, to the prevailing use of research methods that incorporate these assumptions and interests, and to a suspiciously detached spectatorial stance that both denies and oppresses the views and experiences of women and Queers (and other excluded minorities). Part of this critique has involved a thorough critical interrogation of the theoretical traditions of each subject, for example biblical texts and the lives of the religious for one, foundational texts in the more recent traditions, especially those of the so-called founding parents, for the other. New topics have been introduced as worthy of attention, mostly focusing around the cultural aspects of, or, more generally the daily lives of, those who were formerly excluded, and critical readings of texts and historical research developing new insights have led to claims of the need for new methods of enquiry. In the case of sociology, this has led to a lively controversy about empirical research methods as well as theoretical models. In Queer theology, the "methods" debate has been focused on developing new concepts, or putting critical concepts of others to work. It is possible to detect a materialist base for these new interests in both cases, too, in the growing diversity of the university population and its client base, as a result of the cultural autonomy characteristic of modernity.

EMPIRICAL RESEARCH

The role of empirical research has emerged as an important issue. Even the founding parents of sociology felt the need to test their theoretical models against certain forms of empirical data: in Weber's case, historical data on economic activity; in Marx's case, empirical data sometimes derived from official British government sources on wages, prices and living conditions; for Durkheim, in one classic demonstration, social statistics on demographic characteristics and their connections with suicide rates. The argument still persists that without some kind of reference to data we are left only with easy theorizing, or what Adorno (1973) called "identity thinking". These terms relate to the temptations to recognize immediately in the actual world the categories that we have constructed in the theoretical world. To take some famous cases, G. W. F. Hegel far too easily equated Reason with the policies of the Prussian state, while Heidegger was to make a similar mistake, albeit with different categories, with Nazism.

The issue for non-empirical approaches is the status of the concrete claims they make when they comment on the actual social world, when condemning capitalist organizations, say, as we saw with Cixous (in Chapter 3). Are these generalizations not really empirical ones but definitional, so that a capitalist publisher is defined by its practice of excluding women writers? If so, is there any interest in what might be seen as actual publishers or not: is it possible that some at least might be less "capitalist" than others? The same point clearly applies to discussions of politics. Are we defining "the political" or hoping to inform concrete political processes? Is it to be "families" or families, "beliefs" or beliefs? If there is any interest in the concrete and actual practices in these terms there are still choices: to examine or even undertake empirical research or to generalize on the basis of "what is known", or ideology, to use another term.

Of course, it is by no means easy to do, and there are serious temptations to gloss over the problems of empirical research. One trend leads towards unthinking and uncritical positivism, seeing empirical facts as self-sufficient and transparent, or scientism, where rigorously following some version of the scientific method becomes a guarantee of arriving at the truth, much as does the correct pursuit of the ritual for magicians (as Adorno argued; Adorno *et al.* 1976). Positivist results are often seen as being particularly useful for policy-makers and in this they become political and partisan. There can be a blanket rejection of positivism, although it is argued here that sometimes even positivist research can be informative and critical, for example, when it is used to test official policy recommendations on equality of opportunity or social mobility.

The political implications suggest another serious temptation, which arises especially with "standpoint" research, associated with, but not exclusive to, some varieties of feminism and Queer theory. The problem is that obvious standpoints or commitments can help to further a cause, but only for the committed. Any neutrals, waverers or critics are able to point easily to the threats to validity of the research itself, adding to the general scepticism about, and disillusion with, expert knowledge generally in "second modernity" (*Journal of Consumer Culture* 2001). Of course, the insistence on validity in these cases on the part of external critics is also often itself strategic, and it is often naively asserted and seldom applied reflexively. *Ressentiment* and self-interest are not exclusive to activists.

Standpoint epistemology limits theoretical enquiry, and can lead to a premature exhaustion of the possibilities, as Adorno has argued. Jussi Vähämäki and Akseli Virtanen argue that physical exhaustion awaits too in the form of an inevitable "sorrow and disappointment ... [which] derive from materializing a capacity of power, from finding a [political] 'cause'" (2006: 224). This would comply with Deleuze's scepticism towards the value of discussing philosophy with others and encountering only *ressentiment* and self-interest, as mentioned above. The alternative seems to be a controversial "pure" philosophy, devoted only to extending Spinozan "joy", here seen as a personal project of extending one's powers. There are problems with such a "pure" stance too, mostly in terms of making it look aloof and over-specialized in more popular discourses.

One stance developed here is to see empirical work as aimed not at producing some perfect scientific and objective results, but, more modestly, at questioning and criticizing more "common-sense" views about the social world, including those held by politicians and practitioners. Some empirical studies of what we have called "mundane otherness" seem particularly relevant here, in the sense that they are aimed at "making the strange familiar, and the familiar strange", to cite an old slogan, or, more modestly, to deliver "surprise". Agnes Elling *et al.* (2003) suggest a possible modestly "surprising" finding that policies aimed at integrating gay and Queer sportspeople into straight sports clubs would work better the other way around, while Beth Kivel and Douglas Kleiber (2000) found that even the choice of a musical instrument to play had sexual significance, so that playing drums was seen as a straight male behaviour, while saxophones were less straight male than trumpets. The risk is that the very difference of others can also be reduced and domesticated in this way: that their otherness can be accommodated as some kind of empirical variation of the norm, as an exception to the rule, or as some purely private interest that can be tolerated as long as it does not become "harmful".

We might place discussion of body modification in this more ambiguous category. Obesity is widely condemned on the grounds that it causes social harm: excessive public expenditure on healthcare, for example. Again, empirical research, even of the simplest kind, can raise doubts, for example by comparing official figures of costs between different activities. The costs of "treating" obesity are probably the same as, or lower than, the costs of treating malnutrition, or "self-inflicted injury", which includes sports injuries and those arising from gardening or DIY. More promising are studies of the explanations of the obese themselves, which, we argue above, often involve "techniques of neutralization" that can effectively defuse all the state's policies involving official health warnings or shaming attempts, even if we were to support them. Such arguments can generate "surprise" but, with the exception of the openly politicized, they also often concede that obesity is an "injury", a "health problem" or a form of deviant activity, with pejorative undertones.

Again, feminist and Queer theology have taken us beyond this interest in empirical bodies and their part in a politics of identity: studies of mundane otherness, as we have called them. "The body" becomes a far more complex concept, and this helps to place it at the centre of a much more general theoretical and political struggle, as we saw.

The danger of the "imperialism of the same" has been particularly well developed in feminist and Queer theology, where it clearly assumes political importance in trying to break free of heteronormativity. The existing social and cultural systems already acknowledge the difference of women

and Queers to a limited extent, and propose some sort of liberal tolera-
tion of difference and a complementary division of labour. By contrast,
some feminists have been demanding a different sort of equal relationship
even among heterosexuals (e.g. Braidotti 2003, summarizing Irigaray): not
a complementary or a binary one, which will penalize both participants,
but a relationship between fully different equals. Queer theory, and some
feminism, has gone even further in extending this notion beyond the conventionally sexed subject.

However, it would be misleading to see sociological work as simply part of
a phallogocentrist project to construct obedient others. Janice Irvine (2003)
has charted a long history of sociological studies of sexual behaviour rooted
in interactionist traditions. The tradition has long had an interest in sexual
minorities. We have briefly cited one classic – Humphries (1970) – but there
were equally informative studies such as Albert Reiss's 1961 essay "The Social
Integration of Queers and Peers" (cited in Irvine 2003). Theoretical traditions
with which this work is associated are famous for questioning the whole basis
of the category of "deviant", arguing that deviance has no objective basis, but
is defined as such by a collection of rules that can be applied to activity by
powerful "labellers". Queers are people whose main common characteristic
is that their sexual activity has been labelled as deviant.

It is still possible to use this work simply to provoke thought, say in students, or in some audiences for empirical research who imagine that methodological issues are purely technical ones.

CONCEPTUAL CLARIFICATION

If empirical work in sociology is so controversial and limited, why should
it be developed at all? It is certainly easy to see why some philosophical
approaches are so sceptical, and so differently specialized, that they do not
undertake empirical research of their own, and are very cautious about
quoting sociological work. Instead, they operate with a method aimed
at developing and clarifying concepts. It is clearly important to do so,
although outsiders can sometimes see this as unwarranted specialization.

Yet it is clear that it is impossible to rely on empirical research alone if
we wish to go beyond description, and beyond the classically small-scale
studies that characterize modern sociology. One early issue concerned how
to derive scientific laws from empirical data, and there are no agreed procedures: induction is logically flawed, and Popperian falsificationism is ideal-
ist in both the popular and the technical sense.

Beyond empirical patterns lie theoretical connections, which develop
what we have called "the background" in Chapter 5. These refer to underlying processes, mechanisms and energies that cannot be studied empirically,
but which somehow generate the objects of empirical study. To uncover

these underlying processes requires some kind of "transcendental deduction", where the common characteristics of empirical objects, and their empirical variations and differences, are all explained in terms of some generating mechanism operating beyond, behind or above the concrete empirical level. This level transcends, or is immanent to, the empirical, and is not accessed even in empirical generalization.

Deleuze calls this level "the virtual", but for theologians it would be the divine or the sacramental. There are more sociological and cultural notions as well, including "phallogocentrism" for some feminists, and "structuration forces" for some sociologists, as we have seen. Some operation of thought, critique or transcendental logic is required to conceive of and provide access to this level, and the process seems to involve what C. S. Peirce described as technically neither deduction nor induction, but "abduction" (see Richardson & Kramer 2006: 501). Rudy Richardson and Eric Hans Kramer cite Gary Shank (1998), taking Peirce's classic example of drawing beans from a bag as the starting-point to show the form:

> Result. – [We have the experience that] The beans are white [but this experience lacks any real meaning for us].
> Rule. – [The claim that] All the beans from this bag are white [is meaningful in this setting].
> Case. – [Therefore, it is both plausible and meaningful to hypothesize that] These beans are from this bag.

As can be seen, abduction is not a strictly logical process so its conclusions are always disputable, but it involves an explicit and creative attempt to suggest some possible meaning to the wide diversity of empirical experiences encountered and studied. There is no suggestion that one particular variant of the transcendental or immanent can be conclusively established to be the correct one, especially if the transcendental is itself seen as chaotic or groundless; much will depend on both the creative powers of the theorist and their connections with the empirical, through research or through experience.

Nevertheless, it is at the "virtual" level that we can begin to grasp the notion of "radical Otherness", something that is capable at last of resisting the imperialism of the same. In Deleuze's terms, the virtual exhibits intensive forces, not the familiar extensive ones of the empirical world; the radical assertion of difference instead of sameness and analogy; and a quite different zoology with exotics such as multiplicities and series of singularities, and bodies without organs. We find a different conception of time there, and a radical contingency governing the combinations of factors and forces. The empirical world is made up of a particular series of singularities, but other series are equally possible, including divergent ones that would produce quite different worlds if they were actualized. The same conceptions inform

Braidotti's (2003) notion of the "virtual feminine", as that which exists beyond all the empirical manifestations of what she calls "Woman".

These virtual others help us both explain and powerfully critique more reified or ossified conceptions of otherness. The otherness on display in the empirical world is produced by a series of repetitions, not differences. These repetitions are produced by power relations, usually in the form of hierarchies. This empirical world is taken as self-sufficient, all that there is, and empirical methods are sufficient. Systems of metaphysics claim to account for the empirical world but in compromised and tautological and often ideological ways.

But the virtual remains as an excess, a reservoir of additional possibilities, which are equally real. Thus the virtual feminine can be asserted against the claims to self-sufficiency of the current phallogocentric version. Similarly, conventional conceptions of God can also be understood as some kind of objectivist illusion produced by the phallogocentric churches, including their writings and practices, while beneath or behind is a much more dynamic multiplicity. In a Deleuzian version of sacramentalism, empirical bodies can be seen as actualizations or incarnations of this multiplicity.

These arguments draw force by maintaining a relation of radical otherness or difference between the virtual and the empirical, but this produces familiar problems affecting the issue of linking the transcendental back to the empirical level. All is well if the virtual remains as a kind of orienting or inspiring idea or critical belief, but there are problems if we wish to pursue demonstrable connections with the empirical or the political. These are apparent in most of the work we have considered, perhaps illustrated best of all in the feminist material drawing upon Deleuze and Guattari. For one thing, it is not easy to decide on the significance of the particular concepts describing the immanent or virtual: specifically, should feminists be interested in "becoming-woman" or "becoming-minoritarian", to refer back to some other discussions above. We also considered Hindess and Hirst (1975), who offer a close and technical reading of Marx's work but conclude that, for example, the notion of rent was developed in one context (to grasp the specifics of capitalism) and cannot be applied in another context, say, to develop a feudal mode of production. In particular, it cannot be taken as an empirical concept to be tested against historical data: since its function is theoretical, there needs to be considerable modification before we could get to any historical test, so much so that we would be departing from Marxism. It is interesting to explore the suggestion that all two-level analyses must operate in this way, including attempts to "put Deleuze to work" in feminist theory.

Hindess and Hirst themselves think that politics should not be seen as linked to philosophy at all, but should remain as a purely calculative matter, and some feminists might agree (e.g. Fraser 1989). There is sometimes a strange echo of this position in discussion of Deleuzian ethics.

MacCormack (2009) argues that ultimately the point is to establish a position that yields "joy" in the Spinozan sense, adding to human development in a positive way. What is not so well discussed, however, is how this "joy" might itself be established. If it is purely a matter of subjective feeling, this seems to make Deleuzian politics into a personal, even an individual, pursuit, not unlike British utilitarianism. As we know from discussions of that position, serious problems arise when we have to consider social relations, where different sorts of individual joy might conflict, and the difficult matter of priority might be raised. We are supposed to think carefully about our options, and an element of calculation seems necessary.

Exercises of conceptual clarification become crucial to establish what lies in the background and in the foreground, and what is central, for example, what is divine and what is all too human, based on the pursuit of domination or an unresolved *ressentiment*, in Christian theology. We have focused especially on discussions relating to incarnation and corporeality. "Clarification" is perhaps too mild a word for the intense critical effort that goes into explaining how conventional concepts have depended on particular interpretations of religious texts. This has also involved a hermeneutic form of interpretation, tracing specific concepts back to cultural traditions from which they come and rescuing alternative meanings. This sort of critique can develop a specific external reference (to the power structures engaged in theological or theoretical work) and gets close to deploying the notion of ideology in sociological terms, that is, to show how particular theologians in particular social and political contexts incorporated all sorts of dominant, not always explicit, politically loaded assumptions into the very definitions and relations concerned. Using Marxist terminology, this can take "vulgar" (representing the immediate interests of the people concerned) or "scientific" forms (incorporating all sorts of common assumptions and beliefs without criticizing them). Thus we have argued that a crucial role was played by unclarified assumptions in classical Greek metaphysics, for example. More generally, a phallogocentric conceptual system, again combining vulgar and scientific forms, has dominated orthodox understandings of such theological matters as original sin, or the personhood of Christ, just as it has with sociological concepts. Just about any philosophical system can be suspected in this way, and unclarified and political assumptions have been identified even in Deleuze's work, despite his rigorous and systematic attempts to break with conventional thinking. Thus Jardine (1985), for example, suggests that the key notion of the "desiring machine" seems to incorporate some unreflected elements of male fantasies about women. It might also be possible to point to unresolved issues of social-class background in Deleuze's notion of philosophical and cultural tastes.

However, hermeneutic suspicion is a technique that is not always easily confined to the positions of opponents. Paradoxes and "forks" await, especially after reading Gadamer (we have relied on the brief account in

Gadamer 2006), with his suggestion that all positions alike can be seen as involving presuppositions and that all claims to be able to stop hermeneutic circling around these presuppositions must be suspect. Critics might well respond with a demand for reflexivity, a comment that if all positions are bound in a hermeneutic circle, so must be modern hermeneutics itself, and that Gadamer's insistence that there is no abstract truth and no method to attain it can also be located in cultural currents and traditions, stressing postmodern scepticism towards metanarratives. This problem of relativism, when to develop it and when to try to stop it, is a central one in any understanding of otherness it could be suggested.

CONSUMERISM

Two alternative positions, for and against in the simplest terms, have been outlined in Chapter 4, and feminist theology has taken one side, condemning consumerism as an aspect of desacramentalized phallogocentrism, while sociological studies have been used to outline the other, seeing consumerism as a more contested area. However, both disciplines are very familiar with the problems in examining actual routine behaviour such as that displayed in consumerism.

Certain theologies are challenged that suggest modern capitalism can offer spiritual rewards, and that its characteristic institutions, such as the market, can be seen as potentially offering more humanizing and liberating tendencies. The forms of desire that are found in modern consumerism can somehow be converted into a desire for God (again with undertones of Deleuzian politics), and forgiveness will domesticate capitalism. It is fair to say that the conclusions have been largely pessimistic, drawing upon repressive notions such as the liberating effects of sacrifice and inequality, themes found in traditional theology itself. In particular, consumerism invites women to see themselves and their bodies as commodities, or to regulate their bodies with consumer goods of various kinds, and shopping is one of those licensed areas where women are persuaded to invest their power and desire.

It is clear that in later modern or postmodern societies there seems to be much more individual choice in matters of personal identity, as the old social bonds of family, work and religious tradition lose their hold. This can be seen as an engine producing mundane otherness, especially when combined with the highly flexible and sophisticated marketing techniques of modern capitalism. Consumerism has become a major way of pursuing personal identity projects, but the problem is to both display and explain the results.

Consumerism is such a routine and everyday form of behaviour, covering such a wide range of activity, that it is difficult to isolate adequate samples in order to study them using sociological methods, and it is thus almost impossible to produce empirical generalizations. This is clearest, perhaps, when considering consuming the products of the mass media, such as video games, where there never will be an adequate sample or an experimental design that can control all the variables. Indeed, Howard Becker once suggested that this was one reason why funding for such research was so fulsome: the industry itself particularly relished endless careful studies that failed to produce a decisive result, while sponsors with strong views preferred that "researchers, rather than say they hadn't found anything, just say that results were not yet conclusive" (2002: 339). But at the same time, it is clearly dangerous to leave the field to the generalizations and anecdotes of politicians or various "moral entrepreneurs", ever ready to generate a moral panic using undesirable consumer goods as a pretext to sound off about more general political issues.

It is also clear, for example, that consumer behaviour does seem to feature active choice and decision-making, sometimes of a highly skilled nature. The issue really turns on whether such behaviour is a sign of freedom from the cultural manipulations of capitalism, or merely testament to their subtlety. Enough critics can be found to support the latter view, from Adorno's account of the pernicious individualism of the culture industry to feminist analyses of the subordinate positioning of women in consumption. We have mentioned Mulvey's analyses of the positioning effects of modern Hollywood as an example (e.g. Mulvey 1975), but we extended those analyses to consider how advertisements "hailed" and positioned women as objects of the male gaze.

There are certainly hints of this in some of the empirical studies, although the terminology usually refers to a more Marxist problematic of accommodation and resistance. Nevertheless, studies of youth cultures show how young people are able to use consumer products and put them to a much more expressive and aesthetic end. Willis (1990) is perhaps one of the most optimistic here, showing how cheap consumer durables such as posters or clothes (sometimes second-hand ones) can be used even by those on social security to express a lifestyle that denies their official status. The analysis has extended to research on women consumers in particular, including those analyses that stress the sophistication of the female viewer of apparently heterosexist film and television programmes, as we saw with the work of Ang (1985) or hooks (1999). To deny these reported experiences would be to condemn consumers as helpless victims, unable to see through the system that represses them, quite unlike academic theorists, and to subject their accounts to the sort of "symbolic violence" and relations of authority that feminists themselves have been particularly able to denounce.

At the same time, most of the accounts we have considered also suggest that resistance has limits. Youth styles are only "magical solutions" to real political problems (Hall & Jefferson 1976); resisting consumers are able to penetrate some aspects of repressive cultural systems, but their perceptions also display strong "limitations" (Willis 1977) and their rejection of ideological constructs is partial and incomplete: working-class youth cultures displayed strong tendencies towards racism and sexism, for example. Experiments with sexuality among Goth subcultures still failed to break with conventional notions (Wilkins 2004). In general, consuming leisure products can provide "an escape from the constraints of work, a chance to legitimately stand outside the axioms, mores and conventions of society ... Leisure enables us to objectify the rules ... of everyday life and subject them to critical appraisal" (Rojek 2000: 21), but this is only a temporary escape for most consumers.

In particular, and as a manifestation of what we shall call "Rancière's paradox" below, resisting consumers are not able to generalize or theorize about their particular acts, no matter what our populist sympathies might be. Only theorists can operate with a level of analysis that joins up these perceptions and completes them, especially using the sort of transcendental analysis that we mentioned above. This leaves us with a difficult ethical and political issue in justifying the use of theoretical retranslations that are both aspects of symbolic violence and the only productive route towards liberatory politics in general.

POLITICS

We have tried to argue that the political aspects of discussions of otherness are interlinked with empirical research and conceptual formation, at a particularly reflexive level: both disciplines have realized that discussions on research or theory themselves involve political choices. It will be readily noticed, in the chapters above, that the selections are being made from the numbers of arguments, theories and studies actually available. This is inevitable owing to obvious limits of knowledge and expertise, but there is also a choice of which particular varieties of otherness to explore. Issues of sexual otherness are prominent, for example.

It has been suggested that otherness can inform major acts of nation states, including war and mass extermination. These policies are based on the notions of deep and irretrievable otherness, perhaps even absolute Otherness, which are sufficient to disqualify certain groups of people from even the most basic of human rights. If there was any theoretical or philosophical justification, it rested on dubious grounds of differences in "race, blood and soil" for the Nazis, or "objective" class allegiance for Soviet and Chinese regimes. The kind of everyday racism or tendencies towards a fascist personality uncovered in some sociological work should warn us about any current tendencies towards a totally disqualifying otherness in current state policies. At the same time, Deleuzian identification of any hierarchical organization or any kind of conventional thinking as "fascist" (as in Foucault's "Introduction", in Deleuze & Guattari 1984) surely extends and dilutes the term beyond any useful limit.

Sociological work is valuable in explaining the plausibility of divisive common-sense reasoning in these matters, as a kind of primitive positivism. But at the same time, this work leads into some difficult areas concerning the ethical and political warrant of academic specialisms to interpret everyday feelings theoretically or politically. The danger is, clearly, that "symbolic violence" will be the result, with everyday views and common sense seen as offering partial and incomplete insights that need to be criticized and completed by academic specialists. There seem to be two options for theorists. One is to make every attempt to understand and articulate participants' views in the first place. This has led to recommendations such as the deployment of particular seemingly egalitarian or authentic methods, ranging from case-history approaches to autoethnography. Ahmed (2000b: 56) has been particularly critical about the claims here, saying that empathic identification provides an illusory escape from structure: power relations are concealed beneath this "fantasy of togetherness". Ahmed refreshes old methodological advice to avoid "going native" and to record all examples of "strange" findings that do not fit the ethnographic narrative.

For the second option, Bourdieu et al. (1999), for example, suggest making a serious attempt to develop a more rounded understanding of others. The aim would be to articulate a worldview from the point of view of the other, and the researcher uses both theoretical and everyday resources to achieve this task.

Deleuze (1989) has expressed interest in a similar approach developed in the documentary filmmaking of Jean Rouch and Pierre Perrault. Informed by a postcolonial sensibility, this work attempts to develop "free indirect discourse", trying to eliminate colonial associations and terms, and inviting participants to act as deliberate storytellers, participating in the cinematic narrative, and taking a step towards the world of the documentary maker to complement the latter's empathy. What results is "a pure speech act … Neither an impersonal method or a personal fiction, but a collective utterance" (Smith 1997: xliii), produced by both the writer and the people as a form of becoming.

We have explored some of the dangers of partisan or standpoint approaches, and examining actual work often reveals a difficult zone of ambiguity, where theoretical rigour points one way, and political commitment the other. To take one example, Braidotti wants to argue that theoretical accounts of phallogocentrism in Irigaray would suggest that women are completely prevented from any genuine subject position of their own, dominated by "the master discourse of the white, masculine, hegemonic, property owning subject who posits his consciousness as synonymous with a universal knowing subject, and markets a series of 'others' as his onto-logical props" (2003: 51). Later Braidotti refers to heterosexuality as "the very sexual preference that constitutes the majority for the vast majority of women" (*ibid.*: 59). In other words, heterosexuality has changed its value from a form of masculinist domination to a sexual preference for women, perhaps by splitting the category, eventually, and for political reasons, into phallic and non-phallic forms.

The issue of prioritization also emerges as a major issue. There are some positions that imply that no prioritization is needed, that every explora-tion of otherness – whether it be in gardening clubs, church congregations, nightclubs, sex clubs, television programmes or the pursuit of esoteric hobbies – partakes equally in the great struggle for liberation from some all-purpose constraints. This position draws support quite often from poststructuralist positions, which similarly refuse to prioritize particular grand metanarratives. One consequence is compassion fatigue or "posture cramp": not knowing quite where to invest one's efforts first, and possi-bly even allowing others to set the agenda by requiring a response to vari-ous emergencies. For commentators such as Michael Hardt and Antonio Negri (2000), there is a possibility of renewing a Marxist "escalation" sce-nario where people realize that all their struggles actually do line up and, together, exceed the possibilities of capitalism to respond. In a different tradition, this even left a role for intellectuals to develop a master dis-course that would encourage this realization. "Rancière's paradox" awaits us, however.

Classically, Marxism argued that class was the key category, the most important source of identity in capitalism. Not only did exploitation and subsequent class conflict provide the secret of success of capitalism and economic growth, however well disguised, but a successful class struggle would represent a universal good; it would end class societies altogether, leaving a kind of harmless diversity and otherness that would not lead to systematic exploitation. However, other theorists have insisted that other social divisions are just as fundamental as class, although Marxism tends to treat them as epiphenomenal. We have ourselves possibly neglected ethnic otherness, but critical race theory (see Gillborn 2008) insists that "race" divisions are empirically dominant in modern societies, to the extent that inequalities are almost universal in every sphere of social life, and that the more visible aspects of racial difference have always been a major source of fundamental forms of representation in white culture and ideology. A similarly marginalized specialism, but with universalist claims, has been made by Hughes (2002) for the disabled person as a universal signifier, an "other for modernity".

Feminist theory is also central to these debates. A sexual division of labour has dominated social life in families and work in almost every social formation, again despite some controversial appearances and reforms such as the emergence of the "symmetrical family", or the "woman breadwin-ner". Summarizing Irigaray, Braidotti (2003) has described social life as saturated by the products of a "male imaginary", to such an extent that a female imaginary or "virtual female" has never developed and needs to be constructed. This position has been powerfully underpinned by Freudian theory, with the Oedipal triangle as the central mechanism of social discipline, and by French structuralism, especially in the form of Lévi-Strauss's arguments for the universality of the incest principle, where men exchange women in order to preserve social order. The ensuing phallogocentrism can be detected underneath the disguises that permeate the cultural field, including those that display the illusory complementary forms of equality discussed above.

Again, lively debates ensued between Marxists and feminists concerning the issue of priority and interlinkage between class and gender or sex, with positions in both camps claiming universal implications stemming from their specific interests. We have briefly discussed the Marxist claim, but Grosz is perhaps the most explicit defender of the case for sexual difference as primary: drawing on Deleuze, she says that "sexual difference is onto-logical, the very conditions for the emergence of the human ... Race is not reducible to sex, but racial relations are an expression of sexual relations ... [but only] on the biological level", while "class is a very very indirect effect, like an open ended effect of sexual selection, as is ethnicity, geography and all the other particularities that define human life" (Kontturi & Tiainen 2007: 249). However, DeLanda (1999), a major commentator on Deleuze as we have seen, has reminded us that any kind of organic life has had a long prehistory, and that crucial elements such as metals and carbon need to be present to permit the development of the necessary complex molecules: following Grosz to absurdity, we could therefore argue that the key difference at the bottom of all social relations is a chemical one!

A major underpinning for Queer theory lies in the work of Deleuze, we have suggested, with his ontology stressing heterogeneity and the "disjunc-tive", haecceity and the emergence of novelty and hybridity, and multiplicity with its immanence and potential to generate new singularities and actu-alizations. This perspective undoes binaries, including binary distinctions between the sexes, and emphasizes becoming, flow, the contingent and the alleatory. The obvious and immediate "application" is a politics aimed at dereification, the release of the life instinct or Desire, assuming these two are compatible. Such a politics may aim at a very radical dereification of all categories and conceptual grids and of human subjects as we currently know them, as with Brian Massumi (1992).

This gets us close to the original universal liberation notion of poli-tics, with its absence of prioritization. Braidotti is among those who have argued that the female is so effectively excluded by phallogocentrism that women are unable to attain the status of a political subject capable of any action, so the first stage is to develop potency even if this is initially partisan. Goulimari (1999), in a review of a number of feminist positions, denies that poststructuralist interest in becoming-woman can be seen in Jardine's terms as "gynesis" (roughly, a recuperation of feminism to restore that which was previously omitted in abstract philosophy), and elaborates a case for becoming-minoritarian as the key process in liberatory thinking. Goulimari also thinks that minoritarian approaches can form the basis of genuine alliances between women and other oppressed groups rather than offering them a place as a subcategory of the female Subject.

There seems to be far more agreement on the need to preserve some sort of material basis in practice and in the form of the female body, before fully accepting the poststructuralist notion of either fully autonomous theory or gender and sexuality as entirely a matter of performance (see Althaus-Reid & Isherwood 2004: "Introduction"). MacCormack (2009: 91) works with Deleuzian categories to insist on corporeality, not least as a guard against excessively abstract philosophizing, by emphasizing real suffering as an aspect of womanhood, so that becoming woman is not just a happy escape. However, such corporeality takes the form not of a biologically reductive body, nor the body as represented in phallogocentric culture, but that of "a libidinal body without organs". The escape from the determining and limiting effects of organs enables endless hybrid corporeal combinations and this is "inherently queer" (*ibid*.: 86). It also permits tactical alliances both with other minorities and with earlier generations and other tendencies in feminism. It is this that permits feminists to "unfold and find joy in enfleshed affective – ism" (*ibid*.: 95).

As we saw, a search for ground is tempting for anyone wishing to justify their particular project and to distinguish it among the myriads of competing projects, both inside the academy and outside. Deleuze and Guattari (1994) have noted with particular annoyance the tendency for all sorts of commercial agencies, working in advertising, public relations or market research, to offer "concepts" and analyses for discussion, with strategic intents. Politicians also offer instant analyses of social situations, often based on a mixture of anecdotes and received wisdom. Philosophy must break with these colonizing views and avoid in particular the awful process of incorporation or recuperation; suddenly, Deleuzian terms are found on current affairs television programmes, popular discussions about the internet, or advertisements for new insurance companies. Žižek (2004) suggested the same fate would befall Deleuzian categories, too, with "the virtual" becoming another term for the internet, and the "nomadic subject" identified by the modern career portfolio.

We are now in a position to outline what we have called "Rancière's paradox". Writing about aesthetic theory specifically, Jacques Rancière (2002) argued that specialist concepts were required in order to separate adequate theorizing from the more ideological versions found in common sense.

However well intentioned, though, such specialist discussions are likely to meet with popular suspicion or apathy. Their very unconventionality proves alienating and can even cause offence, as Bourdieu (1986) noted in his survey of popular reactions to French avant-garde art. Efforts on the part of theorists to soothingly explain the origins of artistic rejections of convention and to justify their specialist terms and interests will require considerable effort on the part of those being addressed. The effort will involve them having to acquire specialist academic terms, familiarize themselves with scholastic debates, and acquire the necessary insight into academic argument and style. It would be a hard struggle for those lacking adequate cultural capital. It will deliver them over to the domination of academic conventions if not institutions, which will delay their liberation still further, or perhaps postpone it indefinitely. The whole debate raises the suspicion that it is implicitly assumed that the audience for this kind of argument is the university academic body itself.

Obviously, the argument extends to attempts to grasp "difficult" critiques such as those of Deleuze and his collaborators. As Deleuze acknowledges, conventional thinking is closely tied to everyday action, and is supported because it delivers pragmatic results. The decision to reject it, and to embark upon a quest for complex concepts that allude to some world beyond this one, and some abstract Desire that exceeds and even threatens familiar desires for health and security, is clearly going to be an unpopular one. University professors might be able to develop nomadic identities as they roam the continents from one conference to another, and to find themselves in libraries with the time and cultural capital to indulge in voyages of exploration in philosophy, literature and science, but these options are not immediately available to many others. Thinking of themselves as expressions of "libidinal" bodies, or the "virtual feminine" is not going to be seen as being immediately interesting to women immersed in the daily routine.

The alternative has been suggested already: that academic specialisms acquire a much more limited and modest stance, and restrain themselves from attempting to develop a political role or a set of popular "applications" altogether. But this would be to ignore the persuasive powers of what might be called the reified and capitalist forms, however, which classically attempt to represent their perspectives as beyond criticism, as natural or universal. Academic specialisms are precisely capable of demolishing these assertions and claims.

Here we can at last be affirmative about modern universities, perhaps. Deleuze, and possibly Rancière, worked in elite universities, and thus missed the opportunity to attempt to develop a pedagogy in modern "mass" universities. Students in those universities are very often from "non-traditional" backgrounds, and thus can be taken as rather more representative of the general public. In some cases, a highly skilled pedagogy has been developed to build those delicate relations between elite and everyday knowledge that seem essential to overcome the paradox. Such a pedagogy is not always well described, but it involves gauging the optimal level of challenge, reserving the full impact of theoretical knowledge while insisting on a critical assessment of everyday knowledge. Ideally, this would be individualized, enabling a number of specific stages and compromises to be achieved.

Deleuze can be cited even here. Inna Semetsky (2009) identifies a similar "learning paradox" whereby learning based closely on personal experience is limited in its capacity to accommodate anything new, while merely presenting a list of radically new concepts invites adverse reactions, including incomprehension and rejection, so that nothing new is learned that way either. The solution lies in Deleuze's triadic approach involving "percepts", concepts and "affects". These terms are capable of different interpretation, as usual, but Semetsky translates them into familiar Deweyian terms to urge a full consideration of existing perceptions and emotional considerations. Interestingly, Rancière has his own preferred pedagogy (Rancière 1991) based on the techniques of an earlier pedagogue (Joseph Jacotot) who deliberately set out to teach material of which he knew nothing, so that he could learn with the students: this pedagogy involved common efforts to rote learn and memorize as a crucial first step in familiarizing oneself with academic material.

To preserve any sort of pedagogy, critical academics need increasingly to fight their own internal battles, however, and to recast conventional thinking in their own academic specialisms, while resisting reification in the institutions that support them. Perhaps the most difficult tension they will have to manage is that between pursuing radical critique and avoiding total scepticism and cynicism. Poststructuralist philosophy in particular is almost too powerful for this purpose: so critical and self-reflexive that the pointlessness and groundlessness that Deleuze continually warns us about forms a constant horizon. Sociologists and theologians alike have to establish a point at which the groundlessness stops, whatever the risks of dogmatism or incoherence that ensue.

AND RADICAL OTHERNESS?

We have discovered during the writing of the book how otherness works in such a process, as theology wrestles with sociology and vice versa. What has emerged is interesting, as has been noted above: points of agreement and areas of difference. But what of the question of radical otherness? Have we discovered anything beyond liberal ideals of tolerance? What seems to emerge is the strong notion that far from being tolerated and, worse, assimilated, otherness is an essential category because it disrupts the normative at every turn. It is in the struggle with the other that change takes place: all are renamed, as mentioned in the Introduction, and the ongoing unfolding of what all may become is a space of radicalization, even for the divine itself, as we have explored.

Part of the strangeness of the other is that it is an I. As such it is the same as me but once again, as we have seen, the male psychic wishes to expel it in the creation of the phallic symbolic. The working of this phallic posturing attempts to make absolutes out of reality but this becomes more difficult if one is based in an open, alive and engaging enfleshment. As we have seen in feminist theology and its contact with metaphysics, the insistence on flesh has ended with a hybridized God, which allows for more fluidity in those who are followers of the divine. It has also meant that the pilgrim people that Christians like to believe themselves to be are still on a journey but with no particular fixed end in sight. Schneider moves us beyond the One in thinking through theology and this has profound importance in relation to inclusions and exclusions within theology. It is interesting to note also that in psychology, relational analysts are suggesting that psychological health does not lie in a unified self but rather in a multiple self and the ability to stand in the spaces between without losing any of them. There is no longer a push to silence voices but rather an encouragement of calling them all an "I" yet, at the same time, not believing any of them to be the whole story. To do this is to disrupt the demands of any one voice as absolute, even the voices that were once excluded. In short, exclusion is an illusion because nothing leaves the psychic universe, which brings into question the idea of the abject, either inside or out. In this way, otherness is always decentring humans since it is as much an internal reality as an external, which must be lived with. Perhaps what we see developing here is a way by which the co-emerging subject of which Ettinger speaks is not so easily made into the phallic object at birth but can now be nurtured into a healthy psyche with multiple voices at play. It will be interesting to see how this new idea of psychological health will play out in societies and their engagement with strangers.

It is perhaps worth pondering Daly's warning against methodolatry and Rivera's notion of touch. Rivera asks that we attempt to touch and not grasp at the other, since in grasping we are hoping to assimilate or overpower the other, to know the other, which is once again understood to be a way of eliminating otherness. This call to embodiment seems to be one way in which we may avoid the intellectualizing of methods and the categorization that often follows. Bodies are slippery and tend to resist the easy categorization so loved by statisticians and theorists. It is the touch, not the grasp, that allows the flourishing of the other and the growth of all the otherness in that encounter. It is through touch that objectification may be overcome. As Karmen McKendrick puts it, "the body untouched, even the divine body, is just another object" (2004: 173).

BIBLIOGRAPHY

Adorno, T. W. 1973. *The Jargon of Authenticity*. London: Routledge & Kegan Paul.

Adorno, T. W. 2000. *Introduction to Sociology*. Stanford, CA: Stanford University Press.

Adorno, T. W. & M. Horkheimer 1979. *Dialectic of Enlightenment*. London: Verso.

Adorno, T. W., E. Frenkel-Brunswick, D. Levinson & R. Sanford 1964. *The Authoritarian Personality, Part 2*. New York: John Wiley and Sons.

Adorno, T. W., R. Dahrendorf, A. Pilot, H. Albert, J. Habermas & K. Popper 1976. *The Positivist Dispute in German Sociology*. London: Heinemann.

Ahmed, S. 2000a. *Strange Encounters: Embodied Others in Post-Coloniality*. London: Routledge.

Ahmed, S. 2000b. "Who Knows? Knowing Strangers and Strangeness". *Australian Feminist Studies* 15(31): 49–68.

Alliez, É. 2006. "*AntiOedipus*: Thirty Years On (Between Arts and Politics)". In *Deleuze and the Social*, M. Fuglsang & B. Meier Sørenson (eds), 151–68. Edinburgh: Edinburgh University Press.

Althaus-Reid, M. 2001. *Indecent Theology. Theological Perversions in Sex, Gender and Politics*. London: Routledge.

Althaus-Reid, M. 2003. *The Queer God*. London: Routledge.

Althaus-Reid, M. 2005. *From Feminist Theology to Indecent Theology*. London: SCM Press.

Althaus Reid, M. 2007. "Queering the Cross: The Politics of Redemption and the Eternal Debt". *Feminist Theology* 15(3): 289–301.

Althaus-Reid, M. & L. Isherwood (eds) 2004. *The Sexual Theologian: Essays on Sex, God and Politics*. London: T & T Clark International.

Althusser, L. 1966. *For Marx*. Harmondsworth: Penguin.

Althusser, L. 1977a. "Freud and Lacan". In his *"Lenin and Philosophy" and Other Essays*, 2nd edn, 177–202. London: New Left Books.

Althusser, L. 1977b. "Ideology and Ideological State Apparatuses (Notes Towards an Investigation)". In his *"Lenin and Philosophy" and Other Essays*, 2nd edn, 121–76. London: New Left Books.

Anderson, C. 2003. "Violent Video Games: Myths, Facts, and Unanswered. Questions". www.apa.org/science/about/psa/2003/10/anderson.aspx (accessed August 2013).

Anderson, C. & K. Dill 2000. "Video Games and Aggressive Thoughts, Feelings, and Behavior in the Laboratory and in Life". *Journal of Personality and Social Psychology* 78(4): 772–90.

Ang, I. 1985. *Watching Dallas: Soap Opera and the Melodramatic Imagination*. London: Methuen.

167

Atkinson, J. & J. Heritage (eds) 1984. *Structures of Social Action: Studies in Conversation Analysis.* Cambridge: Cambridge University Press.

Bacon, H. 2007. "What's Right With The Trinity? Thinking the Trinity in Relation to Irigaray's Notions of Self Love and Wonder". *Feminist Theology* 15(2): 220–35.

Badiou, A. 2000. *Deleuze: The Clamor of Being.* Minneapolis, MN: University of Minnesota Press.

Baron-Cohen, S. 2003. *The Essential Difference: Men, Women and The Extreme Male Brain.* London: Allen Lane.

Barthes, R. 1973. *Mythologies,* London: Paladin.

Barthes, R. 1977. *Image-Music-Text.* London: Fontana/Collins.

Baudrillard, J. 1987. *Forget Foucault.* New York: Semiotext(e) Foreign Agents.

Baudrillard, J. 1993. *Symbolic Exchange and Death.* London: Sage.

Bay, T. 2006. "I Knew There Were Kisses in the Air". In *Deleuze and the Social,* M. Fuglsang & B. Meier Sørenson (eds), 96–111. Edinburgh: Edinburgh University Press.

Beck, U. 1992. *Risk Society: Towards a New Modernity.* London: Sage.

Becker, H. 2002. "Studying the New Media". *Qualitative Sociology* 25(3): 337–43.

Becker, H., B. Geer & E. Hughes 1995. *Making the Grade: The Academic Side of College Life,* 2nd edn. New Brunswick, NJ and London: Transaction Publishers.

Beezer, A. 1995. "Women and 'Adventure Travel' Tourism". *New Formations* 21: 119–30.

Bell, D. Jr 2001. *Liberation Theology After the End of History.* London: Routledge.

Bellaby, P. & D. Lawrenson 2001. "Approaches to the Risk of Riding Motorcycles: Reflections on the Problem of Reconciling Statistical Risk Assessment and Motorcyclists' Own Reasons for Riding". *The Sociological Review* 49: 368–88.

Benhabib, S. 1984. "Epistemologies of Postmodernism: A Rejoinder to Jean-Francois Lyotard". *New German Critique* (Fall): 103–26.

Benjamin, J. 1983. "Master and Slave: The Fantasy of Erotic Domination". In *Powers of Desire,* A. Snitow (ed.), 75–127. New York: Monthly Review Press.

Bennett, T., S. Boyd-Bowman, C. Mercer & J. Woollacott (eds) 1981. *Popular Television and Film.* London: BFI Publishing in association with the Open University Press.

Bennett, T., M. Savage, E. Silva, A. Warde, M. Gayo-Cal & D. Wright 2008. *Culture, Class, Distinction.* London: Routledge.

Berg, M. 1991. "Luce Irigaray's 'Contradictions': Poststructuralism and Feminism". *Signs; Journal of Women in Culture and Society* 17(1): 49–70.

Bergo, B. 2011. "Emmanuel Levinas". In *Stanford Encyclopedia of Philosophy. Fall 2011 Edition,* A. Zalta (ed.), http://plato.stanford.edu/archives/fall2011/entries/levinas/ (accessed September 2013).

Berkowitz, D. 2006. "Consuming Eroticism: Gender Performances and Presentations in Pornographic Establishments". *Journal of Contemporary Ethnography* 35(5): 583–606.

Bourdieu, P. 1986. *Distinction: A Social Critique of the Judgement of Taste.* London: Routledge & Kegan Paul.

Bourdieu, P. 1988. *Homo Academicus.* Cambridge: Polity.

Bourdieu, P. 1993. *Sociology in Question.* London: Sage.

Bourdieu, P. 2000. *Pascalian Meditations.* Cambridge: Polity.

Bourdieu, P. 2001. *Masculine Domination.* Cambridge: Polity.

Bourdieu, P. & J.-C. Passeron 1979. *The Inheritors: French Students and their Relation to Culture.* Chicago, IL: University of Chicago Press.

Bourdieu, P. & J.-C. Passeron 1990. *Reproduction in Education, Society and Culture,* 2nd edn. London: Sage.

Bourdieu, P., J.-C. Passeron & M. Saint Martin 1994. *Academic Discourse.* Cambridge: Polity.

Bourdieu, P., A. Accardo, G. Balazs, S. Beaud, F. Bonvin, E. Bourdieu, P. Bourgois *et al.* 1999. *The Weight of the World: Social Suffering in Contemporary Society.* Cambridge: Polity.

Braidotti, R. 1994. *Nomadic Subjects: Embodiment and Sexual Difference in Contemporary Feminist Theory*. New York: Columbia University Press.

Braidotti, R. 2003. "Becoming Woman: Or Sexual Difference Revisited". *Theory, Culture and Society* 20(3): 43–64.

Brake, M. (ed.) 1982. *Human Sexual Relations: A Reader. Towards a Redefinition of Sexual Politics*. Harmondsworth: Penguin.

Brock, R. 1988. *Christology by Heart: A Christology of Erotic Power*. New York: Crossroad.

Brock, R. & R. Parker 2008. *Saving Paradise: How Christianity Traded Love of the World for Crucifixion and Empire*. Boston, MA: Beacon Press.

Buchanan, I. 2006. "Practical Deleuzism and Postmodern Space". In *Deleuze and the Social*, M. Fuglsang & B. Meier Sørenson (eds), 135–50. Edinburgh: Edinburgh University Press.

Burgess, I., A. Edwards & J. Skinner 2003. "Football Culture in an Australian School Setting: The Construction of Masculine Identity". *Sport, Education and Society* 8(2): 199–212.

Butler, J. 1990a. *Gender Trouble: Feminism and the Subversion of Gender*. London: Routledge.

Butler, J. 1990b. "Gender Trouble, Feminist Theory and Psychoanalytic Discourse". In *Feminism/Postmodernism*, L. Nicholson (ed.), 324–39. New York: Routledge.

Butler, J. 1994. "Against Proper Objects: Introduction". *Differences: A Journal of Feminist Cultural Studies* 6(2+3): 1–26.

Butler, J. 1999. "Gender is Burning: Questions of Appropriation and Subversion". In *Feminist Film Theory, A Reader*, S. Thornham (ed.), 336–49. Edinburgh: Edinburgh University Press.

Butler, J. 2004. *Undoing Gender*. London: Routledge.

Carrette, J. & R. Young 2005. *Selling Spirituality: The Silent Takeover of Religion*. London: Routledge.

Carrington, B. 1983. "Sport as a Side-track: An Analysis of West Indian Involvement in Extra-Curricular Sport". In *Race, Class and Education*, L. Barton & S. Walker (eds), 40–66. London: Croom Helm.

Cashmore, E. 1987. *The Logic of Racism*. London: Allen & Unwin.

CCCS. 1982. *The Empire Strikes Back: Race and Racism in 70s Britain*. London: Hutchinson.

Chernin, K. 1983. *Womansize: The Tyranny of Slenderness*. London: Women's Press.

Chiapello, E. & N. Fairclough 2002. "Understanding the New Management Ideology: A Transdisciplinary Contribution from Critical Discourse Analysis and the New Sociology of Capitalism". *Discourse and Society* 13(2): 185–208.

Chin, E. 2007. "The Consumer Diaries: Autoethnography in the Inverted World". *Journal of Consumer Culture* 7(3): 335–53.

Chodorow, N. 1979. *The Reproduction of Mothering: Psychoanalysis and the Sociology of Gender*. Berkeley, CA: University of California Press.

Chrisafis, A. 2011. "Paris Show Unveils Life in Human Zoo". www.theguardian.com/world/2011/nov/29/huam-zoo-paris-exhibition (accessed October 2013).

Church Gibson, P. & R. Gibson (eds) 1993. *Dirty Looks: Women, Pornography, Power*. London: BFI Publishing.

Cixous, H., K. Cohen & P. Cohen 1976. "The Laugh of the Medusa". *Signs* 1(4): 875–93.

Clifford, J. 1993. "On Collecting Art and Culture". In *The Cultural Studies Reader*, S. During (ed.), 49–73. London: Routledge.

Clough, P. 1992. *The Ends of Ethnography: From Realism to Social Criticism*. London: Sage.

Cohen, P. 2004. "A Place to Think? Some Reflections on the Idea of the University in the Age of the 'Knowledge Economy'". *New Formations* 53(12): 12–27.

Collins, L. 2002. "Working Out the Contradictions: Feminism and Aerobics". *Journal of Sport and Social Issues* 26(1): 85–109.

Condren, M. 2010. "Relational Theology in the Work of Artist, Psychoanalyst and Theorist Bracha Ettinger". In *Through Us, With Us, In Us: Relational Theologies in the 21st Century*, L. Isherwood & E. Bellchambers (eds), 230–63. London: SCM Press.

Cook, P. (ed.) 1985. *Cinema Book*. London: British Film Institute.

Cooley, C. H. 1972. "Looking-glass Self". In *Symbolic Interaction: A Reader in Social Psychology*, 2nd edn, J. G. Manis & B. N. Meltzer (eds), 231–3. Boston, MA: Allyn & Bacon.

Coward, R. 1977. "Class, Culture and the Social Formation". *Screen* 18(1).

Craib, I. 1992. *Anthony Giddens*. London: Routledge.

Critcher, C. 2000. "'Still Raving': Social Reaction to Ecstasy". *Leisure Studies* 19: 145–62.

Crook, S. 1991. *Modernist Radicalism and its Aftermath: Foundationalism and Anti-Foundationalism in Radical Social Theory*. London: Routledge.

Crook, S., J. Pakulski & M. Waters 1992. *Postmodernization: Change in Advanced. Society*. London: Sage.

Crossley, N. 2005. "Mapping Reflexive Body Techniques: On Body Modification and Maintenance". *Body and Society* 11(1): 1–35.

Daly, M. 1981. *Gyn/Ecology: The Metaethics of Radical Feminism*. London: Women's Press.

De Certeau, M. 1984. *The Practice of Everyday Life*. Berkeley, CA: University of California Press.

De Chardin, T. 1970. *Hymn of the Universe*. London: Collins.

de Haardt, M. 2010. "Monotheism as a Threat to Relationality". In *Through Us, With Us, In Us: Relational Theologies in the 21st Century*, L. Isherwood & E. Bellchambers (eds), 181–96. London: SCM Press.

Deem, R. 1986. *All Work and No Play*. Milton Keynes: Open University Press.

DeLanda, M. 1999. "Deleuze and the Open-Ended Becoming of the World". *Manuel DeLanda Annotated Bibliography*. www.cddc.vt.edu/host/delanda/pages/becoming.htm (accessed September 2013).

DeLanda, M. 2002. *Intensive Science and Virtual Philosophy*. London: Continuum.

DeLanda, M. 2006. *A New Philosophy of Society: Assemblage Theory and Social Complexity*. London: Continuum.

Deleuze, G. 1989. *Cinema 2: The Time-Image*. London: Athlone Press.

Deleuze, G. 1990. *The Logic of Sense*, M. Lester (trans.), C. Boundas (ed.). New York: Columbia University Press.

Deleuze, G. 1995. *Negotiations*, M. Joughin (trans.). New York: Columbia University Press.

Deleuze, G. 1997. *Essays Critical and Clinical*, D. Smith & M. Greco (trans.). Minneapolis, MN: University of Minnesota Press.

Deleuze, G. 1999. *Foucault*, S. Hand (trans.). London: Continuum.

Deleuze, G. 2000. "The Brain Is The Screen: An Interview with Gilles Deleuze". In *The Brain is the Screen: Deleuze and the Philosophy of Cinema*, G. Flaxman (ed.), 365–76. London: University of Minnesota Press.

Deleuze, G. 2004. *Difference and Repetition*, P. Patton (trans.). London: Continuum.

Deleuze, G. no date. "Lectures on Spinoza". http://deleuzelectures.blogspot.com/2007/02/on-spinoza.html (accessed September 2013).

Deleuze, G. & F. Guattari 1984. *Anti-Oedipus: Capitalism and Schizophrenia*. London: Athlone Press.

Deleuze, G. & F. Guattari 1994. *What is Philosophy?* London: Verso.

Deleuze, G. & F. Guattari 2004. *A Thousand Plateaus*. London: Continuum.

Deleuze, G. & C. Parnet 1987. *Dialogues*. London: Athlone Press.

Denzin, N. 2006. "Analytic Autoethnography, or Déja-Vu all Over Again". *Journal of Contemporary Ethnography* 35(4): 419–28.

Dews, P. 1987. *Logics of Disintegration*. London: Verso.

Dillon, K. & J. Tait 2000. "Spirituality and Being in the Zone in Team Sports: A Relationship?" *Journal of Sport Behaviour* 23(2): 91–100.

Douglas, K. 1994. *The Black Christ*. New York: Orbis.

During, S. (ed.) 1993. *The Cultural Studies Reader*. London: Routledge.

Durkheim, E. 1961. *Moral Education*. New York: The Free Press of Glencoe.

Durkheim, E. 1964. *The Rules of Sociological Method*, 2nd edn. London: Collier Macmillan.

Dyer, R. 2002. *The Culture of Queers*. London: Routledge.

Eco, U. 1981. *Role of the Reader: Explorations in the Semiotics of Texts*. London: Hutchinson.

Eiesland, N. 1994. *The Disabled God: Toward a Liberatory Theology of Disability*. Nashville, TN: Abingdon Press.

Elling, A., P. De Knop & A. Knoppers 2003. "Gay/Lesbian Sport Clubs and Events: Places of Homo-Social Bonding and Cultural Resistance?" *International Review for the Sociology of Sport* 38(4): 441–56.

Elliott, J. 1986. "Democratic Evaluation as Social Criticism: Or Putting the Judgment Back Into Evaluation". In *Controversies in Classroom Research*, M. Hammersley (ed.), 228–37. Milton Keynes: Open University Press.

Ellis, C. & A. Bochner 2006. "Analyzing Analytic Autoethnography: An Autopsy". *Journal of Contemporary Ethnography* 35(4): 429–49.

Elsaesser, T. 1985. "Narrative Cinema and Audience-Oriented Aesthetics". In *Popular Television and Film*, T. Bennett, S. Boyd-Bowman, C. Mercer & J. Wollacott (eds), 237–84. London: BFI Publishing in association with Open University Press.

Elson, D. (ed.) 1979. *Value: The Representation of Labour in Capitalism*. New York: Humanities Press.

Ettinger, B. 2006. *The Matrixial Borderspace*. Minneapolis, MN: University of Minnesota Press.

Ettinger, B. 2007. "Matrixial Subjectivity and the Matrixial Subject". Lecture. www.youtube.com/watch?v=mdkbYsjlMA8 (accessed October 2013).

Ettinger, B. 2010. "(M)Other Re-spect: Maternal Subjectivity, the *Ready-made mother monster* and The Ethics of Respecting". *Studies in the Maternal* 2(1) www.mamsie.bbk.ac.uk/back_issues/issue_three/mother_respect.html (accessed September 2013).

Evans-Pritchard, E. & E. Gillies 1976. *Witchcraft, Oracles and Magic Among the Azande*. Oxford: Oxford University Press.

Falk, P. 1994. *The Consuming Body*. London: Sage.

Faulkner, K. 2002. "Deleuze *In Utero*: Deleuze-Sartre and the Essence of Woman". *Angelaki* 7(3): 25–43.

Ferguson, C. 2007. "The Good, the Bad and the Ugly; a MetaAnalytic Review of the Positive and Negative Effects of Violent Video Games". *Psychiatric Quarterly* 78: 309–16.

Fiorenza, E. 1983. *In Memory of Her*. London: SCM Press.

Firestone, S. 1993. *The Dialectics of Sex: The Case for Feminist Revolution*. London: Quill.

Fisher, J. 2002. "Tattooing the Body, Marking Culture". *Body and Society* 8(4): 91–107.

Fiske, J. 1989. *Reading the Popular*. London: Unwin Hyman.

Foster, P. 1993. "Case Not Proven: An Evaluation of a Study of Teacher Racism". In *Gender and Ethnicity in Schools: Ethnographic Accounts*, P. Woods & M. Hammersley (eds), 216–23. London: Routledge.

Foster, P., M. Gomm & M. Hammersley 2000. "Case Studies as Spurious Evaluation: The Example of Research on Educational Inequalities". *British Journal of Educational Studies* 48(3): 215–30.

Foucault, M. 1970. "Theatrum Philosophicum". www.generation-online.org/p/fpfoucault5. htm (accessed September 2013).

Foucault, M. 1977. *Discipline and Punish: The Birth of the Prison*. Harmondsworth: Penguin.

Foucault, M. 1980. *Power/Knowledge Selected Interviews and Other Writings 1972–1977*. Brighton: Harvester Press.

Frankfurt Institute for Social Research 1974. *Aspects of Sociology*. London: Heinemann.

Fraser, N. 1989. *Unruly Practices: Power Discourse and Agenda in Contemporary Social Theory*. Cambridge: Polity.

Frisby, D. 1984. *Georg Simmel*. London: Tavistock.

Fullagar, S. 2002. "Narratives of Travel: Desire and the Movement of Feminine Subjectivity". *Leisure Studies* 21: 57–74.

Fuller, S. 2003. *Kuhn vs Popper. The Struggle for the Soul of Science*. Colchester: Icon Books.

Gadamer, H.-G. 2006. "Classical and Philosophical Hermeneutics". *Theory, Culture and Society* 23(1): 29–56.

Gannon, S. 2006. "The (Im)Possibilities of Writing the Self-Writing: French Poststructural Theory and Autoethnography". *Cultural Studies ó Critical Methodologies* 6(4): 474–95.

Gardiner, M. 2000. *Critiques of Everyday Life*. London: Routledge.

Gebara, I. 1999. *Longing for Running Water*. Minneapolis, MN: Fortress Press.

Gelsthorpe, L. 1992. "Response to Martyn Hammersley's Paper 'On Feminist Methodology'". *Sociology* 26(2): 213–18.

Geraghty, C. 1991. *Women and Soap Operas*. Cambridge: Polity.

Giddens, A. 1991. *The Consequences of Modernity*. Cambridge: Polity in association with Blackwell.

Gillborn, D. 2008. *Racism and Education: Coincidence or Conspiracy?* London: Routledge.

Gilligan, C. 1982. *In a Different Voice: Psychological Theory and Women's Development*. Cambridge, MA: Harvard University Press.

Gimlin, D. 2007. "Accounting for Cosmetic Surgery in the USA and Great Britain: A Cross-Cultural Analysis of Women's Narratives". *Body and Society* 13(1): 41–60.

Giroux, H., R. Simon *et al.* 1989. *Popular Culture Schooling and Everyday Life*. South Hadley, MA: Bergin & Garvey.

Glaser, B. & A. Strauss 1967. *The Discovery of Grounded Theory: Strategies for Qualitative Research*. New York: Aldine de Gruyter.

Goffman, E. 1963. *Stigma*. Harmondsworth: Penguin.

Goldacre, B. 2012. *Bad Pharma: How Drug Companies Mislead Doctors and Harm Patients*. London: Fourth Estate.

Goldman, R. & S. Papson 1998. *Nike Culture*. London: Sage.

Goldthorpe, J., C. Llewellyn & C. Payne 1980. *Social Mobility and Class Structure in Modern Britain*. Oxford: Clarendon Press.

Goody, D. 2007. *Globalization, Spirituality and Justice*. New York: Orbis.

Goss, B. 2002. *Queering Christ: Beyond Jesus Acted Up*. Cleveland, OH: Pilgrim Press.

Gottdiener, M. 1995. *Postmodern Semiotics: Material Culture and the Forms of Postmodern Life*. Cambridge, MA: Blackwell.

Goulimari, P. 1999. "A Minoritarian Feminism? Things to Do With Deleuze and Guattari". *Hypatia* 14(2): 97–120.

Graham, E. 2002. *Representations of the Post/Human: Monsters, Aliens and Others in Popular Culture*. Manchester: Manchester University Press.

Grau, M. 2004. *Of Divine Economy: Refinancing Redemption*. London: T&T Clark.

Grau, M. 2012. *Rethinking Mission in Postcolony*. London: Continuum.

Grey, M. 1989. *Redeeming the Dream: Feminism, Redemption and the Christian Tradition*. London: SPCK.

Grey, M. 2003. *Sacred Longings: Ecofeminist Theology and Globalisation*. London: SCM Press.

Griffiths, R. 2004. *Born Again Bodies*. Berkeley, CA: University of California Press.

Guattari, F. 1995. *Chaosmosis: An Ethico-Aesthetic Paradigm*. Sydney: Power Publications.

Habermas, J. 1974. *Theory and Practice*. London: Heinemann.

Habermas, J. 1976. *Legitimation Crisis*. London: Heinemann.

Habermas J. 1984. "The French Path to Postmodernity: Bataille Between Eroticism and General Economy". *New German Critique* 33: 79–102.

Habermas, J. 1987. *The Theory of Communicative Action, Volume Two: The Critique of Functionalist Reason*. Cambridge: Polity in association with Blackwell.

Hall, S. & T. Jefferson (eds) 1976. *Resistance Through Rituals*. London: Hutchinson.

Hall, S., C. Critcher, T. Jefferson, J. Clarke & B. Roberts 1978. *Policing the Crisis: Mugging, the State and Law and Order*. London: Macmillan.

Hammersley, M. 1992. "On Feminist Research". *Sociology* 26(2): 187–206.

Hammersley, M. 1994. "On Feminist Sociology: A Response". *Sociology* 28(1): 293–300.

Hammersley, M. 1997. "Educational Research and Teaching: A Response to David Hargreaves' TTA lecture". *British Educational Research Journal* 23(2): 208–319.

Hammersely, M. 2000. "The Relevance of Qualitative Research". *Oxford Review of Education* 26(3 & 4): 393–405.

Hammersley, M. 2004. "Action Research: A Contradiction in Terms". *Oxford Review of Education* 30(2): 165–81.

Hammersley, M. 2005. "What Can the Literature on Communities of Practice Tell Us About Educational Research? Reflections on Some Recent Proposals". *International Journal of Research and Method in Education* 28(1): 5–21.

Hampson, D. 1996. *Swallowing a Fishbone: Feminist Theologians Debate Christianity*. London: SPCK.

Haraway, D. 2003. "A Cyborg Manifesto: Science, Technology, and Socialist-Feminism in the Late Twentieth Century". http://www.egs.edu/faculty/donna-haraway/articles/donna-haraway-a-cyborg-manifesto/ (accessed October 2013).

Hardt, M. & A. Negri 2000. *Empire*. London: Harvard University Press.

Hargreaves, J. 1986. *Sport, Power and Culture*. Cambridge: Polity.

Harris, D. 1987. *Openness and Closure in Distance Education*. Barcombe: Falmer Press.

Harris, D. 1992. *From Class Struggle to the Politics of Pleasure: The Effects of Gramscianism on Cultural Studies*. London: Routledge.

Harris, D. 1996. *A Society of Signs?* London: Routledge.

Harris, D. 2004. *Key Concepts in Leisure Studies*. London: Sage.

Harris, D. no date. "Social Mobility in the UK: Some Debates". www.arasite.org/mmedia/socialmobility/index.htm (accessed September 2013).

Harrison, B. 1999. "Feminist Ethics and Post Modernism". Keynote lecture, Academy of Religion, Boston, 20 November.

Harrison, L., L. Azzarito & J. Burden 2004. "Perceptions of Athletic Superiority: A View from the Other Side". *Race Ethnicity and Education* 7(2): 149–66.

Hebdige, D. 1979. *Subcultures: The Meaning of Style*. London: Methuen.

Hebdige, D. 1988. *Hiding in the Light*. London: Comedia/Routledge.

Hellwig, M. K. 1992. *The Eucharist and the Hunger of the World*. Oxford: Sheed & Ward.

Helstein, M. 2003. "That's Who I Want To Be. The Politics and Production of Desire Within Nike Advertising to Women". *Journal of Sport and Social Issues* 27(3): 276–92.

Herring, S. 2003 "Gender and Democracy in Computer-Mediated. Communication". http://ella.slis.indiana.edu/~herring/ejc.txt (accessed September 2013).

Heyward, C. 1982. *The Redemption of God: A Theology of Mutual Relation*. Washington, DC: University of America Press.

Heyward, C. 1989. *Touching Our Strength: The Erotic as Power and the Love of God*. San Francisco, CA: HarperCollins.

Heyward, C. 2002. *God in the Balance: Christian Spirituality in Times of Terror*. Cleveland, OH: Pilgrim Press.

Heyward, C. 2003. "Crossing Over: Dorothee Soelle and the Transcendence of God". In *The Theology of Dorothee Soelle*, S. Pinnock (ed.), 221–38. London: Trinity Press International.

Hindess, B. 1977. *Philosophy and Methodology of the Social Sciences*. Hassocks: Harvester Press.

Hindess, B. & P. Hirst 1975. *Pre-Capitalist Modes of Production*. London: Macmillan.

Hirst, P. 1977. "'Economic Classes and Politics". In *Class and Class Structure*, A. Hunt (ed.), 125–54. London: Lawrence & Wishart.

Hodgson, N. & P. Standish 2009. "Uses and Misuses of Poststructuralism in Educational Research". *International Journal of Research & Method in Education* 32(3): 309–26.

Hoffman, E. 1998. *Lost in Translation*. London: Vintage.

Honeycutt, K. 1999. "Fat World/Thin World: 'Fat Busters', 'Equivocators', 'Fat Boosters' and the Social Construction of Obesity". In *Interpreting Weight: The Social Management of Fatness and Thinness*, J. Sobal & D. Maurer (eds), 165–85. New York: Aldine de Gruyter.

Honneth, A. 1985. "An Aversion Against the Universal: A Commentary on Lyotard's *Postmodern Condition*". *Theory Culture and Society* 2(3): 147–56.

Hoogland, R. 2002. "Fact and Fantasy: The Body of Desire in the Age of Post Humanism". *Journal of Gender Studies* 11(3): 213–31.

hooks, b. 1999. "The Oppositional Gaze: Black Female Spectators". In *Feminist Film Theory: A Reader*, S. Thornham (ed.), 307–19. Edinburgh: Edinburgh University Press.

Hopper, E. 1981. *Social Mobility: A Study of Social Control and Insatiability*. Oxford: Blackwell.

Howie, G. & J. Jobling (eds) 2009. *Women and the Divine: Touching Transcendence*. London: Palgrave.

Hua Liu, C. & R. Matthews 2005. "Vygotsky's Philosophy: Constructivism and its Critics Examined". *International Education Journal* 6(3): 386–99.

Hubbard, P. 2005. "Accommodating Otherness: Anti-Asylum Centre Protest and the Maintenance of White Privilege". *Transactions of the Institute of British Geographers* 30(1): 52–6.

Hughes, B. 2002. "Bauman's Strangers: Impairments and the Invalidation of Disabled People in Modern and Post-Modern Cultures". *Disability and Society* 17(5): 571–84.

Humphries, L. 1970. *Tearoom Trade: A Study of Homosexual Encounters in Public Places*. London: Gerald Duckworth.

Husserl, E. 1973. *Cartesian Meditations*, D. Cairns (trans). The Hague: Martinus Nijhoff.

Irigaray, L. 1985. *This Sex Which Is Not One*, C. Porter & C. Burke (trans.). Ithaca, NY: Cornell University Press.

Irvine, J. 2003 "'The Sociologist as Voyeur': Social Theory and Sexuality Research 1910–1978". *Qualitative Sociology* 26(4): 428–56.

Isherwood, L. 1999. *Liberating Christ: Exploring Christologies of Contemporary Liberation Movements*. Cleveland, OH: Pilgrim Press.

Isherwood, L. 2001. *Introducing Feminist Christologies*. Sheffield: Sheffield Academic Press.

Isherwood, L. 2004. "Fucking Straight and the Gospel of Radical Equality". In *The Sexual Theologian*, M. Althaus-Reid & L. Isherwood (eds), 47–57. London: T&T Clark International.

Isherwood, L. 2005. "Incarnation In Times of Terror: Christian Theology and Challenge of September 11th". *Feminist Theology* 14(1): 69–81.

Isherwood, L. 2007. "What's God Got To Do With It?" *Feminist Theology* 15(3): 265–74.

Jardine, A. 1985. *Gynesis Configurations of Women and Modernity*. Ithaca, NY: Cornell University Press.

Jeffreys, S. 2003. *Unpacking Queer Politics*. Cambridge: Polity.

Jervis, J. 1999. *Transgressing the Modern: Explorations in the Western Experience of Otherness*. Oxford: Blackwell.

Johnston, J. & J. Taylor 2008. "Feminist Consumerism and Fat Activists: A Comparative Study of Grass Roots Activism and the Dove Real Beauty Campaign". *Signs: Journal of Women in Culture and Society* 33(4): 941–66.

Journal of Consumer Culture 2001. "Interview with Ulrich Beck". *Journal of Consumer Culture* 1(2): 261–77.

Jung, L. S. 2004. *Food For Life: The Spirituality and Ethics of Eating*. Minneapolis, MN: Fortress Press.

Keenan, W. 2003. "Rediscovering the Theological in Sociology: Foundations and Possibilities". *Theory, Culture and Society* 20(1): 19–42.

Keller, C. 2003. *Face of the Deep: A Theology of Becoming*. London: Routledge.

Keller, C. 2008. *On the Mystery: Divinity in Process*. Minneapolis, MN: Fortress Press.

Keller, C. 2012. "The Energy We Are: A Meditation in Seven Pulsations". In *Cosmology, Ecology and the Energy of God*, D. Bowman & C. Crockett (eds), 11–25. New York: Fordham Press.

Kibby, M. & B. Costello 2001. "Between the Image and the Act: Interactive Sex Entertainment on the Internet". *Sexualities* 4(3): 353–69.

Kivel, B. & D. Kleiber. 2000. "Leisure in the Identity Formation of Lesbian/Gay Youth: Personal, but Not Social". *Leisure Sciences* 22: 215–32.

Kjølsrød, L. 2003. "Adventure Revisited: On Structure and Metaphor in Specialized Play". *Sociology* 37(3): 459–76.

Kontturi, K.-K. & K. Tiainen 2007. "Feminism, Art, Deleuze and Darwin: An Interview with Elizabeth Grosz". *NORA–Nordic Journal of Women's Studies* 15(4): 246–56.

Korte, A-M. & M. de Haardt (eds) 2009. *The Boundaries of Monotheism: Interdisciplinary Explorations into the Foundations of Western Monotheism*. Leiden: Brill.

Kristeva, J. 1974. *About Chinese Women*, A. Barrows (trans.). New York: Boyars.

Kuhn, A. & A.-M. Wolpe (eds) 1978. *Feminism and Materialism*. London: Routledge & Kegan Paul.

Kuhn, T. 1970. *The Structure of Scientific Revolutions*, 2nd edn. Chicago, IL: University of Chicago Press.

Laclau, E. & C. Mouffe 1987. "Post-Marxism Without Apologies". *New Left Review* 166: 79–106.

Land, C. 2006. "Becoming-Cyborg: Changing the Subject of the Social". In *Deleuze and the Social*, M. Fuglsang & B. Meier Sørenson (eds), 112–32. Edinburgh: Edinburgh University Press.

Lasch, C. 1982. *The Culture of Narcissism*. London: Sphere.

Lather, P. 2000. "Against Empathy, Voice and Authenticity". *Kvinder, Køn & Forskning* 4: 16–25.

Latour, B. 1987. *Science in Action*. Cambridge, MA: Harvard University Press.

Latour, B., P. Jensen, T. Venturini, S. Grauwin & D. Boullier 2012. "The Whole is Always Smaller than its Parts: A Digital Test of Gabriel Tarde's Monads". www.bruno-latour.fr/sites/default/files/123-WHOLE-PART-FINAL.pdf (accessed September 2013).

Latour, B., S. Woolgar & J. Salk 1986. *Laboratory Life: The Construction of Scientific Facts*. Princeton, NJ: Princeton University Press.

Law, J. (ed.) 1993. *A Sociology of Monsters: Essays on Power, Technology and Domination*. London: Routledge.

Lehtonen, T.-K. & P. Mäenpää 1997. "Shopping in the East Centre Mall". In *The Shopping Experience*, P. Falk & C. Campbell (eds), 136–65. London: Sage.

Lévi-Strauss, C. 1977. "Structural Analysis in Linguistics and in Anthropology". In his *Structural Anthropology*, vol. 1, 31–54. Harmondsworth: Peregrine Books.

Lewis, M. 2008. "New Strategies of Control: Academic Freedom and Research Ethics Boards". *Qualitative Inquiry* 14: 684–99.

Lotringer, S. & C. Marrazi 1980. "The Return of Politics". In *Autonomia: Post Political Politics*, S. Lotringer & C. Marrazi (eds), 8–21. New York: Semiotext(e).

Lukes, S. 1974. *Power: A Radical View*. London: Macmillan.

Lukes, S. 1975. *Emile Durkheim, His Life and Work: A Historical and Critical Study*. Harmondsworth: Penguin.

Lutz, F. W. 1988. "Witches and Witchfinding in Educational Organizations". In *Culture and Power in Educational Organisations*, A. Westoby (ed.), 328–44. Milton Keynes: Open University Press.

MacCabe, C. 1981. "Realism and the Cinema: Notes on Some Brechtian Theses". In *Popular Television and Film*, T. Bennett, S. Boyd-Bowman, C. Mercer & J. Wollacott (eds), 216–35. London: BFI Publishing in association with Open University Press.

MacCormack, P. 2009. "Feminist Becomings: Hybrid Feminism and Haecceitic (Re) Production". *Australian Feminist Studies* 24(59): 85–97.

Magee, B. 1974. *Popper*. London: Fontana.

Marcuse, H. 1972. *Negations*. Harmondsworth: Penguin.

Marshall, J. 2003. "The Sexual Life of Cyber-Savants". *Australian Journal of Anthropology* 15(2): 229–48.

Marx, K. 1843. *Contribution to a Critique of Hegel's* Philosophy of Right: *Introduction*. www.marxists.org/archive/marx/works/1843/critique-hpr/intro.htm (accessed September 2013).

Marx, K. 1844. *Critique of Hegel's Dialectic and General Philosophy*. www.marxists.org/archive/marx/works/1844/epm/3rd.htm#s5 (accessed October 2013).

Marx K. 1852. *The Eighteenth Brumaire of Louis Bonaparte*. www.marxists.org/archive/marx/works/1852/18th-brumaire (accessed September 2013).

Marx, K. 1858. *The Grundrisse, Notebook VII*. www.marxists.org/archive/marx/works/1857/grundrisse/ch14.htm (accessed September 2013).

Marx, K. 1875. *Critique of the Gotha Programme*. http://www.marxists.org/archive/marx/works/1875/gotha/ (accessed December 2012).

Marx, K. 1881. *Notes on Adolph Wagner's* Lehrbuch der politischen Ökonomie, *2nd edn*. www.marxists.org/archive/marx/works/1881/01/wagner.htm (accessed September 2013).

Marx, K. 1954. *Capital*, vol. 1. London: Lawrence & Wishart.

Massumi, B. 1992. *A User's Guide to Capitalism and Schizophrenia: Deviations from Deleuze and Guattari*. Cambridge, MA: Swerve Editions.

McClintock, A. 1993. "Maid to Order: Commercial S/M and Gender Power". In *Dirty Looks: Women, Pornography, Power*, P. Church Gibson & R. Gibson (eds), 207–32. London: BFI Publishing

McKendrick, K. 2004. *Word Made Skin: Figuring Language at the Surface of Flesh*. New York: Fordham Press.

McLaren, P. & R. Smith 1989. "Televangelism as Pedagogy and Cultural Politics". In *Popular Culture Schooling and Everyday Life*, H. Giroux, R. Simon *et al.*, 147–74. South Hadley, MA: Bergin & Garvey.

Mennell, S. 1985. *All Manners of Food*. Oxford: Blackwell.

Merton, R. 1968. *Social Theory and Social Structure*. New York: Free Press.

Miah, A. 2000. "Virtually Nothing: Re-evaluating the Significance of Cyberspace". *Leisure Studies* 19(3): 211–24.

Miles, S. 1998. "McDonaldization and the Global Sports Store: Constructing Consumer

Meanings in a Rationalized Society". In *McDonaldization Revisited: Critical Essays on Consumer Culture*, M. Alfino, J. Caputo & R. Wynyard (eds), 53–66. Westport, CT: Praeger.

Morris, M. 1988. "Banality in Cultural Studies". *Discourse* X(2): 3–29.

Morris, M. 1993. "Things to Do with Shopping Centres". In *The Cultural Studies Reader*, S. During (ed.), 295–319. London & New York: Routledge.

Morss, J. 2002. "The Several Social Constructions of James, Jencks and Prout: A Contribution to the Sociological Theorisation of Childhood". *International Journal of Children's Rights* 10: 39–54.

Morton, N. 1985. *The Journey is Home*. Boston, MA: Beacon Press.

Mueller-Volmer, K. (ed.) 1985. *The Hermeneutics Reader*. Oxford: Blackwell.

Mulvey, L. 1975. "Visual Pleasure and Narrative Cinema". *Screen* 16(3): 58–69.

Mynott, E. 2000. "Analysing the Creation of Apartheid for Asylum Seekers in the UK". *Community, Work and Family* 3(3): 311–31.

New Left Review (eds) 1975. *Marx: Early Writings*. Harmondsworth: Penguin.

Oduyoye, M. 2001. *Introducing African Women's Theology*. Sheffield: Sheffield Academic Press.

O'Murchu, D. 2004. *Evolutionary Faith*. Maryknoll, NY: Orbis Books.

Orbach, S. 1979. *Fat is a Feminist Issue*. London: Hamlyn.

Paglia, C. 1994. *Vamps and Tramps: New Essays*. Harmondsworth: Penguin.

Pakulski, J. & M. Waters 1996. "The Reshaping and Dissolution of Social Class in Advanced Societies". *Theory and Society* 25(5): 667–91.

Palmer, R. 1969. *Hermeneutics*. Evanston, IL: Northwestern University Press.

Parin, P. 1978. *Der Wildspruch im Subject*. Frankfurt: Syndikat.

Petrella, I. 2006. *The Future of Liberation Theology: An Argument and Manifesto*. London: SCM Press.

Pine, J. & J. Gilmour 1999. *The Experience Economy: Work is Theatre and Every Business a Stage*. Boston, MA: Harvard Business School Press.

Pitts, V. 1998. "'Reclaiming' the Female Body: Embodied Identity, Work, Resistance and the Grotesque". *Body and Society* 4(3): 67–84.

Plummer, K. 1982. "Symbolic Interactionism and Sexual Conduct: An Emergent Perspective". In *Human Sexual Relations: A Reader. Towards a Redefinition of Sexual Politics*, M. Brake (ed.), 233–44. Harmondsworth: Penguin.

Plumwood, V. 2002. *Environmental Culture: The Ecological Crisis of Reason*. London: Routledge.

Pohl, C. 1999. *Making Room: Recovering Hospitality as a Christian Tradition*. Grand Rapids, MI: William Eerdmans.

Popper, K. 1963. *Conjectures and Refutations: The Growth of Scientific Knowledge*. London: Routledge & Kegan Paul.

Poulantzas, N. 1975. *Classes in Contemporary Capitalism*. London: New Left Books.

Quintaneiro, T. 2006. "The Concepts of Figuration or Configuration in Norbert Elias's Sociological Theory". http://socialsciences.scielo.org/pdf/s_tsoc/v2nse/scs_a02.pdf (accessed September 2013).

Ramazanoglu, C. 1992. "On Feminist Methodology: Male Reason versus Female Empowerment". *Sociology* 26(2): 207–12.

Ramazanoglu, C. (ed.) 1993. *Up Against Foucault: Explorations of Some Tensions Between Foucault and Feminism*. London: Routledge.

Rambuss, R. 1998. *Closet Devotions*. Durham, NC: Duke University Press.

Rancière, J. 1991. *The Ignorant Schoolmaster: Five Lessons in Intellectual Emancipation*. Stanford, CA: Stanford University Press.

Rancière, J. 2002. "The Aesthetic Revolution and its Outcomes: Emplotments of Autonomy and Heteronomy". *New Left Review* 14 (March–April): 133–51.

Reay, D. 2003. "A Risky Business? Mature Working-Class Women Students and Access to Higher Education". *Gender and Education* 15(3): 301–17.

Reed, E. 2010. *Work for God's Sake: Christian Ethics in the Workplace*. London: SCM Press.

Richardson, R. & E. Kramer 2006. "Abduction as the Type of Inference that Characterizes the Development of a Grounded Theory". *Qualitative Research* 6(4): 497–513.

Ritzer, G. 1993. *The McDonaldization of Society*. Thousand Oaks, CA: Pine Forge.

Ritzer, G. 1999. *Enchanting a Disenchanted. World: Revolutionizing the Means of Consumption*. Thousand Oaks, CA: Pine Forge Press.

Ritzer, G. 2007. *The Globalization of Nothing 2*. London: Sage.

Ritzer, G. & T. Stillman 2001. "The Postmodern Ballpark as a Leisure Setting: Enchantment and Simulated De-McDonaldization". *Leisure Sciences* 23: 99–113.

Rivera, M. 2007. *The Touch of Transcendence: A Postcolonial Theology of God*. Louisville, KY: Westminster John Knox Press.

Rojek, C. 2000. *Leisure and Culture*. Basingstoke: Macmillan.

Rossiter, P. 2007. "Rock Climbing: On Humans, Nature, and Other Nonhumans". *Space and Culture* 10(2): 292–305.

Rubenstein, M.-J. 2012. "The Fire Each Time: Dark Energy and the Breath of Creation". In *Cosmology, Ecology & the Energy of God*, D. Bowman & C. Crockett (eds), 26–42. New York: Fordham Press.

Ruether, R. R. 1983. *Sexism and God-Talk*. London: SCM Press.

Scatamburlo-D'Annibale, V. & P. McLaren 2003. "The Strategic Centrality of Class in the Politics of 'Race' and 'Difference'". *Cultural Studie ⇔ Critical Methodologies* 3(2): 148–75.

Schneider, L. 2008. *Beyond Monotheism: A Theology of Multiplicity*. London: Routledge.

Schreiter, R. 1998. "'Who is a Local Theologian?" In *Urban Theology*, M. Northcott (ed.), 24–9. London: Cassell.

Schutz, A. 1971. *Collected Papers I: The Problem of Social Reality*. The Hague: Martinus Nijhoff.

Schutz, A. 1972. *The Phenomenology of the Social World*. London: Heinemann.

Screen (ed.) 1993. *Screen Reader on Sexuality*. London: BFI Publications.

Seid, R. 1994. "Too Close to the Bone: The Historical Context for Women's Obsession with Slenderness". In *Feminist Perspectives on Eating Disorders*, P. Fallon, M. A. Katzman & S. C. Wooley (eds), 3–16. New York: Guildford Press.

Sellers, W. & N. Gough. 2010. "Sharing Outsider Thinking: Thinking (Differently) with Deleuze in Educational Philosophy and Curriculum Inquiry". *International Journal of Qualitative Studies in Education* 23(5): 589–614.

Semetsky, I. 2009. "Deleuze as a Philosopher of Education: Affective Knowledge/Effective Learning". *The European Legacy* 14(4): 443–56.

Shank, G. 1998. "The Extraordinary Ordinary Powers of Abductive Reasoning". *Theory & Psychology* 8(6): 841–60.

Silva, E. 2000. "The Cook, the Cooker and the Gendering of the Kitchen". *Sociological Review* 48(4): 612–29.

Simmel, G. [1908] 1950. "The Stranger". In *The Sociology of Georg Simmel*, K. Wolff (ed.), 402–8. New York: Free Press.

Simon, B. 2011. "Not Going to Starbucks: Boycotts and the Outsourcing of Politics in the Branded World". *Journal of Consumer Culture* 11(2): 145–67.

Smith, D. 1997. "Introduction". In G. Deleuze, *Essays Critical and Clinical*, D. Smith & M. Greco (trans.), xi–lvi. Minneapolis, MN: University of Minnesota Press.

Soelle, D. 1996. *Theology for Sceptics: Reflections on God*. Philadelphia, PA: Fortress Press.

Soelle, D. 2001. *The Silent Cry: Mysticism and Resistance*. Minneapolis, MN: Augsburg Fortress.

St Louis, B. 2004. "Sport and Common-Sense Racial Science". *Leisure Studies* 23(1): 31–46.

Stanworth, M. 1984. "Women and Class Analysis: A Reply to Goldthorpe". *Sociology* 18(2): 159–70.

Stone, K. 2005. *Practicing Safer Texts: Food, Sex and Bible in Queer Perspective*. New York: T&T Clark.

Stuart, E. 2000. "Disruptive Bodies: Disability, Embodiment and Sexuality" In *The Good News of the Body: Sexual Theology and Feminism*, L. Isherwood (ed.), 166–84. Sheffield: Sheffield Academic Press.

Suthwell, C. 2004. *Unzipping Gender, Sex, Cross Dressing and Culture*. Oxford: Berg.

Sweetman, P. 1999. "Anchoring the (Postmodern) Self? Body Modification, Fashion and Identity". *Body and Society* 5(2–3): 51–76.

Sykes, G. & D. Matza 1957. "Techniques of Neutralisation: A Theory of Delinquency". *American Sociological Review* 22: 664–70.

Taylor, B. & D. Tilford 2000. "Why Consumption Matters". In *The Consumer Society: A Reader*, J. Schor & D. Holt (eds), 463–87. New York: New Press.

Thanem, T. & S. Linstead 2006. "The Trembling Organisation: Order, Change and the Philosophy of the Virtual". In *Deleuze and the Social*, M. Fuglsang & B. Meier Sørenson (eds), 39–57. Edinburgh: Edinburgh University Press.

Thompson, J. 1983. *Critical Hermeneutics. A Study in the Thought of Paul Ricoeur and Jürgen Habermas*. Cambridge: Cambridge University Press.

Thornton, S. 1995. *Club Cultures: Music, Media and Subcultural Capital*. Cambridge: Polity.

Thweatt-Bates, J. 2012. *Cyborg Selves: A Theological Anthropology of the Posthuman*. Ashford: Ashgate.

Tomlinson, A. (ed.) 1990. *Consumption, Identity and Style*. London: Routledge & Kegan Paul.

Townshend, J. 2004. "Laclau and Mouffe's Hegemonic Project: The Story So Far". *Political Studies* 52: 269–88.

Tuori, S. & S. Peltonen 2007. "Feminist Politics: An Interview with Sara Ahmed". *NORA– Nordic Journal of Women's Studies* 15(4): 257–64.

Tyler, I. 2006. "'Welcome to Britain': The Cultural Politics of Asylum". *European Journal of Cultural Studies* 9: 185–99.

Vähämäki, J. & A. Virtanen 2006. "Deleuze, Change, History". In *Deleuze and the Social*, M. Fuglsang & B. Meier Sørenson (eds), 207–28. Edinburgh: Edinburgh University Press.

Vanier, J. 1989. *Community and Growth*. Mahwah, NJ: Paulist Press.

Walker, A. 1993. *Possessing the Secret of Joy*. New York: Harcourt Brace Jovanovich.

Ward, G. 2004. "On the Politics of Embodiment and the Mystery of All Flesh". In *The Sexual Theologian*, M. Althaus-Reid & L. Isherwood (eds), 71–85. London: T&T Clark.

Warde, A. 2005. "Consumption and Theories of Practice". *Journal of Consumer Culture* 5(2): 131–53.

Warde, A., D. Wright & M. Gayo-Cal 2007. "Understanding Cultural Omnivorousness. Or the Myth of the Cultural Omnivore". *Cultural Sociology* 1(2): 143–64.

Warner, M. 1993. "Tongues Untied: Memoirs of a Pentecostal Boyhood". *Village Voice Literary Supplement* 112 (February): 13–15.

Weber, M. 1985. *Protestant Ethic and the Spirit of Capitalism*. London: Unwin Hyman.

Weick, K. 1988 "Educational Organisations as Loosely Coupled Systems". In *Culture and Power in Educational Organisations*, A. Westoby (ed.), 156–73. Milton Keynes: Open University Press.

Westoby, A. (ed.) 1988. *Culture and Power in Educational Organisations*. Milton Keynes: Open University Press.

Wilkins, A. 2004. "'So Full of Myself as a Chick': Goth Women, Sexual Independence, and Gender Egalitarianism". *Gender and Society* 18(3): 328–49.

Williams, D. 1993. *Sisters in the Wilderness: The Challenge of Womanist God Talk*. Maryknoll, NY: Orbis.

Williamson, J. 1978. *Decoding Advertisements: Ideology and Meaning in Advertising*. London: Marion Boyars.

Willis, P. 1977. *Learning to Labour: How Working-Class Kids Get Working-Class Jobs*. Farnborough: Saxon House.

Willis, P. 1978. *Profane Culture*. London: Routledge & Kegan Paul.

Willis, P. 1990. *Common Culture*. Milton Keynes: Open University Press.

Willis, P. & M. Trondman 2000. "Manifesto for *Ethnography*". *Ethnography* 1(1): 5–16.

Winch, P. 1958. *The Idea of a Social Science and Its Relation to Philosophy*. London: Routledge & Kegan Paul.

Windeatt, B. (trans) 1985. *The Book of Margery Kempe*. Harmondsworth: Penguin.

Women's Studies Group 1978. *Women Take Issue: Aspects of Women's Subordination*. London: Hutchinson.

Woods, P. & M. Hammersley (eds) 1993. *Gender and Ethnicity in Schools: Ethnographic Accounts*. London: Routledge.

Woodward, I., M. Emmison & P. Smith 2000. "Consumerism, Disorientation and Postmodern Space: A Modest Test of an Immodest Theory". *British Journal of Sociology* 51(2): 339–54.

Young, J. 1971. *The Drugtakers: The Social Meaning of Drug Abuse*. London: McGibbon & Kee.

Young, J. 1975. "Working Class Criminology". In *Critical Criminology*, I. Taylor, P. Walton & J. Young (eds), 63–94. London: Routledge and Ketan Paul.

Young-Eisendrath, P. 1999. *Women and Desire: Beyond Wanting to be Wanted*. London: Piatkus.

Žižek, S. 2004. *Organs Without Bodies*. London: Routledge.

INDEX